M000251981

The War on the
Eastern Front

Defending Moscow in the summer of 1941.

The War on the Eastern Front

The Soviet Union 1941–1945
A Photographic History

Alexander Hill

Foreword by David Stahel

Pen & Sword
MILITARY

First published in Great Britain in 2021 by
PEN & SWORD MILITARY
an imprint of Pen & Sword Books Ltd
Yorkshire – Philadelphia

Copyright © Alexander Hill, 2021

ISBN 978-1-52678-610-4

The right of Alexander Hill to be identified as the author of this work has been asserted
by him in accordance with the Copyright, Designs and Patents Act 1988.

A CIP catalogue record for this book is available from the British Library.

All rights reserved. No part of this book may be reproduced or transmitted in any form or
by any means, electronic or mechanical including photocopying, recording or by any
information storage and retrieval system, without permission from the Publisher in writing.

Typeset by Concept, Huddersfield, West Yorkshire, HD4 5JL.
Printed and bound in England by CPI Group (UK) Ltd, Croydon CR0 4YY.

Pen & Sword Books Ltd incorporates the Imprints of Aviation, Atlas, Family History,
Fiction, Maritime, Military, Discovery, Politics, History, Archaeology, Select, Wharncliffe
Local History, Wharncliffe True Crime, Military Classics, Wharncliffe Transport,
Leo Cooper, The Praetorian Press, Remember When, White Owl, Seaforth Publishing and
Frontline Books.

For a complete list of Pen & Sword titles please contact
PEN & SWORD BOOKS LTD
47 Church Street, Barnsley, South Yorkshire, S70 2AS, England
E-mail: enquiries@pen-and-sword.co.uk
Website: www.pen-and-sword.co.uk
or
PEN & SWORD BOOKS
1950 Lawrence Rd, Havertown, PA 19083, USA
E-mail: uspen-and-sword@casematepublishers.com
Website: www.penandswordbooks.com

Contents

Acknowledgements

Although the acknowledgements for this book are shorter than for some of my other works, I would like to take the opportunity to thank a few key individuals, without whom this project would not have come to fruition. First of all, I would certainly like to thank Ralph Gibson of RIA-Novosti (branded as Sputnik in the West) for making this project possible at all by making the selection of photographs presented here available to me at a viable cost. Having drawn on Sputnik's excellent photo archive for a number of other projects, I was keen to see more of the photos I had come across be published in the West as part of a publication such as this one. Ralph's enthusiasm for and commitment to the project when I proposed it to him has certainly been a valuable asset.

Having obtained the photographs for this book, I then sought out a publisher. Rupert Harding of Pen & Sword had asked me on a number of occasions over the years whether I'd like to write a book for them, and in this instance I was happy to oblige. Rupert successfully made the case for the book with his colleagues, and has been supportive of the whole endeavour from start to finish.

I would also like to thank Sarah Cook for her competent editing of my manuscript for the publisher, and the typesetter Noel Sadler for doing such a great job at showing off the photos in this book. Also to be thanked is Aaron Bates for his willingness to take a look at the proofs to look for any errors that might have made their way into the text. David Stahel kindly agreed to write a foreword for the book, and I very much appreciate the time and effort both Aaron and David have put in.

As is the convention with such books, I am pointing out that any errors or omissions are of course my responsibility. To close, I hope that you appreciate reading and browsing this book as much as I have selecting the photos and writing the captions!

Alexander Hill
Okotoks, Alberta
February 2021

Foreword

As an 18-year-old first-year history undergraduate I discovered the Nazi-Soviet War on the shelves of my university library. From the beginning I was gripped by the impossible scale, the frightful brutality and the mysterious absence of this unknown war in my decidedly Anglo-American education of the Second World War. I waded through the dense histories of Albert Seaton (*The Russo-German War*) and John Erickson (*The Road to Stalingrad*) without always understanding what I was reading. The military ranks, units and structures were assumed knowledge that I didn't possess. I'd never heard of most of the place-names and even major cities like Stalingrad were nowhere to be found in the family atlas. The cast of German and Soviet generals was too great to make sense of – I could never remember who was where or what they commanded. It was like some terribly overblown epic with a hopelessly convoluted plot and an unrelenting overindulgence in violence. Nevertheless, I felt compelled to read on because underlying all that I did not know was the one thing that I did – these horrific events were all real. Armies of millions of men battered away at each other for years in Eastern Europe to decide the outcome of the greatest war in history. Although I didn't know it then, my discovery of the Nazi-Soviet War was something of a rupture in my young life. My early fascination never really subsided and the old refrain that the more knowledge one has the more questions one asks was never more true.

As many devoted readers will know, studying the history of this war can be a solitary path. More than once I've been asked if the subject matter does not, at times, depress me. Perhaps it should. Perhaps the understandable aversion most people feel towards these events is part of what keeps us from repeating them. But I'm also sure that reading and writing about them provides its own essential warning from history. Books, army files, official papers, military documents, letters and diaries might record the fate of millions, but they are consumed in isolation and experienced individually. If nothing else, war is a highly emotional encounter, impossible to fully appreciate through history, but perhaps only in hindsight earning an essential objectivity. Giving voice to this past – or in the current context giving it a face – is a responsibility governed by a strict discipline of study that informs all of the very best histories and historians. Alexander Hill is one who has mastered this craft and here he brings to light a new and exciting collection of photographs that tell their own story of the Red Army's war, sometimes in ways words cannot. It is an invaluable record that charts some remarkable dimensions to this conflict and stands among the very best visual records of this great war. While we each experience the Nazi-Soviet War in unique ways, in an increasingly polarized world perhaps the simplicity of the static image reminds us of what the people who made up the Soviet Union sacrificed to defeat the scourge of Nazism.

David Stahel
The University of New South Wales, Canberra
April 2021

Introduction

The Great Patriotic War of 1941–1945 was both a traumatic and a formative experience for many tens of millions of the citizens of the Soviet Union. The figure of 27 million that is now commonly given for Soviet war-related deaths does not do justice to the collective suffering that the war brought on the Soviet peoples – a figure that includes many millions of Soviet Jews killed as part of the Final Solution or Holocaust. In the aftermath of the war, for a Soviet survivor not to have known of someone who had lost their life would have been the exception rather than the norm – a far cry from the situation for the Western Allies. The war might have ended in 1945, but as Belorussian Nobel Laureate Svetlana Alexievich recalled in *The Unwomanly Face of War*, her post-war childhood in many ways revolved around the memory of one war and preparations for the next one, with the absence of men thanks to the war a stark reality. She recalled:

> The village of my postwar childhood was a village of women. Village women. I don't remember any men's voices … They weep. Their songs are like weeping.
>
> In the school library half of the books were about the war. The same with the village library, and in the nearby town … Now I know the reason why … We were making war all the time, or preparing for war. Remembering how we made war.[1]

Although during the Cold War the Soviet contribution to the defeat of the Axis alliance was played down in the West, since the collapse of the Soviet Union in 1991 this has been less so. Western readers now have far greater access to a broader range of quality historical work on the Soviet experience of its part of the Second World War – still known today in Russia and many former Soviet republics as the Great Patriotic War. This broader range of work has been made possible to a large extent by the opening up of Soviet-era archives, and those archives have included not only historical documents but also photographs. This book takes advantage of this greater post-Soviet availability of Soviet photographs to provide what is arguably the most comprehensive photographic history of the Great Patriotic War available outside the former Soviet Union.

The photographs used in this book have been provided by the Russian news agency RIA-Novosti – now known in the West as Sputnik. The organisation on which RIA-Novosti is founded has been through many incarnations over the years, but can ultimately be traced back to the *Sovinformbiuro* of the period of the Great Patriotic War. The Soviet Information Bureau (*Sovetskoe informatsionnoe biuro* in Russian – typically shortened to *Sovinformbiuro*) was formed on 24 June 1941 two days after the German-led invasion of the Soviet Union had begun on the orders of the Communist Party of the Soviet Union and Soviet government. The *Sovinformbiuro* was to be an umbrella organisation to provide official information and sanctioned reporting on the war for both the Soviet people and foreign news outlets. Within the Soviet Union daily radio reports on the war by the *Sovinformbiuro* that began on 25 June 1941 ran until 15 May 1945 and were listened to by millions, with their announcer Iurii Levitan becoming a household name. Also becoming household names were many of the journalists who worked under the auspices of the *Sovinformbiuro*, including Konstantin Simonov, Mikhail Sholokhov and Il'ia Ehrenburg. Less famous, but no less significant in their work, were the many photographers also working ultimately for the *Sovinformbiuro* who took thousands of pictures and risked their lives to get their photographic record of the war. Photographers such as Max Alpert, Evgenii Khaldei and Mikhail Trakhman did not become household names in the same way as their literary counterparts, but with their cameras made what is arguably an as significant, if not more so, contribution to chronicling the war as their counterparts armed with their typewriters. Many of their photographs were published at home or abroad – being provided to foreign news outlets and governments as well as the Soviet press. Many of the pictures that were taken were, however, far too raw or honest in their portrayals of what was going on at the front or in the rear for them to be published during the war or during the Soviet period. Although some of those photographs have since then found their way into publications in the West, many have not, and certainly not as part of a single-volume collection such as this.

In its twenty-four chapters this book uses the photographs in the archives of the RIA-Novosti press agency inherited from the *Sovinformbiuro* to chart the course of the Soviet Union's wartime experiences. It does so starting with Soviet preparations for war in the 1930s and the small-war precursors to the Great Patriotic War of the late 1930s and 1940, before examining in some detail the titanic struggle that was the Great Patriotic War itself. It concludes with a final chapter looking at the aftermath of the war and its commemoration. Each chapter is provided with an introduction to set the scene for the photographs in that chapter, with each photograph being provided with a caption – some relatively brief but many providing more significant detail on what the photograph shows or on the context in which it is to be understood. In providing the reader with the introductions and captions, I have made use of much of my own work, with page references to those works provided in brackets in the text. In particular I have referred to *The Red Army and the Second World War* (Cambridge University Press, 2017), abbreviated as RASWW, and *The Great Patriotic War of the Soviet Union, 1941–45: A documentary reader* (Routledge, 2009), abbreviated as GPW. I have also made reference on occasion to other sources, and those references are provided in the short list of endnotes at the end of the book. For those looking to delve deeper into the content of particular chapters, in addition to being able to follow up on references in my own and other works that have been referenced, I have provided a Further Reading section by chapter at the end of the book with some suggestions for those wanting more detail on a particular topic or theme.

This collection of photographs is a testimony to the sacrifices made by the Soviet peoples in the defeat of Nazi Germany and her allies. As such, it seemed appropriate that its publication be linked to another recent memorialisation of the efforts of the Soviet peoples, namely the Soviet War Memorial in London. As part of the marking of the 50th Anniversary of Allied victory over Nazi Germany, the Russian Embassy in London asked the UK Society for Co-operation in Russian and Soviet Studies to organise services at the graves of Soviet service personnel in the UK. That request soon developed into a plan to erect a national memorial to Soviet citizens who lost their lives in the war against Nazi Germany and her allies, and which has ultimately resulted in the physical memorial that now stands in Geraldine Mary Harmsworth Park adjacent to the Imperial War Museum in Southwark, London. When I agreed to write this book for Pen & Sword, the publisher kindly agreed to make a donation to the Soviet War Memorial Trust. As part of that contract, the Soviet War Memorial Trust also has the opportunity to purchase copies of the book at a trade price and sell them as part of its ongoing fundraising efforts to maintain the memorial and organise events and educational activities relating to it. If you have purchased this book through them, you will have made a further contribution to the ongoing work of the trust by doing so.

Regardless of any political turmoil in governmental relations between the former Allies in the war against the Axis, it is important to remember and celebrate the wartime alliance between the Soviet Union and Western allies, and the sacrifices made by the Soviet peoples in securing victory. This book will hopefully contribute to maintaining that memory of events and the people who participated in them.

Alexander Hill
Okotoks, near Calgary, Canada
1 February 2021

'Wait for me'

By Konstantin Simonov

Simonov's 1941 wartime poem 'Wait for me' is undoubtedly one of the most famous pieces of artistic work to come out of the Great Patriotic War (see p. 186). The original Russian version, along with this author's own very liberal translation of the poem that aims to get across the original's sentiments as best as possible in English, are reproduced here. Alongside the photographs in this book, Simonov's poem is a memorial to the sacrifices made by the Soviet people during the Great Patriotic War.

Жди меня, и я вернусь.
Только очень жди,
Жди, когда наводят грусть
Желтые дожди,
Жди, когда снега метут,
Жди, когда жара,
Жди, когда других не ждут,
Позабыв вчера.
Жди, когда из дальних мест
Писем не придет,
Жди, когда уж надоест
Всем, кто вместе ждет.
Жди меня, и я вернусь,
Не желай добра
Всем, кто знает наизусть,
Что забыть пора.
Пусть поверят сын и мать
В то, что нет меня,
Пусть друзья устанут ждать,
Сядут у огня,
Выпьют горькое вино
На помин души ...
Жди. И с ними заодно
Выпить не спеши.
Жди меня, и я вернусь,
Всем смертям назло.

Wait for me, and I'll be back.
Only be sure to wait,
Wait, when the pollen-laden rains
bring forth their gloom,
Wait, when the snow is swirling,
Wait, in the baking sun,
Wait, when others can wait no more,
And when yesterday has been forgotten.
Wait, when letters fail to arrive
from places far away,
Wait, when those waiting with you
Cannot wait another day.
Wait for me, and I'll be back,
Do not harbour enmity,
For those who do not fail to tell you,
That the time has come to forget.
Let my mother, and my son,
convince themselves that I am gone,
Let my friends tire of waiting,
Sitting round the fire,
Drinking bitter wine
Reminding themselves of the past ...
Wait! Do not hasten to join with them
In drinking to one now gone.
Wait for me, and I'll be back.
Death will not have his wicked way.

Кто не ждал меня, тот пусть
Скажет: – Повезло.
Не понять, не ждавшим им,
Как среди огня
Ожиданием своим
Ты спасла меня.
Как я выжил, будем знать
Только мы с тобой, –
Просто ты умела ждать,
Как никто другой.

Let those who did not wait for me
Say simply that he cheated death.
They will not understand,
Not having waited, how
in the face of strife it was you,
You that saved me.
Only you and I will know,
How it was that I survived,
For solely you knew how to wait,
You, and you alone.

Chapter 1

The Red Army Prepares for War

The Great Patriotic War of the Soviet Union of 1941–1945 was fought by a Soviet Red Army that in many senses had been preparing for war for more than a decade when the German-led Axis invasion began on 22 June 1941. Although it was the October Revolution and Civil War in Russia of 1917–1921 that brought the Bolsheviks to power, in some ways the real revolution or a second revolution in Russia took place under Stalin. The collectivisation of agriculture and rapid industrialisation of the Soviet Union under Stalin undoubtedly led to a revolutionary transformation in the lives of many Soviet citizens, and particularly the peasantry, for whom many authors suggest that collectivisation of agriculture brought about a second serfdom. This second revolution not only advanced the goals of the October Revolution in leading to a growth in the proletariat or urban working class, but also in strengthening Soviet power. The collectivisation of agriculture in the Soviet Union that began in earnest in 1929 was geared to paying for industrialisation, and industrialisation was to a considerable extent about military power. In February 1931 Stalin gave what has become a famous and seemingly prescient speech to industrial managers, in which he pointed out:

> One feature of the history of Old Russia was the continual beating she suffered because of her backwardness. She was beaten by the Mongol Khans. She was beaten by the Turkish beys. She was beaten by the Swedish feudal lords. She was beaten by the Polish and Lithuanian gentry. She was beaten by the British and French capitalists. She was beaten by the Japanese barons. All beat her – because of her backwardness: because of her military backwardness, cultural backwardness, political backwardness, industrial backwardness, agricultural backwardness. They beat her because it was profitable and could be done with impunity ...
>
> That is why we must no longer lag behind ...
>
> We are fifty to a hundred years behind the advanced countries. We must make good this distance in ten years. Either we do it, or they crush us. [GPW, p. 9]

Although the Soviet Union still lacked concrete threats at this point beyond a vague notion that the capitalist powers would seek to undermine it, the expansion of Soviet military capabilities need not only have had a defensive purpose, but could also have allowed the Soviet Union to spread revolution by force of arms should conducive circumstances arise. Such an eventuality was something considered in the economic planning process – a powerful Red Army would be valuable regardless of the circumstances. Ultimately, according to Marxist-Leninist theory, the Russian Revolution would only be secure if there was revolution elsewhere, and the Soviet Union was committed to helping that along. Japanese expansion in the Far East, starting with Manchuria in 1931, soon gave the Soviet Union a concrete threat to focus on, although the Japanese threat alone was hardly existential. What was to become existential was the threat from fascism in Europe, and in particular the threat from a Nazi Germany that made it plain that eastward expansion was on its agenda, and that the Treaty of Versailles was not going to impede its territorial ambitions.

By 1936 the Red Army was arguably the most powerful army in Europe, although the purges launched against the Red Army and wider Soviet society in 1936–1938 did much to undermine gains that had been made. It is in many ways ironic that purges launched to supposedly make Stalin's regime more secure in the face of largely imagined foreign-backed internal opposition did so much to weaken the Red Army at the end of the 1930s. Perhaps fortunately for the Soviet Union, war with Nazi Germany was delayed by the signing of the Nazi-Soviet Pact and associated protocols of August–September 1939. Although during the spring of 1941 the Red Army was in the throes of expansion and reorganisation, it was back on a track towards greater military effectiveness. This improvement was thanks to some soul searching about the Red Army's performance in some of the small wars it was involved in during the late 1930s and 1940, and particularly the war with Finland of 1939–1940. These small wars preceding the Great Patriotic War will be considered in Chapters 2 and 3. This first chapter takes us more broadly through the 1930s and up to 1941 in visually highlighting key elements in the development of the Red Army and Soviet preparations for future war during the period prior to the beginning of the Great Patriotic War.

Sputnik 28932. It is perhaps appropriate that in this first photograph captured First World War-vintage 'Rikardo' Type B tanks (British Mark Vs) of the Red Army are shown on parade in Red Square on 7 November 1930 – the date of the 13th anniversary of the Russian Revolution according to the new post-revolutionary calendar. The First World War had been the final factor weakening the Tsarist regime in Russia to such an extent that it collapsed. That at the beginning of the new decade the Red Army was using such tanks in a parade highlights just how far behind the British and French the Soviet Union was at the start of the 1930s in terms of the development of armoured vehicles. At this time Weimar Germany was not allowed tanks under the Treaty of Versailles of 1919, although was secretly involved in developing tanks with the Soviet Union after Germany and the Soviet Union had come to terms under the 1922 Treaty of Rapallo. The Soviet Union's Tsarist predecessor had fought the First World War without any tanks at all – with the first tanks seeing action on Russian soil during the 1917–1921 Russian Civil War. Nonetheless, at the time this photograph was taken the first of the Soviet Union's Five-Year Plans was under way, and mass production of the first Soviet tanks was on the horizon. Stalin – now clearly the Soviet Union's leader – was determined that the Soviet Union would be able not only to defend itself, but perhaps even export its revolution abroad by force of arms. What the Soviet Union would also develop during the early 1930s was a military doctrine in which the new tanks would play a central role as the Red Army moved from relying on cavalry as the principle manoeuvre arm, to the tank.

Sputnik 21824. Here cavalry of the Central Asian Military District are shown on the move some-where in Kazakhstan in 1932. Despite the development of tanks, the cavalry would continue to rival the armoured forces within the Red Army in terms of prestige until the mid-1930s. Cavalry had proven well-suited to the manoeuvrings of the Russian Civil War when the railway and the horse had proven so essential for all sides. Cavalry also proved valuable in the post-Civil War Red Army for many reasons, including the fact that many of the Red Army's territorial and regular forces were more familiar with the horse than the combustion engine, where most recruits were poorly educated peasants. Cavalry also proved valuable in the counter-insurgencies conducted by Soviet forces during the interwar period, including against the Basmachi resistance movement that was initially largely neutralised on Soviet soil in the early 1920s but that saw a resurgence in the late 1920s and early 1930s. Basmachi forces were able to briefly operate against the Soviet Union from Afghan territory at the end of the 1920s, during the suppression of which Soviet cavalry operated within northern Afghanistan.

Sputnik 87898. A key proponent of the cavalry arm within the Red Army was Semen Budennii, pictured here as Marshal of the Soviet Union in June 1938 as the so-called 'Great Purges' raged within Soviet society and the Red Army. Budennii's hostility towards Marshal Mikhail Tukhachevskii – who was an early victim of the purges of the Red Army in June 1937 – was not something that Budennii concealed, and seems to have at least in part been as a result of Tukhachevskii's support for the mechanisation of the Red Army as part of the development of the concepts of 'Deep Battle' and 'Deep Operations'. 'Deep Battle' – and its larger-scale compatriot 'Deep Operations' – shared much with the later much-vaunted German Blitzkrieg, whereby tanks, supported by artillery, aircraft and even airborne forces, would punch through enemy defences and break into the rear, where they would paralyse the enemy response to the offensive operations. Despite the deaths of Tukhachevskii and many of his colleagues, Budennii was unable to halt the mechanisation of the Red Army even if his position within the chain of command no doubt played a part in the continued importance of the cavalry arm in the Red Army into the Great Patriotic War.

Sputnik 3324617. The Soviet armed forces in 1930 were not only dependent on equipment manufactured before the revolution in terms of tanks and other equipment for the army, but also for naval forces. Here 'Novik' Class destroyers are shown with what appears to be a Polikarpov R-1 aircraft on manoeuvres during the summer of 1930. These vessels had been built or laid down by the Tsarist regime, with the Bolsheviks completing a number of such vessels after the revolution. In 1930 Bolshevik naval power was limited to the Baltic and Black Seas, but the 1930s would see the emergence of flotillas that would become fleets in both the north and Far East. Although ambitious Soviet plans for naval development during the 1930s would not come to fruition because increasing attention had to be paid to the readying of ground and air forces for war on the Eurasian landmass, the Soviet Navy would by the start of the Great Patriotic War be equipped with a mixture of ships of both Tsarist and Soviet construction. The Polikarpov aircraft in the photo was one of the first mass-produced aircraft in the Soviet Union, although it was derived from flyable British Airco/ de Havilland D.H.4 aircraft captured during the Russian Civil War. The 1930s would see the mass production of genuinely Soviet aircraft.

Sputnik 60300. By 1936 the Red Army had been, particularly materially, transformed. Tanks such as the T-26s shown here on exercises in the spring of that year in the Krasnoiarsk region in Siberia were available in their thousands. More than a thousand early T-26s had been produced by the end of the First Five-Year Plan in 1932, with 1936 alone seeing the manufacture or completion of just over 1,300 more [RASWW, p. 37]. Whether the tanks and their crews – as part of formations of increasing size – were capable of putting 'Deep Operations' or even 'Deep Battle' into effect was, however, another matter. Notice the rail-like aerial around the turret on the lead and second tanks in this picture. Most of the remaining tanks lack radio communications, meaning that communication between the command tanks and the remainder of the unit would mean reliance on visual signals. If a command tank was to be knocked out, in all probability a unit would be unable to communicate with its headquarters. Communications would be one of a number of impediments to the implementation of 'Deep Battle'. Soon, however, as Tukhachevskii and those of his colleagues who were the architects of 'Deep Battle' were purged, the Red Army would move temporarily towards a focus on the tank as primarily being a means of supporting the infantry. Manoeuvres such as those shown here were often not particularly realistic in recreating anything like actual wartime conditions. Tightly choreographed, such manoeuvres during the 1930s were more about impressing foreign observers and the top brass rather than preparing troops for the chaos of battle.

(*Opposite*) Sputnik 3029276. Another shot of a T-26 from 1936, this time taken during manoeuvres in the summer of that year in the Moscow region. Other than showing off some of the relatively ornate woodwork on this peasant's cottage and indeed providing a close-up of the front portion of the tank, the picture in many ways encapsulates key contrasts in the Soviet Union at the time. One contrast evident in this picture is between industrialisation and the development of a modern Red Army and the continued existence of a peasant majority that in many ways was living under a new serfdom in the form of collectivisation. Also, as many young people were receiving an education denied to their forebears and often looked towards a new life in the growing cities and urban settlements, something of a chasm existed in Soviet society not just between the urban and rural, but between younger and older generations. Note that this tank has a radio aerial indicating a command vehicle. Note also the machine gun mounted alongside the very respectable-for-the-time main armament in the form of a relatively high-velocity 45mm gun capable of penetrating more than 35mm of vertical armour at a range of 1km with an armour-piercing round.

(*Above*) Sputnik 103315. An impressive array of Soviet TB-3 bombers in early 1934. In the 'Deep Battle' and 'Deep Operations' schema the heavy bomber was to play its part in the breakthrough and exploitation by ground forces by hitting enemy communications and infrastructure deeper in the enemy rear, and thus contributing to the degradation of the enemy's ability to deal with a Soviet penetration of their lines. Alongside tanks the TB-3 heavy bomber was often used to symbolise the transformation and modernisation of the Soviet armed forces during the mid-1930s. Used as both a bomber and transport aircraft for paratroops, the TB-3 was when introduced an advanced design that would establish a configuration for heavy bombers that would be the norm throughout the period of the piston-engined aircraft. Although still in service at the beginning of the Great Patriotic War – and consequently compared to Allied heavy bombers available during the early part of the Second World War – its contemporaries in terms of design were the somewhat antiquated Curtiss B-2 and Handley-Page Heyford bombers that were vastly inferior. As with other aircraft types, any Soviet advantages in terms of capabilities gained through being pioneers in new design features had been lost by the end of the decade. However, whereas the Soviet Union would introduce new fighter aircraft during the Great Patriotic War that would match or exceed the capabilities of those of their opponents, the Soviet heavy bomber force would not advance beyond the already inadequate at the time of series production pre-war successor to the TB-3, the Pe-8.

(*Above*) Sputnik 3045682. Often shown jumping from modified TB-3 bombers, this photo of September 1935 shows Soviet paratroopers descending towards and having landed on open terrain in the Kiev region of the Ukraine. Like the bomber aircraft from which they would typically jump, at this time the Soviet Union was ahead of its would-be competitors in terms of the development of airborne forces. In the 'Deep Battle' schema such troops dropped en masse in the enemy rear would in theory be used to further paralyse any enemy response to the breakthrough of ground forces. Subsequently, only rarely during the Great Patriotic War were Soviet paratroops employed in their intended role, where their opponents and allies had taken an idea that the Soviet Union had pioneered and developed it. Soviet enthusiasm for airborne forces would, however, return with something of a vengeance during the Cold War.

(*Opposite, above*) Sputnik 5781688. One area in which the Soviet Union had considerable pre-revolutionary stocks of weaponry that would still be useful in future wars was in light and medium artillery. In addition, the Soviet Union would manufacture Tsarist-era guns in order to get production under way before new designs could be produced. This photo shows a 122mm Model 1910/1930 gun with horses and limber on parade in Red Square in Moscow on the 18th anniversary of the Revolution in 1935. Soviet production of this gun differed from the earlier Tsarist version in terms of the sights, and in the modified carriage on the Soviet production model that was in fact simplified. Only some of the guns would end up with metal wheels with rubber tires, without which they could only be towed at a maximum speed of 6km/h! Although the Red Army strove towards greater mechanisation, the infantry divisions in particular continued to rely on the horse into and throughout the Great Patriotic War. This gun equipped the artillery regiments of many infantry divisions at the beginning of the Great Patriotic War.

(*Overleaf*) Sputnik 24690. Although the Red Army put considerable existing stocks of artillery to good use – and produced their own versions of Tsarist-era guns – the addition of modern artillery for the Red Army was a key goal for the military elements of the five-year plans for Soviet industry of the 1930s. Indeed, in 1929 the Communist Party had dictated that the Red Army should have technology more advanced than that of potential opponents by the end of the First Five-Year Plan in three key areas – for aircraft, tanks and artillery. [RASWW, p. 39] Although it would take a little longer to reach this point than proposed, as the T-26 tank and TB-3 bomber suggest, by the mid-1930s the Soviet Union was providing the Soviet armed forces with modern military equipment that exceeded foreign equivalents in terms of capability. To a lesser extent such a claim could be made regarding some of the newer artillery pieces being provided to the Red Army. Here, B-4 guns are shown on parade in Red Square in Moscow, this time on 1 May 1936, with the photograph being taken from the Kremlin side of the square. Such heavy artillery – very much suited for siege work and clearly developed in the light of First World War experience – absorbed considerable industrial resources at a time when there were very many competing demands for them. Although of little use early in the Great Patriotic War, as photographs later in this book will show, they had value in Finland in 1939–1940 in breaking through the Mannerheim Line defences, and again in urban warfare as the Red Army fought its way through fortified German towns and cities later in the Great Patriotic War.

(*Opposite, below*) Sputnik 5783245. This parade shot – taken in Red Square on 7 November 1938 on the 21st anniversary of the revolution – shows T-37 light amphibious tanks. Although the Soviet Union had in excess of 11,000 tanks in service by February 1938, many of these tanks were lighter models that had little value by that time when facing contemporary anti-tank weapons. At this point the Red Army had nearly 4,000 of these T-37 and similar T-38 tanks in service. [RASWW, p. 119 and p. 601 n. 36] Although in theory useful for reconnaissance – for which their amphibious capability was a particular asset – the absence of radios would in many cases mean that getting reconnaissance information back to those who could use it in a timely manner would be a significant problem. At the end of the 1930s the Soviet Union was looking to switch productive capacity to more heavily armoured and armed tanks.

(*Above*) Sputnik 2389825. During the 1930s not only were the five-year plans increasingly focused on the defence sector, but Soviet society was increasingly focused on the prospect of future war. In addition to those subject to compulsory military service receiving military training with the Red Army, Soviet citizens could receive some sort of military preparation – even if rudimentary – through the civil defence organisation typically known by the abbreviation form of its title, OSOAVIAKHIM. This picture shows civil defence training in progress in the spring of 1939 in the Ukraine. The threat of the use of chemical weapons seems to have been something of a recurring theme in such preparations, with the gas mask a far from unusual accoutrement to such activities. Although the value of such training was in many instances probably limited, OSOAVIAKHIM did offer programmes – sometimes in collaboration with the Komsomol or youth wing of the Communist Party – that were apparently popular with young people and that gave a select few the opportunity to learn to fly or receive parachute training.

(*Above*) Sputnik 662684. A key component in developing a modern, mechanised Red Army was education – be that prior to entering the Red Army or during service within it. Although this photograph shows students of the Military Academy for Motorisation and Mechanisation on 28 June 1941, the academy was created back in 1932. By the end of the 1930s not only were new recruits into the Red Army receiving longer educations than their predecessors the previous decade before donning their uniforms, but were far more likely to receive specialised military education beyond basic training once in the Red Army. Military commanders were much more likely to receive additional education as they progressed in rank than in the past, with the Academy of the General Staff created in 1936 being at the apex of the Red Army educational system. [RASWW, pp. 20, 49]

(*Opposite*) Sputnik 7381. Ironically, given the drive to increase educational levels within the Red Army during the 1930s, by the beginning of 1940 the purges of the Red Army in 1937–1938 had left a clique of senior military leaders in positions of authority who were poorly educated in military matters. This state of affairs was epitomised by People's Commissar for Defence and head of the armed forces, Kliment Voroshilov, who had no formal military education at all! After the débâcle in Finland covered in Chapter 3, Voroshilov was removed from his position as head of the armed forces, and there were signs that his clique was losing authority to younger commanders with more military education, such as the two Soviet military leaders shown here during exercises in the Kiev Military District in September 1940: Marshal Semen Timoshenko (*left*) and General Georgii Zhukov (*right*). Timoshenko and Zhukov amongst others would oversee something of a transformation in Red Army training and manoeuvres immediately prior to the Great Patriotic War away from the superficial and choreographed towards a better approximation of combat conditions. Zhukov would go on to become a Marshal of the Soviet Union and the only person in the Soviet Union other than Leonid Brezhnev to receive the prestigious Hero of the Soviet Union award four times.

Sputnik 634863. This photograph shows the new, more realistic training of the Red Army immediately prior to the Great Patriotic War. Here soldiers of the 70th Rifle Division advance through a smokescreen in the Leningrad region on 10 May 1941. Note the junior commander leading his troops – in distinct uniform and with only a pistol – making him a desirable target for any enemy soldier but particularly a sniper. During the Great Patriotic War the tendency would be for junior officers to look more like the soldiers they were fighting with to mitigate the risk of them being singled out for particular enemy attention. At the time this photograph was taken, although Stalin was attempting not to provoke Nazi Germany into attacking the Soviet Union by clearly mobilising for war, this was nonetheless brought about by a certain realisation of the possibility of German attack in the near future. A significant part of the Red Army was mobilised during this period, even if the Soviet Union had not ordered a general mobilisation. Although Stalin would subsequently suppress the notion that a German attack was imminent, nonetheless the Red Army continued to move units and formations to the West in late May and early June 1941 as it prepared for war – just not by Hitler's timetable. Having seen action in the war against Finland in 1939–1940, the 70th Rifle Division would begin the Great Patriotic War as a reserve division for forces facing the Finns, before being thrown into the maelstrom below Leningrad in early July as the Red Army sought to halt the German advance towards the city.[2]

Chapter 2

Preludes to the Main Event: the Soviet Union's Small Wars of the 1930s

As the Red Army grew during the second half of the 1930s and readied itself for future war, it would have a number of opportunities to fight against a range of opponents, from German and Italian-backed Nationalist forces in Spain to Japanese forces in China. Although few Soviet troops would participate in the Spanish Civil War, Soviet military equipment that included tanks and aircraft – often with 'volunteer' Soviet crews – would get its first meaningful combat testing from 1936. The following year Soviet 'volunteer' aircrews would for the first time face the Japanese in the Far East as Japan foolhardily expanded its commitments on the continent from Manchuria to the whole of China. As if the fighting with Chinese forces wasn't enough, local Japanese commanders took it upon themselves to pick fights with the Soviet Union both in 1938 on the Manchurian border with Soviet Far Eastern territory, and in 1939 on the Manchurian border with Soviet-backed Mongolia. In all of these instances Soviet lives were lost, but experience was accrued – with some of it even leading to meaningful and positive changes to wider Soviet preparations for future war in Europe. A good example here is in the development of tanks, where experience in the late 1930s highlighted how speed provided little defence alone for tanks with only weak armour against contemporary anti-tank guns, leading ultimately to the development and introduction of the KV-series and T-34 tanks for the

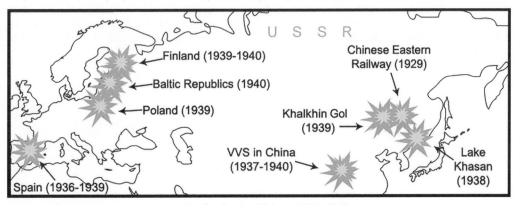

Soviet military engagements outside the Soviet Union, 1929–1940.

beginning of the next decade. All of this was unfortunately taking place under the cloud of the Great Purges of the Red Army in 1937–1938 that would hamper not only Red Army operations but also the processing of combat experience that was being accrued. This chapter looks at the nature of Soviet participation in some of those conflicts, and in particular in the fighting against Japan on the Soviet and Mongolian borders in 1938–1939.

Sputnik 6226. Soviet cameraman and later director Roman Karmen with Republican troops in September 1936 during the early phases of the Spanish Civil War. Karmen made his way to Spain slightly ironically via Berlin and then Paris – the latter stop required him to obtain a Spanish visa since at that time the Soviet Union didn't even have diplomatic relations with Spain. Of note apparently en route was Karmen's first encounter with bananas – which he had never tried before – and in Berlin the sight of 'live fascists'![3] The Spanish Civil War was undoubtedly a major milestone for Soviet fears of actual rather than imagined war on the European continent. With their interventions in the Spanish Civil War it became apparent that Nazi Germany and fascist Italy were going to be able to support the Nationalist rebels in Spain without meaningful sanction by Britain and France. If Britain and France were not going to act against fascism in Europe then a showdown between fascism and Soviet communism was becoming all the more likely. The Soviet Union did provide some support to the Republican government in Spain, with Soviet military personnel serving alongside Republican forces as pilots, tank crew and advisers for example, although as 'volunteers' nominally not serving as Red Army personnel. However, Stalin was keen not to provoke either all-out war with the fascist powers, or perhaps more importantly at this point a falling-out with Britain and France, who it was hoped would be willing to join the Soviet Union in curtailing fascist ambitions in Europe. There was certainly a relationship between the Spanish Civil War and the Great Purges in the Soviet Union, where the former seems to have provoked Stalin to believe that it was necessary to put his domestic house in order if there was an increasing threat of a war that his enemies might use as an opportunity to undermine or overthrow him.

Sputnik 104299. This Soviet poster of 1938 by artist Boris Prorokov is nominally concerned with the 24th International Day of Youth associated with the Young Communist International and International Union of Socialist Youth. The caption reads 'For peace, freedom and democracy, against fascism and war!' Those fighting fascism in the poster are a young Spanish republican and Chinese soldier. In 1937 Japanese forces, having invaded Manchuria in 1931, invaded the remainder of China. Once again, as in Spain, relatively small numbers of Soviet 'volunteers' would fight alongside the Chinese, with Soviet aircraft and aircrews being the most significant contribution.

Sputnik 59244. In this picture Soviet commanders are shown surveying the scene at Lake Khasan on the Soviet-Manchurian border at the end of July 1938, at the beginning of the Lake Khasan incident. The Lake Khasan border incident saw significant localised fighting between Soviet and Japanese forces that ended in the Soviet Union being able to assert its border claims after a two-week period of conflict. Although typically described as a border incident because the fighting over boundaries was geographically so constrained, this incident was far from being a skirmish, with a significant part of a Soviet corps (39th Rifle Corps) being committed against a sizeable portion of a Japanese division (19th Division).

(*Above*) Sputnik 44392. A slightly later photograph showing Red Army soldiers near Lake Khasan in early August 1938, at which point Japanese troops were occupying higher ground that they had seized from Soviet border troops at the end of July. That Soviet forces were successful in asserting Soviet claims on territory in the region owed more to a lack of Japanese commitment to the fighting than to Soviet competence. During the summer of 1938 the purges of the Red Army were still in full swing and had hit Soviet forces in the region hard, and undoubtedly had an impact on Soviet military effectiveness. Nonetheless, local Japanese commanders did not receive the same level of support from their superiors as their Soviet counterparts, where Japanese leaders higher up the chain of command were keen to prevent an escalation in the fighting. Japanese forces were not only outnumbered during the Lake Khasan fighting, but also operating without air support, and would eventually withdraw from the battlefield after having been pushed back at heavy cost for the Red Army rather than being resoundingly defeated. During the fighting near Lake Khasan at least 717 Soviet troops were killed, with a further 75 missing, along with 2,752 wounded. On the Japanese side in the region of 526 were killed and 913 wounded. [RASWW, p. 88]

(*Opposite*) Sputnik 40949. A Soviet Red Banner is flown over Zaozernaia Hill towards the end of the Lake Khasan fighting, where a ceasefire was implemented the following day on 11 August. The terrain over which the fighting took place is shown well in this photo, with a combination of low-lying wet terrain and craggy outcrops higher up being far from suitable for the deployment of tanks. Nonetheless, the Red Army would deploy the tanks of the 2nd Mechanized Brigade along with those organic to the 32nd Rifle Division during the fighting. Given the terrain it is unsurprising that, despite the limited number of anti-tank weapons on the Japanese side, as Soviet tanks advanced on 6–7 August after Japanese positions had been softened up by Soviet bombers only 'individual tanks made it to their objectives, but very few made it back. They got stuck in the marshes …'. In order to prevent their capture by the Japanese 'four to five tanks were bombarded by their own artillery'. According to one Soviet source the Red Army lost twenty-four tanks outright with a further fifty-six damaged during fighting that in many ways did not show the Red Army in a favourable light. [RASWW, pp. 88–9]

(*Opposite, above*) Sputnik 61242. The following year another border incident – nominally between the Japanese and Mongolians – escalated into significant if localised fighting between Soviet, Mongolian and Japanese forces at Khalkhin Gol. This time, however, the terrain was far better suited to Soviet mechanised forces. Here, Soviet tankers are shown prior to combat operations with their BT-series tanks during an early period in the fighting. Although relatively lightly armoured, the BT-7s shown here were both capable of high speeds on suitable terrain and armed with a potent 45mm gun developed from the 45mm 20-K gun of the early 1930s. In the 'Deep Battle' schema of the mid-1930s such tanks were to be tasked with exploiting a breakthrough in enemy lines, but by the late 1930s it was becoming clear to Soviet military leaders that in practice designating tanks for specific battlefield roles did not always fit in with front-line needs and the availability of vehicles. At Khalkhin Gol such tanks would not only operate semi-independently as intended when they were conceived, but also in combination with and at the pace of the infantry (a photograph of which is available in RASWW, p. 99). Of note in this picture are the covers on some of the M1936 helmets being worn – something that was certainly not standard issue but fits in with a growing Soviet awareness of the need for camouflage and *maskirovka* ('concealment').

(*Opposite, below*) Sputnik 601334. The first of two shots of Soviet BT-series tanks at Khalkhin Gol, this time on the move. In this photo there is a mixture of earlier BT-5 and more recent BT-7 tanks, the former with the armour on the turret less well sloped. Although such tanks performed well enough at Khalkhin Gol against an opponent poorly prepared for anti-tank warfare, by the time German forces led the Axis invasion of the Soviet Union in June 1941 they were looking increasingly outdated compared to the modern anti-tank weapons typically available to German forces. At the beginning of April 1941 the Red Army would still have nearly 2,500 of the basic version of the BT-7 in service, along with approaching 2,000 equipped with radios – to which can be added nearly 1,500 earlier BT-5 and more than 500 BT-2 tanks.[4] Most of these tanks would be lost during the summer and autumn of 1941.

(*Above*) Sputnik 38695. Another shot of BT-series tanks 'in action' during the initial stages of the fighting at Khalkhin Gol. This photograph – apparently showing tanks hull-down behind the ridge of some shallow hills – gives a good sense of the terrain at Khalkhin Gol that would serve the Red Army so well and allow their tanks to successfully operate on the flanks of the Japanese forces. Although the Japanese would employ their own tanks early on, during the later stages of the fighting they would operate without armoured units. With relatively few anti-tank guns, in such terrain the Japanese had relatively few ways in which to effectively counter such Soviet tanks that had proven far more vulnerable in the face of light anti-tank guns in fighting over less tank-friendly terrain in Spain.

(*Opposite*) Sputnik 42389. The official caption for this photograph notes that it shows the commissar for an artillery *divizion* (not to be confused with division) giving the troops a political pep talk very early on in the Khalkhin Gol fighting on 5 June 1939. Their artillery piece is, once again as in Chapter 1, a 122mm Model 1910/1930 gun. Not only did the Red Army have a clear superiority in armour at Khalkhin Gol – and particularly during the later phases of the fighting – but enjoyed a superiority in artillery for most of the fighting as well. During what was in many ways a nineteenth-century set-piece battle fought with twentieth-century weapons, Soviet artillery was often firing directly on visible Japanese positions and from prepared Soviet positions – making fire control far easier than it would often be against German forces in more fluid circumstances in the near future.

(*Above*) Sputnik 39615. The Soviet infantry at Khalkhin Gol also had advantages over their Japanese counterparts, one of which was having a far more effective heavy machine gun than the Japanese Type 3 or 92. The ubiquitous Maxim Model 1910/1930 had served some of these Red Army men's fathers and grandfathers during the First World War, and like the similar British Vickers gun would serve them well during the Second World War. Although rather cumbersome, in a sustained fire role from defensive positions such machine guns continued to be as deadly to infantry as they had been in the First World War as long as they were kept supplied with ammunition. Note that the infantrymen behind the machine gunners are equipped only with rifles – submachine guns had yet to be adopted by the Red Army. Despite the increasingly modern weaponry being deployed in battle, the infantryman had still to be prepared to fight with his bayonet as affixed to the rifle in the right foreground of this picture.

(*Above*) Sputnik 41139. In overall command of Soviet forces at Khalkhin Gol prior to the arrival of Georgii Zhukov was Komandarm 2nd Rank Gregorii Shtern. Shtern was something of a rising star in the Red Army in the late 1930s, and the evidence suggests that he was at least a competent military leader. He had been the Head Soviet Adviser to Republican forces in Spain during 1937 and into early 1938, before commanding Soviet forces at Lake Khasan later that same year. Further promotion and a role as co-ordinator of Soviet forces in the Far East during the Khalkhin Gol

fighting followed, and he was awarded the prestigious title of Hero of the Soviet Union after the successful conclusion of the fighting there. Whilst his reputation was a little tarnished during the fighting in Finland in early 1940, this does not seem to have damaged his career, and he would command Soviet forces in the Far East from June 1940 through to the beginning of June 1941. Although Shtern had survived the period of intense purging of the Red Army command of 1937–1938, the purges continued at a reduced tempo into the first months of the Great Patriotic War. Despite having been awarded the title Hero of the Soviet Union less than two years earlier, Shtern was arrested on 7 June 1941 and executed in late October of that year, having been accused of the usual crime of participation in a Trotskyist conspiracy against Stalin and of spying for the Germans. That these charges lacked substance is evidenced by the fact that he was posthumously rehabilitated in 1954 after Stalin's death. The purging of the Soviet military leadership prior to the Great Patriotic War would undoubtedly hamper Soviet efforts to prepare for what was seen as the inevitable showdown with Nazi Germany. Note the attempts at camouflage of the position in this picture, where at Khalkhin Gol Red Army forces showed elements of a penchant for *maskirovka* that would be evident during the Great Patriotic War.

(*Above*) Sputnik 43033. A radio operator from an artillery unit joins the Young Communist organisation, the Komsomol, during the period of the Khalkhin Gol fighting. In the background are a pair of BA-20 armoured cars. Such armoured cars would play a meaningful role in the fighting in ensuring communications between Soviet units. Despite the contained nature of the Khalkhin Gol fighting, and opportunities for the use of field telephone communications, such communications were always subject to damage in the fighting, and the Red Army was poorly provided for with radios. In such circumstances communication between units and higher level command was frequently dependent on runners and commanders physically moving around the battlefield – often making use of armoured cars to provide at least some safety. Such armoured cars – with limited ground clearance – still had reasonable mobility on the grassland at Khalkhin Gol, although would largely be replaced by more mobile vehicles during the Great Patriotic War. A fairly staggering 133 Soviet armoured cars were lost at Khalkhin Gol, including 19 BA-20. [RASWW, p. 103]

(*Above*) Sputnik 40071. In command of Soviet forces during the later phases of operations on the ground at Khalkhin Gol – that is commanding the 57th Special Army Corps – was future Marshal of the Soviet Union Georgii Zhukov, seen here with other commanders in the Khalkhin Gol area. Although Soviet success here contributed to Zhukov's meteoric rise in the Red Army in the late 1930s and early 1940s, in his post-career memoirs he does not make much of his leadership at Khalkhin Gol. Whilst events there were certainly overshadowed by the Great Patriotic War, it is reasonable to surmise that Zhukov knew that success at Khalkhin Gol did not equate to battlefield success against the German Wehrmacht. At Khalkhin Gol the Japanese were outnumbered in terms of key indices such as artillery, and in general did not receive the relatively lavish material support that Red Army forces enjoyed, and were also ill-equipped for the sort of mechanised warfare that the Red Army and the Wehrmacht were preparing to fight in the late 1930s. The fighting at Khalkhin Gol was also constrained to a limited area, over which it was relatively easy to exercise command even with poor communications. Thus it is perhaps apparent why Zhukov seemed reticent to blow his own trumpet over a success that would soon be overshadowed by defeats at the hands of the Wehrmacht during the summer of 1941.

(*Opposite, above*) Sputnik 41135. Soviet pilots play dominoes during the early phases of the fighting at Khalkhin Gol. In the background their I-16 fighter aircraft stand waiting. When introduced in 1934, and particularly when up-engined, the I-16 was an advanced and capable aircraft. Flown by some of the better Soviet pilots available and operating over a confined area that did not tax Soviet command-and-control capabilities, Soviet air support at Khalkhin Gol proved relatively effective. Later model I-16s could certainly more than hold their own against the Ki-27 aircraft fielded by the Japanese, and continued to be a useful aircraft into the Second World War.

(*Opposite, below*) Sputnik 56153. One of the most significant Soviet achievements at Khalkhin Gol was logistical – sustaining a large force at a considerable distance from the Soviet European heartland. By the time Soviet forces launched their 20 August offensive that would lead to Japanese defeat, the 1st Army Group at Khalkhin Gol would consist of in the region of 57,000 troops. Communications both with and within Mongolia were poor, with the nearest railhead to Khalkhin Gol being some 700km away. One thing that the Soviet Union could do very well, however, was

focus effort and resources on a particular problem – and particularly where that was the only pressing problem at a given time. More than 6,000 motor vehicles allotted to the 57th Special Corps alone would help keep the corps fighting, at a time when the Red Army as a whole had a total of only 272,000 motor vehicles of all types. Aircraft had their role to play in the Soviet effort at Khalkhin Gol, where aircraft such as this licence-built DC-3 – in Soviet service the Li-2 – were used to fly in key personnel and supplies and fly out wounded, as shown here. In addition to losing nearly 10,000 killed, missing or who died from wounds in situ, a further 15,000 or more Soviet troops were wounded. From a similar strength force in terms of manpower, the Japanese would lose at least 8,000 killed and a slightly higher number wounded. [RASWW, pp. 102–5]

Chapter 3

Débâcles in Poland and Finland

More significant for the development of the Red Army than the Spanish Civil War or fighting against the Japanese in the Far East in 1937–1939 was the war against Finland, fought by the Soviet Union in late 1939 and early 1940. In August and September 1939 the Soviet Union signed the Molotov-Ribbentrop or Nazi-Soviet Pact and associated protocols that saw the Soviet Union and the Third Reich agree to carve up Poland and divide Eastern Europe into spheres of influence. For the Soviet Union the signing of the Pact was clearly a means to an end – to buy time before what was seen as an inevitable showdown with Nazi Germany. Just what the Soviet Union was buying time for has, however, been the subject of some debate. Soviet and post-Soviet Russian scholars have tended to portray the signing of the Pact as a measure simply designed to deflect German attentions from a peacefully inclined Soviet Union only interested in its own defence. That this defence seems to have required territorial acquisition – be that the eastern regions of Poland forcibly acquired in September 1939, or the Baltic Republics in June 1940 – was typically brushed over both at the time and in subsequent Soviet histories. Soviet defence also apparently required the acquisition of territory close to Leningrad from Finland, where Bolshevik leaders could remember how Finnish territory had been a springboard for German forces back in February 1918. It was the acquisition of this territory in particular during a costly war lasting from the end of November 1939 through to mid-March 1940 that provoked considerable soul-searching in the Soviet Union as to how the Red Army could be a better fighting force. During the war in Finland the Red Army lost in excess of 70,000 killed or died during casualty evacuation, with a further at least 16,292 who died in hospital and 39,369 missing in action and largely assumed killed. As such, the Red Army lost more than 125,000 troops in a very localised war against a much smaller and in many senses less well-equipped force, although the nearly 25,000 Finnish soldiers killed, missing and died from wounds speaks to the intensity of the fighting. [RASWW, p. 167] What Western accounts of the war tended to ignore was that the Red Army that performed so dismally in Finland in late 1939 had already shown improvement by the end of the war in mid-March 1940, and would continue to improve as the German invasion of 22 June 1941 approached. The more realistic training portrayed in Chapter 1 was just one of the results of the war with Finland.

Although Stalin and the Soviet leadership fully expected to go to war with Germany at some point in the future, after the signing of the Nazi-Soviet Pact it was hoped this would not be for some time. It was certainly hoped that Germany would get bogged down in war against Britain and France for a protracted period of time, allowing the Red Army to be readied for the inevitable showdown. Whether this showdown was supposed to involve the Soviet Union attacking Germany first is unclear, but there is certainly evidence that this was seen as a distinct possibility. In reality, Germany defeated British and French forces on the continent far more quickly than had been hoped for in Moscow. As Germany readied itself for war against the Soviet Union – despite not having knocked the British out of the war – Stalin seems to have tried to convince himself that Hitler would not be foolish enough to attack the Soviet Union. Certainly, with an 'active' Western Front and whilst the Soviet Union was providing Germany with the sort of raw materials it could hope to acquire if it invaded the Soviet Union, a German invasion did not seem to be a wise course of action to a Stalin who was assuming that Hitler was operating according to the logic of Realpolitik. Stalin, it seems, underestimated the role that ideology played in German foreign policy – an underestimation that would cost the Red Army dearly.

Sputnik 101829. In this photograph Soviet forces are shown passing through the village of Molochanka in what in Soviet terms was western Belorussia, in Polish terms eastern Poland, sometime after 17 September 1939. The Soviet invasion of Poland, which began on 17 September 1939, was hurriedly organised to take advantage of an opportunity offered by the Nazi-Soviet Pact signed only weeks before. The resulting Soviet advance was poorly organised. The photograph here shows an interesting mix of mechanised and horse-drawn elements of the Red Army. Throughout the Great Patriotic War Soviet infantry divisions would rely primarily on the horse. The armoured cars are BA-10 models, essentially a lightly armoured tank on wheels armed with a for the time potent 45mm gun. Although such armoured cars continued to be used throughout the Great Patriotic War, they were increasingly replaced in a reconnaissance role by either foreign-supplied light armoured vehicles or light tanks. The Red Army would meet only sporadic resistance as it occupied the eastern part of Poland, and particularly so in the border regions where the population was more likely to be ethnically Belorussian or Ukrainian.

Sputnik 25895. The official caption for this photo reads 'German military personnel chat with the commander of a Soviet tank regiment somewhere near Brest' – the date given being 20 September 1939. This clearly staged photo does not do justice to what must in many senses have been an uncomfortable meeting. Prior to the Nazi-Soviet Pact Nazi Germany had been vilified in the Soviet press, and all of a sudden it was effectively allied to the Soviet Union. What would now be termed 'friendly fire' incidents between German and Soviet forces can also not have helped the atmosphere as Soviet and German forces met. [e.g. RASWW, pp. 128–9] Whilst military personnel could easily find common ground through their professions, the ideological contexts in which the two armed forces were operating were very different.

(*Above*) Sputnik 432036. Another meeting apparently taking place on 20 September 1939, this time between Soviet and Polish soldiers. Whether this gathering continued to be quite as cordial as it appears after the photograph was taken is unclear. With much of the Polish armed forces fighting German forces, there were few Polish troops to oppose the Soviet advance. There were, however, a number of relatively small engagements between Soviet and Polish forces that led to losses on both sides. Because resistance was typically light – and perhaps because Soviet troops believed the propaganda that they would be met with open arms by those they were 'liberating' during their rapid advance – when there was meaningful resistance Soviet casualties were sometimes far from trivial. According to one count of Soviet casualties during the 'liberation' of Western Belorussia and the Ukraine, Soviet forces lost 852 killed or died during casualty evacuation, 144 missing and 2,002 wounded during active operations. [RASWW, p. 129] The tank behind the soldiers in the picture is an early model T-26 (Model 1932) with two small turrets with a machine gun in each. Of limited value as such tanks were by the start of the Second World War, there were still more than 1,000 of them in service with the Red Army at the beginning of April 1941 out of more than 1,600 manufactured.[5]

(*Opposite, above*) Sputnik 432037. This photograph in many ways highlights the complex inter-national situation in Eastern Europe in late 1939. Here Soviet troops are shown on the streets of Wilno – later Vilnius – apparently on 20 September 1939. At this time Wilno was part of Poland, having been effectively seized by Polish forces from the fledgling independent Lithuanian state in 1920. By the end of October 1939 the city would be handed over to Lithuanian control by Soviet forces, after Lithuania had 'invited' Soviet troops into the country that month under the auspices of a mutual assistance treaty imposed on it by the Soviet Union. At the end of the summer of 1940 the Soviet Union would compel Lithuania to join the Soviet Union as the Lithuanian Soviet Socialist Republic. The territories of the Baltic Republics were soon to be militarised by the Red Army as airfields and other military infrastructure was hurriedly constructed. Whether the Baltic Republics were intended as forward defensive positions for the Soviet Union or as a springboard for offensive operations westwards was to depend on circumstances. Any intention that the Baltic Republics would serve the latter function would, however, be quashed by Nazi Germany.

(*Left*) Sputnik 494034. This final photo relating to the Soviet invasion of Poland is dated 3 November 1939, and the caption reads 'a peasant tells a Red Army lieutenant of the location of a hostile element during the period of the liberation of Western Belorussia'. This combination of caption and date certainly suggests that the Red Army troops in the photo are engaged in the suppression of real or perceived opposition to Soviet rule after Polish territory had been formally incorporated into the Soviet Union. The lieutenant is still wearing a *Budenovka* hat, first introduced during the Russian Civil War. Such hats continued to be worn into the early period of the Great Patriotic War.

Sputnik 45612. Nazi Germany received considerable quantities of raw materials from the Soviet Union after the signing of the Nazi-Soviet Pact and associated economic agreements. Here, at Peremishl', a Soviet official signs over a shipment of oil to his German counterparts in February 1940. The fact that Nazi Germany was receiving such shipments right up until the German invasion of June 1941 was seen by Stalin as one of the reasons why Hitler would not actually order an invasion of the Soviet Union. That Hitler did just that – and despite the continued state of war between Nazi Germany and Britain – highlighted the extent to which ideology rather than prag-matism was informing German decision-making.

(*Above*) Sputnik 45604. A Soviet 203mm B-4 gun fires on Finnish positions in late 1939. Finnish forces could not hope to compete with the Red Army in terms of firepower, and such super-heavy Soviet artillery was used with some success to reduce Finnish fortifications, and particularly those of the so-called Mannerheim defence line. Soviet artillery was particularly potent when fired over open sights – that is when the crew could see the target – rather than being fired indirectly. Indirect fire required not only far greater training, but also the communications equipment for observers to relay instructions to the guns. During the Great Patriotic War Soviet forces would continue to use artillery in a direct-fire role far more frequently than their opponents or allies.

(*Overleaf*) Sputnik 45601. Soviet scouts receive instructions from a commander sometime in late 1939 on Finnish territory. Take note of their clothing – a far cry from the white camouflage smocks that are iconic for Soviet forces operating in winter during the Great Patriotic War. A reconnaissance soldier of the 17th Independent Ski Battalion operating against the Finns retrospectively recalled what he thought about the suitability of his equipment for his scouting role, writing: 'What sort of Scouts are we!?' – 'we are asses or camels loaded up and unable to turn around ... Our kit hampered us – we were neither manoeuvrable nor particularly mobile and operating in biting frost and deep snow!'[RASWW, p. 142] At least some of their Finnish opponents were far better equipped for operating away from the roads in the deep snow of the forest. In early January 1940 one Soviet staff officer noted that Red Army troops were all too often 'frightened by the forest and cannot ski', with some of the troops committed in Finland having being transferred from areas of the Soviet Union that did not offer similar conditions to those being experienced in Finland in winter. [RASWW, p. 145]

(*Below*) Sputnik 40453. These Red Army snipers – also pictured in late 1939 – are better equipped for the conditions than the scouts pictured in the previous photograph. After the débâcle of the early phase of the war in Finland – when such clothing was in short supply – the Red Army would make great efforts to be better equipped for winter warfare in the future, be that in terms of having the right clothing available, to actually training in winter conditions rather than solely during the summer. It was Finnish snipers – or 'cuckoos' as they were known to Soviet troops – who would develop a fearsome reputation during the Soviet war against Finland that would contribute to the Soviet penchant for sniping during the Great Patriotic War.

Sputnik 60383. Another area in which the Red Army would become much more capable during the Great Patriotic War was in conducting river crossings. Here Red Army forces have bridged a river in Karelia at the very end of 1939. The absence of specialised bridging equipment is very much evident, with the large number of vehicles backed up on the 'friendly' side of the river suggesting that getting across the river was a slow process. Few Soviet vehicles at this time were four- or all-wheel drive, further hampering the Soviet advance.

Sputnik 5658622. Soviet horse artillery on the move in Finland in late 1939. Soviet forces in Finland were very much road-bound thanks to the terrain, few four- or all-wheel drive vehicles, and a mindset that limited the willingness of Soviet commanders to move away from the few roads that were available. Long and slow-moving Soviet columns were very vulnerable to attack by Finnish forces from the flanks, with many Soviet troops perishing in the withering cold after they had been isolated from their comrades by Finnish troops.

Sputnik 5659460. A photo very much capturing the cold of the so-called Winter War. Here Red Army soldiers are wearing *Budenovka* hats and great coats in Finland in late 1939. Looking little different than some of their predecessors during the Russian Civil War, they would suffer and die in Finland by the tens of thousands at the hands of both the Finns and the cold.

(*Above*) Sputnik 872655. Here a Soviet T-28 tank is shown in Finland later in the war in early February 1940, by which point the Red Army was starting to get its house in order. Not only were the infantry starting to use far more appropriate small unit tactics against fortified Finnish positions, but the Red Army was deploying tanks with some effect where Finnish ranged anti-tank weapons were few. The Soviet Union had developed a number of multi-turreted tanks during the 1930s, with the T-28 being the most numerous. Although on paper they seemed a good idea, in practice these multi-turreted tanks were not only unwieldy in terms of size, but could not be provided with strong armour if they were not to become even less mobile than they already were. Co-ordination of the fire of multiple turrets was also something that in practice proved extremely difficult for an overtaxed tank commander, and the multi-turreted tank concept was finally abandoned by the Red Army after the war in Finland. The bulk of Soviet stocks of such tanks were expended during the first days of the Great Patriotic War.

(*Overleaf*) Sputnik 54203. Here Soviet forces enter Riga in June 1940. Although Soviet troops had been based in the Baltic Republics since the autumn of 1939, a full Soviet occupation of the Baltic Republics did not take place until the following summer, after the defeat of Anglo-French forces in France. During the same period Soviet forces would also occupy Bessarabia further south. After Soviet forces moved into the Baltic Republics the Red Army would have to expend considerable resources in developing the infrastructure for the basing of troops that previously had been based further east. The development of this infrastructure and indeed fortifications along the border with Nazi Germany was far from complete when Axis forces launched Operation Barbarossa – the invasion of the Soviet Union – on 22 June 1941.

(*Below*) Sputnik 61676. Although taking place in late August 1941, this photo of Soviet troops entering Tabriz in Iran is included in this chapter for the sake of coherence given that this chapter has Soviet pre-war or in this case early-war expansion as a theme. Britain and the Soviet Union jointly invaded Iran at the beginning of the Great Patriotic War, and in doing so secured for the Allies what would become an important conduit for Western Allied assistance to the Soviet Union during the second half of the Second World War. Soviet and British troops would pull out of Iran in 1946. Note how the soldiers pictured here are equipped with the helmet that would be used by the bulk of Soviet troops during the Great Patriotic War, the then new Model 1939/1940 helmet.

Chapter 4

'Barbarossa'

Despite preparations for future war that had lasted more than a decade, and specifically from 1936 for a war against Nazi Germany, the Soviet Union was caught off guard by the Axis invasion of 22 June 1941 – codenamed 'Barbarossa'. Regardless of whether Soviet intentions were purely defensive, or Soviet military expansion and reorganisation was geared towards offensive operations westwards at some point in the future, the Red Army was not ready to fight in June 1941. Stalin had certainly convinced himself to at least some extent that Hitler would be foolish to attack the Soviet Union that summer, although Soviet forces had nonetheless massed in the border regions, for what purpose remains unclear. That a significant proportion of the Soviet Union's vast mechanised forces were concentrated along the Soviet border with Nazi Germany and her allies – with divisions in many instances only partially manned and with insufficient supplies – put them in a very vulnerable position that German forces would quickly exploit. Very few contemporary Soviet photos exist of those mechanised forces that summer that would fight some of the largest tank battles in history in the Ukraine, in part because their defeat was so complete. Ordered to counter-attack against the advancing Axis forces rather than attempting some sort of orderly retreat, the Red Army lost not only thousands of tanks and other pieces of equipment, but millions of soldiers caught in vast German encirclements that would take Axis forces weeks to fully reduce. Nonetheless, the Red Army that fought the Axis advance that summer was undoubtedly tactically at least more capable than it would have been had Soviet forces gone to war back in 1938 or 1939, and was starting to receive an increasing amount of new equipment that would be the match or superior to even the latest German equivalents – the T-34 tank being the iconic example. Behind those Soviet forces destroyed in the border regions lay a second echelon, soon to be joined by fresh if often poorly trained and equipped units that were the result of a full mobilisation of the Red Army and the creation of new units. The hundreds of thousands who would be killed or taken prisoner only to die in German camps were in many ways lives squandered, but at the same time they exacted a steady toll on advancing Axis forces that would gradually contribute to a degradation of Axis combat capabilities. At a cost of hundreds of thousands of lives, Hitler's plans to defeat the Soviet Union in a single crushing blow that summer were thwarted.

The Axis on the offensive – the Great Patriotic War from 22 June 1941 to 19 November 1942.

Sputnik 62161. The first photo in the first chapter of those dealing with the Great Patriotic War is perhaps surprisingly of a German: Alfred Liskow. Liskow – a German communist born in Kolberg in 1910 – would during the evening of 21 June 1941 desert from his unit and swim across the Bug river to Soviet positions and inform his captors of the German invasion to come that forthcoming morning. By the time his testimony had been pushed up the Soviet chain of command, the wheels of a Soviet response to the imminent threat of invasion were starting to turn as Soviet forces were all too late put on a higher state of alert. Many Soviet units would not receive these orders before the first German bombs fell and German forces launched themselves eastwards. Despite his heroism, Liskow's fate in Soviet hands is uncertain. Although used as a willing propaganda tool by the Soviet side – with this photograph appearing in the Soviet press – it seems that his critical stance over the activities of the Soviet-sponsored Communist International or Comintern prior to the war might have played a role in the fact that he did not survive to see the defeat of Nazi Germany.

Sputnik 2172. Some of the Soviet wounded of the first days of the war make their way back from the front line. Although it is unclear where and exactly when this picture was taken, it no doubt shows a typical scene being repeated across the front. If lucky, these two soldiers were able to escape the encirclements that would see so many of their compatriots end up in German PoW camps, and in which they would all too often not survive the winter of 1941/1942 as a result of wilful neglect.

Sputnik 65718. Another image from the first days of the war, this time by a different photographer, showing a Soviet soldier having his wounds dressed with the assistance of Soviet civilians. This photograph, and the next concerning refugees, gives some sense of the chaos at the front during the first days of the war.

Sputnik 432. A long line of refugees retreats from the fighting on the horizon during the first days of the war, in this case somewhere in the Ukraine. As the summer progressed, Soviet civilians were discouraged from retreating with the Red Army unless their evacuation was a sanctioned part of the relocation of Soviet industry to the east. Such a policy certainly meant that disruption caused to forces moving to the front by refugees moving in the opposite direction was minimised, but at a cost. As a result of such a policy a peak of more than 70 million Soviet citizens would find themselves living on Axis-occupied territory. Those who were able would be expected to join or assist the Communist underground or Soviet partisan units operating near where they lived. As shown in Chapter 9, many did join the partisans, and many lost their lives not only resisting foreign occupation but also in German and Axis retribution against the civilian population for the activities of the underground and partisans nearby or as part of the Final Solution to the Jewish Question – the Holocaust.

(*Above*) Sputnik 662757. New recruits for the Red Army in Moscow on 23 June 1941. Although the Axis invasion prompted a full mobilisation and successive waves of conscription into the Red Army, at the beginning of the war in the cities in particular there was no shortage of volunteers for the Red Army. Although keen to harness this initial enthusiasm to defend the Motherland, the authorities did, however, have to make sure not to allow the volunteering of skilled workers to denude the factories of personnel who were likely to be of greater service in the rear. Sadly many volunteers would be thrown into action with only limited training as the Red Army's need for replacements took precedence over desirable training regimens.

(*Opposite, above*) Sputnik 594348. This second picture of new recruits for the Red Army was taken on 24 June in Moscow, and shows them being provided with their uniforms. The scale of Soviet losses during the summer and autumn of 1941, combined with stocks lost to the enemy and damage done to production by the war, would mean that many items of clothing for the Red Army would soon be in relatively short supply. Long boots as shown here that used a lot of leather would soon no longer be available for distribution to mere rank-and-file conscripts. As the war progressed the Western Allies would provide many millions of pairs of boots for the Red Army.

(*Opposite, below*) Sputnik 662733. In this picture, also taken on 23 June, recently mobilised Red Army troops are shown heading towards the front. Note that they are equipped with both the Model 1936 and Model 1939/1940 helmets. The sign on the left reads, 'Our task is righteous, the enemy will be crushed, victory will be ours!' This is a quote from the end of Soviet foreign minister Viacheslav Molotov's address to the Soviet people of the previous day, announcing the beginning of the war. [See GPW, p. 43 for the introduction to this speech] That Stalin didn't make that speech was no doubt noted by some, and contributed to the notion in some Western Cold War-era literature on the war that Stalin was somehow incapacitated at the beginning of the war. Stalin was indeed briefly incapacitated at the very end of the month after he had become aware of the capture of the Belorussian capital Minsk by German forces and the poor state of the forces of the Western Front on the key Moscow axis. However, the evidence available suggests that Stalin had soon recovered from his apparently short-lived depressive state in good time in order to give his first speech of the war to the Soviet people on 3 July. [See GPW, pp. 49–50].

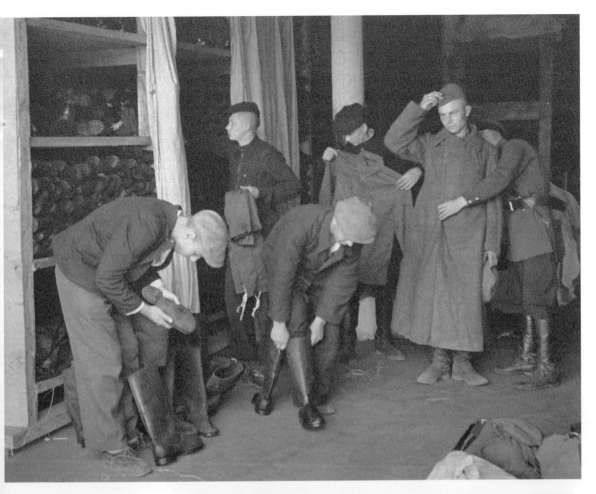

НАШЕ ДЕЛО ПРАВОЕ.
ВРАГ БУДЕТ РАЗБИТ.
ПОБЕДА БУДЕТ
ЗА НАМИ!

Sputnik 601169. BA-10 armoured cars near the Romanian border early in the war. The Axis advance in the south began after that in the centre and north, giving Soviet forces in the region a chance to prepare for combat. Consequently the Axis advance was slower in the south, creating a situation where Axis forces in the centre were soon significantly further east than those in the south. A halt of the Axis advance in the centre and transfer of resources to north and south helped the Soviets achieve a rare operational success in the summer of 1941 in the centre at El'nia in early September.

Sputnik 2517. A cavalry unit of Pavel Belov's 2nd Cavalry Corps near Tiraspol' in Moldavia on 11 July 1941. According to the war diary for what would become the 1st Guards Cavalry Corps, Belov's corps was on the defensive along the river Raut or Reut, a tributary of the Dnestr.[6] Tiraspol' was on Romanian territory prior to Bessarabia being ceded to the Soviet Union in June 1940. In early August the city was occupied by Romanian troops fighting as part of the Axis, and was then incorporated into Transnistria. In the foreground a Maxim machine gun is mounted on a horse-drawn carriage, together known as a *tachanka*. The crew appear to be watching for aircraft, at a time when the Luftwaffe typically had air superiority over the battlefield.

Sputnik 612. Taken on 5 August 1941, this photograph shows a Soviet sailor chatting with an Odessan militiaman prior to the point at which the port of Odessa was encircled on its landward sides by Axis forces. In many Soviet cities threatened by Axis forces such workers' militia were hastily organised and thrown into their defence alongside the Red Army. Although many Soviet citizens had either served in the Red Army or had some sort of pre-conscription military training, such militia units were no substitute for regular Red Army units.

Sputnik 59232. This very evocative picture shows Red Army soldiers in action somewhere near Odessa after it had been encircled on its landward sides by Axis forces but before it had been captured by the enemy. The siege of Odessa would in fact last from early August until mid-October 1941, with Soviet naval forces initially bringing in troops and supplies by sea and later evacuating them as the prospects of holding out deteriorated.

Sputnik 6046555. A third picture taken near Odessa in late August 1941 showing sailors hitching a ride on a 'Komsomolets' artillery tractor. Such tractors had been produced prior to the war with the intention of providing the Red Army's light artillery – including anti-tank guns – with a motorised means to more rapidly deploy than if they were towed by horses. In all, 7,780 were manufactured between 1937 and 1941.[7] Most 'Komsomolets' tractors were lost during 1941 and not replaced as Soviet industry focused its productive effort on the production of tanks. Such light armoured tractors would be largely replaced in the towing role with either lorries of either Soviet or US manufacture, or other vehicles supplied under Lend-Lease. Sailors were frequently called on to fight on land during the Great Patriotic War, with substantial numbers not only participating in the defence of such port cities as Odessa and Leningrad, but also participating in the fighting further inland for cities such as Stalingrad.

Sputnik 76. The official caption for this photograph reads 'Soldiers of one of the units of the 20th Army (Western Front) engaged in battle on the banks of the Dnepr River, west of Dorogobuzh.' Dorogobuzh is in the Smolensk region, the scene of prolonged and intense fighting. The historic town of Dorogobuzh was almost equidistant between Smolensk and Viaz'ma on the key Moscow axis – the former captured by German forces on 16 July, the latter associated with of one of the major German encirclements of Soviet forces in October 1941, during operations that will be considered in Chapter 5. To the south of Dorogobuzh was the town of El'nia, briefly liberated by Soviet forces in early September only to be recaptured by German forces at the beginning of the following month. The troops shown here were quite possibly involved in those early September Soviet offensive operations. Dorogobuzh would fall to the Wehrmacht very early on during renewed German offensive operations in early October, and the 20th Army was subsequently caught in the Viaz'ma encirclement – the second time it had been encircled that summer. The troops in the picture are clearly in rather pristine uniforms, suggesting that they were relatively fresh troops and even that this was perhaps their first taste of combat. Note also their lack of helmets – not unusual during this period of the war and something that was relatively typical for Soviet forces throughout the war. Whilst at times there were shortages of helmets, even when they were available some Soviet troops chose not to wear them for reasons of comfort. Without a helmet such troops were of course at a significantly greater risk of suffering often fatal head injuries due to shrapnel in particular.

Sputnik 1228. Red Army troops are once again shown in action here in September 1941 in the Smolensk region. The official caption notes that they are shown in action fighting for heights on the right bank of the Dnepr river. As in the previous photo, they appear to be relatively fresh troops, and are similarly not wearing helmets. Note the commander on the left who does not have a rifle – making it plain to German snipers and other combatants that he is an officer. The Red Army – as many other armies – would as the war progressed move away from allowing junior officers to single themselves out in such a fashion.

Sputnik 2066. The artillery piece shown here is in action in early September 1941 somewhere close to the dam of the Dnepr Hydroelectric Station constructed during the first of the Soviet Union's Five-Year Plans in southern Ukraine, at what had been Aleksandrovsk, later Zaporizhia. The gun shown is a relatively modern piece for the time: an M-10 Model 1938 122mm Howitzer. Such artillery pieces, of which well over 3,000 had been produced by the end of 1941 alone, would serve throughout the Great Patriotic War. Some of the examples captured by German forces were used to make up German artillery units. It is quite possible that such was the fate of this particular weapon.

Chapter 5

On the Moscow Axis

By the end of September 1941 Axis forces – primarily German – had destroyed much of the Red Army that had existed in June 1941. By the end of what in Soviet terms was known as 'The Kiev Strategic Defensive Operation' that ran from 7 July through to 26 September 1941, the Red Army had lost more than 600,000 troops as 'irrecoverable losses' in the Ukraine, with the South-Western Front alone losing more than 500,000. [RASWW, p.247] 'Irrecoverable losses' were, as the term suggests, those losses which the Red Army could not reasonably expect to get back, meaning not only those killed, but also those missing and taken prisoner by the enemy. Of the more than 600,000 troops lost in the Kiev region in an encirclement of epic proportions, the vast majority were lost as prisoners of war. However, although Axis forces had captured much of the western part of the Soviet Union as well, they had not destroyed the Soviet ability to create and equip new units – as well as transfer units from the Far East that had been guarding against the possibility of further Japanese aggression in the region.

During the pause in the German advance on the key central axis towards Moscow in the late summer of 1941, the Soviet Union managed to throw fresh forces into the distant defence of the capital. When the German advance on Moscow resumed in earnest on 2 October 1941 these troops would ensure that the German advance would be fiercely, if not necessarily coherently, resisted. Soon, as the previous month near Kiev, hundreds of thousands of Soviet troops would be encircled in pockets of resistance near Briansk and Viaz'ma as German forces showed their operational superiority. German successes on the Moscow axis would see a state of siege declared for Moscow on 16 October, with plans being made for the evacuation of the Soviet government to the east. However, operational superiority alone would not win the war for Germany as often stubborn Soviet resistance, fatigue, both losses of and wear-and-tear on equipment, and issues with extended supply lines across territory not cleared of roving bands of Red Army personnel cut off from their lines took their toll on German forces. All of these factors would prove an impediment to the German advance even without the onset of the rainy season in the autumn, that would see the German advance literally bogged down in the face of mud and Soviet resistance by the end of October. By the time the German advance on Moscow could be resumed in earnest in early November the Red Army had once again been able to throw new units in front of German forces. By the end of November increasingly small German spearheads sought to punch through to the Soviet capital but to no avail, as the Red Army found the strength to launch local counter-attacks that would soon snowball into a major counter-offensive. The German Blitzkrieg had been halted, and the much-vaunted Wehrmacht would be thrown back from the gates of the Soviet capital. This chapter examines the Soviet defence of Moscow from the start of renewed German offensive operations towards Moscow at the beginning of October 1941 – Operation 'Typhoon' – to the weekend of 5–7 December when localised Soviet counter-attacks became something much more significant.

(*Below*) Sputnik 77. Red Army troops of an undisclosed unit defend a bridge from dug-in positions sometime around the very beginning of October 1941 in the Smolensk region. These quite possibly fresh troops would soon find themselves in the maelstrom of battle as German mechanised forces punched through Soviet lines and raced eastwards, leaving the infantry to 'mop up' often encircled Soviet forces left in their wake. Clearly at the point that this photograph was taken the weather had not yet taken a turn for the worse – although the temperature had clearly dropped from the summer the leaves were still on many trees and the first snows had yet to fall.

(*Opposite, above*) Sputnik 2551. Less than two weeks later than in the previous photograph and the weather had clearly shifted, bringing the first snow to the battlefields on the Moscow axis. This photograph is dated 10 October, and shows Soviet tanks moving up to the front through a village somewhere in the Moscow region. Both tanks are T-26s – the lead tank a later model and the second tank an earlier one. Note the whitewash applied to the tanks as camouflage in the new weather conditions. During this period of the fighting on the Moscow axis the Red Army would throw almost any tanks it had available into the fray in a desperate attempt to halt German forces on defence lines that had been constructed to protect Moscow.

(*Opposite, below*) Sputnik 3500. Muscovites involved in the construction of a defensive line somewhere outside Moscow during October 1941. Thousands of civilians were mobilised to construct the series of defensive lines for the protection of the capital in what was not only arduous work, but work also made more onerous by the deteriorating weather conditions. Note that both men and women alike are involved in digging these positions.

Sputnik 616433. This is a relatively rare photograph in that it shows Soviet motorcycle troops early in the war, in this case on 16 October somewhere in the Moscow region. Both German and Soviet forces – but particularly the former – would make use of the motorcycle in a reconnaissance role early in the war. Later in the war the use of the motorcycle in this role was not as frequent for German forces, with armoured cars and other armoured vehicles being preferred, in part because of the greater protection from the enemy that they offered. Soviet use of the motorcycle seems actually to have increased by the mid-war period. By the date this photograph was taken German forces had breached the Mozhaisk line defending Moscow – about halfway between the city and Viaz'ma – and the evacuation of the Soviet capital had been set in motion the previous day.

Sputnik 601158. Although this picture might be confused with pictures showing the famous parade held in Moscow on 7 November 1941 to celebrate the anniversary of the Russian Revolution, it was in fact apparently taken on 23 October. It shows Soviet artillery on its way to the front through the streets of Moscow. Of note are the older artillery pieces being towed by lorries: it was not only older tanks but also other equipment that would be thrown into action in defence of Moscow. Note that the guns have wooden-spoked wheels, which would reduce the speed they could be safely towed to little more than a fast march.

Sputnik 604269. Although taken during the summer of 1941, this photograph was selected because it so effectively symbolises Moscow and indeed the Soviet Union at war. Clearly shown in the background is the Kremlin in all its glory, pictured underneath threatening clouds. The anti-aircraft gun in the foreground is being crewed by both men and women. During the period with which this chapter is concerned Moscow would come under frequent air attack.

(*Opposite, above*) Sputnik 279. The German assault on Moscow in the autumn of 1941 saw two German pincers seek to encircle the Soviet capital from the north-east and south. The defence of the south hinged to a large extent on the defence of the town of Tula. Early in the war Soviet forces had made little use of built-up areas for defence, but were soon ordered to do so more frequently. Whilst defending urban areas meant that the civilian population would suffer more from the ravages of war in their locale, the defence of urban areas sapped German strength and proved to be a great leveller in combat between the Red Army and the Wehrmacht. Here an anti-aircraft gun is being used in a ground defence role somewhere in what are probably the outskirts of Tula at the end of November 1941.

(*Opposite, below*) Sputnik 2558. Here Soviet troops are shown dug-in covering a street close to the centre of Tula on the same day as Sputnik 279 above. The soldier on the right is armed with an anti-tank rifle – a weapon used by the Red Army well into the Great Patriotic War even as other armies had all but abandoned the concept. Soviet anti-tank rifles were more effective than shorter versions in service with other armies, but were still unable to penetrate the armour of increasingly well protected tanks. Such anti-tank rifles did continue to have value against lighter armoured vehicles, and were also used at times for sniping – including against aircraft!

(*Above*) Sputnik 5686100. Soviet enthusiasm for the anti-tank rifle is well illustrated in this picture of a tank destruction unit pictured somewhere on Russian territory during November 1941. To some extent the PTRD anti-tank rifle was used to make up for insufficient anti-tank guns in Soviet rifle divisions in late 1941, although they were a poor substitute.

(*Left*) Sputnik 431876. A poster by Soviet artist Boris Mukhin simply stating 'We will defend [our] native Moscow!', with the text accompanied by a soldier, a militiaman, a sailor and a woman serving in an unconfirmed role in defence of Moscow. There were in fact relatively few sailors involved in the defence of Moscow, but the poster is in keeping with Soviet propaganda stemming from the Revolution and Civil War in portraying not only different services but also civilians in a militia role, at the time of the Revolution having been known as the Red Guard.

(*Above*) Sputnik 669661. These KV-1 tanks are shown on a street in Moscow just after the famous parade held on 7 November 1941 to celebrate the anniversary of the October Revolution (being celebrated on the appropriate day in the new calendar). The parade in 1941 was notable because it took place when Moscow was officially under siege, and where the Red Army units involved frequently found themselves dispatched to the front line soon after having paraded through Red Square. Holding the parade in such circumstances represented a propaganda coup for Stalin and the Soviet leadership, which would go some way to convincing those at home and abroad that the Soviet Union was not finished. These KV-1 tanks would have been particularly in demand at the front line at this time, representing – along with the T-34 – the best of the Soviet tanks then available. The KV-1 tank was almost impervious to the lighter anti-tank and tank guns then in use with the German Wehrmacht, often requiring the expenditure of considerable resources on the part of German forces for their neutralisation. Most famously these tanks would be stopped by the infamous 88mm German anti-aircraft gun in one of its increasingly numerous guises. Fortunately for the Wehrmacht, production of the KV-1 was only just picking up speed when German forces invaded the Soviet Union, and only 368 of all modifications were on hand as of 1 April 1941.[8]

(*Opposite, above*) Sputnik 390. This photograph once again shows Soviet anti-tank troops armed with anti-tank rifles, also in November 1941. The location in this instance is somewhere near the small town of Zvenigorod to the immediate west of Moscow. This picture is particularly suitable for inclusion here in the sense that it gives a good feel for some of the terrain being fought over in late 1941 on the Moscow axis, where between settlements there were frequent and often sizeable forested areas that often were far from good tank country. The picture also makes it plain that winter conditions hampered the activities of both sides, the icy conditions here making climbing this piece of steeper ground that bit more difficult.

(*Opposite, below*) Sputnik 58848. By late November 1941 it was far more likely than it had been only weeks before that Soviet troops would be fielding captured German equipment against its previous owners, as Soviet troops were by now more frequently getting the better of their German opponents in the increasingly small-scale engagements on the approaches to Moscow. Here one 'Sergeant Zhruravlev' is pictured with his gun crew using a captured 5cm PaK 38 anti-tank gun against German forces. The capture of these guns with ammunition by Soviet crews would have been a boon in late 1941 at a time when the Red Army was short of anti-tank guns.

(*Above*) Sputnik 5822580. This photograph, taken on 20 November 1941, actually shows Soviet troops in action on the streets of Rostov-on-Don in the far south of the Soviet Union rather than near Moscow. It was here, rather than at Moscow, that German forces suffered their first obvious reverse, as they were pushed back from the Caucasus in late November 1941. They would soon also suffer a similar fate not only on the outskirts of Moscow but near Tikhvin, east of Leningrad. Note that the Soviet troops in this picture are still only equipped with rifles, as the sub-machine guns that would become almost ubiquitous in the Red Army were still not available in large numbers. Being equipped only with rifles would put Soviet troops at a disadvantage against German forces in some situations where German troops at least had some MP 40 sub-machine guns for use at relatively close quarters.

(*Opposite*) Sputnik 2549. The final picture in this chapter gives what is in many senses a taste of things to come on a larger scale in Chapter 8: the Red Army on the attack. In this photograph Soviet cavalry are shown on the attack somewhere near Moscow on 2 December 1941. By this time Soviet forces were increasingly frequently engaged in local offensive operations that would soon snowball into a wider offensive near Moscow during the weekend of 5–7 December. Cavalry undoubtedly had a useful role to play over the vast expanses of the Soviet Union and Eastern Europe, and would continue to be employed by the Red Army through to the end of the war. As will be further discussed in Chapter 8, the horse offered considerable mobility to light forces even in winter. Whilst creating a dramatic impression, cavalry charges such as this one were, however, only very rarely effective against any sort of organised opposition – the horse was best left as a means of transport, not of assault. In one particularly egregious instance in mid-November two regiments of the 44th Cavalry Division charged dug-in German troops of the 106th Infantry Division near Musino on the approaches to Klin to the north-east of Moscow. One German observer described some of the cavalry as offering 'an unbelievably beautiful sight on a clear sunny winter landscape' as they went into the attack 'with gleaming sabres above their heads'. The massacre that seems to

have followed was in stark contrast to such words, offering 'a nightmarish performance' for the German soldiers. [RASWW, p. 311] Total losses for the 44th Cavalry Division from 16 November to 21 December 1941 were a horrendous 3,299 men (of whom 405 were reported as killed and 1,624 missing) and 3,595 horses (of which 1,830 were reported as killed and 1,471 missing).[9]

Chapter 6

Leningrad Besieged

During the summer and autumn of 1941 Axis forces destroyed much of the pre-war strength of the Red Army. Millions of Red Army personnel found themselves trapped in multiple instances of encirclement on the Moscow axis, both during the first weeks of the war and in October. In the south the encirclement of mid-September near Kiev ripped the heart out of Soviet forces in that region, not only facilitating the advance of Axis forces towards the Caucasus, but removing a southern threat to the German advance on Moscow. In the north, however, both on the axis of advance towards Leningrad and in the Arctic in the far north, Red Army forces did not suffer the encirclements of their colleagues to the south. On the Leningrad axis the Red Army was pushed back towards what had been the capital prior to the winter of 1918, but in relatively good order by the standards of the summer as a whole. In many ways this is explained by the geography of the region, where the combination of lakes, forest and marshes was not suited to the broad mechanised sweeps possible in the centre and particularly on the open steppe in the south. On the Leningrad axis, having the Baltic Sea as a flank further limited German opportunities for manoeuvre. Nonetheless, despite the Soviet authorities having formed defensive lines to protect Leningrad from the south – and having thrown poorly trained militia units into their defence in a desperate attempt to stem the German advance – by 8 September German forces had reached Lake Ladoga to the east of Leningrad and cut the city's land communications with the remainder of the Soviet Union. With the Finns having reoccupied Karelian territory to the north as part of their 'continuation war' with the Soviet Union, Leningrad was hemmed in and under siege.

Although German plans for the invasion of the Soviet Union – Operation 'Barbarossa' – had slated Leningrad for capture by German forces, after they had reached the outskirts of the city in September 1941 plans changed. Fighting for the city would undoubtedly have proven costly for German forces, and the decision was made instead to lay siege to the city and starve, shell and bomb it into submission before ultimately levelling it. The siege of Leningrad had begun, and would drag on until January 1943 before limited land communications with the Soviet heartland were restored, and January 1944 before the siege could be said to have been fully lifted. During that period more than a million of its inhabitants would die – many of muscle wastage caused by starvation or of illnesses that in other circumstances they might very well have survived. The vast majority of those who died did so during the winter of 1941/1942, during which the deaths of so many made it more feasible to feed the remainder. During this period being a soldier was for once something of a saving grace, since rations for front-line troops were better than for other categories of Leningrad's defenders and inhabitants. For much of the war – as the dramas of the Battles of Moscow, Stalingrad and Kursk were fought elsewhere – Leningrad held out stubbornly, relying to a large extent on its own resources. There were, however, numerous attempts to lift the siege, a number of which failed because they were far too ambitious in their aims and went far beyond trying to simply punch a corridor through to the city. This chapter is concerned with the siege of Leningrad, and illustrates not only events leading up to and the siege itself, but also the eventual relief of the city.

(*Opposite, above left*) Sputnik 715710. This first photo was taken on 29 June 1941, and shows children being evacuated from the city of Leningrad into the rural areas around it. Although at this time the threat to the city from German forces to the south was not acute, Finnish forces were moving towards the city from the north. Leningrad's vulnerability in 1918 when it was Petrograd certainly provided a precedent for seeing it as vulnerable in 1941, and that was at a time when aerial bombing of cities was in its infancy. According to statistics for the city's Evacuation Commission, from 29 June to 27 August 395,091 children were evacuated from the city, but because of enemy action 175,400 were returned to Leningrad. Additionally during the same period 164,320 'workers and administrative personnel' were evacuated, along with industrial concerns that were relocated to safer areas to the east, as well as an additional 104,691 residents. Although this meant that 488,703 had been evacuated from the city, 147,500 were evacuated to Leningrad from the Soviet Baltic Republics and Karelia. [GPW, pp. 150–1] Subsequently some of those from within Leningrad were evacuated by boat or by air before Lake Ladoga had frozen over, or across the ice road that during the winter months linked Leningrad to Soviet-controlled territory.

(*Opposite, above right*) Sputnik 802. With the city cut off from the remainder of Soviet territory, Soviet soldiers of the 115th Rifle Division are pictured here awaiting an enemy counter-attack after they had secured positions on the left bank of the Neva river near Leningrad during the latter half of September 1941. The division had previously been based in Karelia, but had been pushed back on Leningrad by the Finns. With the division reinforced, two battalions of the division then took part in operations to seize a bridgehead over the Neva river to the south-east of the city during the night of 19/20 September 1941. During 6–7 October the remainder of the division was transferred across the Neva to participate in fighting on the bridgehead that would see the division take heavy losses. A printed version of the division's history for the first year of the war makes specific note of the poor rations available to its troops during this period given the food situation in Leningrad, and of the 'exhaustion and physical weakness of soldiers and commanders who had just left Leningrad hospitals'.[10]

(*Opposite, below*) Sputnik 770. Soviet militia are shown here in action somewhere on the outskirts of Leningrad during October 1941, after the city had been encircled by enemy forces. At this time Stalin clearly did not expect that the siege would last as long as it eventually would. General Zhukov had been given command of the Leningrad Front in early September, but by the point this photograph was taken had probably headed back to the Moscow region to take command of what would become the Western Front there. Such militia units were hastily thrown into action both near Moscow and Leningrad, where they took heavy losses. Militia divisions lacked not only some of the training and equipment afforded to regular divisions, but also the same level of support from artillery and other units. In addition to their rifles, these militiamen do at least seem to have a hand grenade each, placed on the ground in front of them ready to be used to repel an enemy attack.

(*Above*) Sputnik 323. Soviet sailors of the Baltic Fleet on their way to the front, also sometime during October 1941. By this point, with the city encircled, their ships were bottled up in the Gulf of Finland with little to do than provide fire-support for ground forces with their guns. Such fire-support did not require all of their crews, meaning that many of the sailors could be sent to the front as ground troops. Their footwear is far from ideal for ground forces, and they also lack helmets and greatcoats.

(*Opposite, above*) Sputnik 637272. In many ways better provided for are these Soviet reinforcements heading towards the front in late October 1941. They are photographed here not far from the famous Winter Palace in the centre of Leningrad, marching past the former Tsarist Admiralty building. Note once again the absence of helmets, and the fact that they are all armed only with rifles – typical for this period of the war. It is unclear whether these soldiers are part of a militia or a regular army unit.

(*Opposite, below*) Sputnik 286. Soviet troops with a camouflaged F-22 (76.2mm Divisional Gun Model 1936) divisional artillery piece sometime in early November 1941 during the 2nd Siniavino Operation – one of many attempts to lift the siege of Leningrad. Although the snow on the ground suggests colder temperatures, the churned-up road is testimony to how bad conditions could get for the mobility of either side during the autumn. The slightly higher temperatures near Leningrad would mean that such conditions were more likely to last longer on that sector of the front than near Moscow. The F-22 gun in this picture entered service in 1936 as a modernised version of an earlier model, with the Red Army receiving 2,932 of these guns by the end of 1939. Most of these guns were either destroyed or captured during the fighting in 1941, making their presence in a photograph one indicator of its date. German forces would use some of these guns on tank destroyers where into 1942 German forces faced a shortage of guns with ballistic characteristics sufficient to deal with the armour of the KV-series and T-34 tanks.

(*Opposite, above*) Sputnik 60024. Although many sailors of the Baltic Fleet were sent as infantry to the front line of the ground war, some at least were required to man their ships' guns so that they could operate in support of ground forces in the defence of Leningrad. In the event of German forces looking likely to seize the city, plans had been made to scuttle the Baltic Fleet. Here the destroyer *Opitnii* is shown at her mooring in Leningrad providing fire-support to the Red Army in February 1942. Given that her 'main armament' was reportedly removed from the ship at this time, we can assume that she lacks her forward gun mount, which would explain why pictures of her during this period only show her rear guns that were pointing in the right direction for her to provide fire-support from her berth! This particular vessel was the first in a class that never went into series production, and in fact this ship entered service and left it as a floating battery.[11]

(*Opposite, below*) Sputnik 666681. The aircraft in the foreground of this photograph is an I-16 fighter of the 7th Fighter Air Corps of the Soviet Air Defence forces (PVO) shown in October 1941. In the background Li-2 transport aircraft – originally given the designation PS-84, but in both cases a Soviet-manufactured DC-3 'Dakota' – take off. These aircraft were used in increasing numbers to fly people and supplies in and out of the city, and were particularly valuable during the period when Lake Ladoga was icing up and hence was not navigable by boats, but when the ice wasn't yet solid enough for vehicles to drive on. The German Luftwaffe of course attempted to interdict this supply route into the city, meaning that fighter aircraft such as that pictured here had to be allocated for the defence of the air corridor.

(*Above*) Sputnik 62127. This next photograph shows Li-2 aircraft flying over Lake Ladoga in March 1942. The official caption for this photograph suggests that the aircraft were carrying food, which was indeed one of the categories of goods being flown into the city. Throughout the year these flights allowed food and other key items to be brought into the city quickly. In an order by the Soviet State Defence Committee – the highest organ of Soviet government during the war – of 20 September 1941, a list of items to be flown into the city included fuses for shells, parts in short supply for military vehicles, communications equipment and precious metals for production purposes. [GPW, p. 145]

Sputnik 324. This bleak picture shows a street in Leningrad in April 1942. The couple in the foreground are, according to the official caption, delivering the body of a relative to the cemetery. By this point the death rate in the city was slowing, in part because the available food now had to feed fewer people, given how many tens of thousands had died over the winter. In total, Soviet sources suggest that more than a million deaths in Leningrad during the siege were attributable to starvation, malnutrition and resultant illnesses, enemy activity and other causes relating to the siege – that is, deaths that would not or might not have happened were it not for the siege.

Sputnik 58262. Soviet troops fire flamethrowers in the Leningrad region in September 1942. The Red Army had dedicated units equipped with flamethrowers even during the first year of the war, such as the flamethrower company that was part of a unit formed to destroy German forces in the Kaluga area near Moscow and liberate the town at the end of 1941. [RASWW, p. 312] The Soviets tended to concentrate weapons types in particular units, as illustrated by the antitank rifles in Sputnik 5686100 in Chapter 5 (see p. 61). This certainly simplified resupply.

Sputnik 741. Here Soviet troops are shown with what the official caption suggests is a captured German howitzer near Leningrad during mid-1943. The howitzer in the picture seems, however, to be a 305mm Howitzer Model 1939 of Soviet production, suggesting that it may have been first captured by German forces from the Red Army. Such weapons were a feature of the siege of Leningrad, with German forces employing significant artillery assets in order to 'reduce' the city. The Soviet side responded with its own artillery assets, which of course included the heavy artillery on the ships of the Baltic Fleet.

(*Above*) Sputnik 5635. Pictured here are SU-122 self-propelled guns near the Narva Triumphal Arch in Leningrad sometime during the mid-war period. The arch was constructed to celebrate the Russian victory over Napoleon in 1814. Given that these self-propelled guns were not produced in Leningrad, it is quite probable that they found their way into the city via the corridor punched through along the southern shore of Lake Ladoga during January 1943. Although the Soviet Union had experimented with self-propelled guns prior to the war, it was really the German StuG III self-propelled gun that highlighted their utility when considering the labour and other inputs required to build them compared to a tank, as well as their low profiles and the possibility of adding additional armour where there wasn't the weight of a turret to contend with. These SU-122 guns were produced in late 1942 and early 1943 on the T-34 chassis, before being replaced in production by superior self-propelled guns for the remainder of the war.

(*Opposite, above*) Sputnik 602168. This photograph once again shows Soviet sailors being readied for the front line near Leningrad, but in this case in 1943 on the island of Kronstadt off the city. As is apparent here, later in the war Soviet sailors were being provided with Red Army uniforms and equipment for service as ground troops, rather than going into action in their rather unsuitable naval uniforms. The unit here is apparently the 260th Naval Infantry Brigade, with the picture taken in November 1943.

(*Opposite, below*) Sputnik 448. Although a narrow land corridor had been punched through to Leningrad from the remainder of Soviet territory in January 1943, this corridor was still subject to German artillery bombardment. Soviet sources tend to see the final end to the blockade as having been in January–February 1944, when most of the Leningrad region was liberated from Axis forces. Here Soviet infantry dismount from now aged BA-10 armoured cars at Krasnoe Selo near Leningrad on 19 January 1944. Just as German forces had been unable to encircle large numbers of Soviet troops in the region as they advanced on Leningrad, so Soviet forces were unable to do the same thing as they liberated the region.

Chapter 7

The Soviet Navy at War

As noted in the previous chapter, the Soviet navy's Baltic Fleet was bottled up in Leningrad for much of the war – this after having taken heavy losses as it retreated from forward bases in the Baltic Republics, with the retreat from Tallinn in late August 1941 being a particular débâcle. In the south, the second largest Soviet naval force, the Black Sea Fleet, also suffered heavy losses during the early phases of the war as it too was pushed back from forward bases such as Odessa and its principal base at Sevastopol' all the way to the Caucasus region. Although the Soviet navy had a significant force of cruisers and antiquated battleships, there were no dramatic encounters between Soviet and German capital ships off any of the Soviet coastlines. Because of this, and the fact that the principal fighting was clearly taking place on land, the Soviet navy has often been all but dismissed in Western histories of the Great Patriotic War. To dismiss the Soviet navy to the extent to which is the case in so many Western histories is, however, to ignore the fact that significant elements of the Soviet naval forces saw considerable action during the war not only during retreats in the face of the German and Axis advance, but also in support of the war on land. In the far north, where the Soviet Northern Fleet was not bottled up in its ports, vessels of the Northern Fleet saw action not only in the defence of Allied convoys to the Soviet Union, but also in landing operations against the German coastal flanks. In the Black Sea the retreat from Odessa and Sevastopol' was a protracted affair that saw vessels of the Black Sea Fleet provide significant support to ground forces and the besieged port cities, as well as support for substantial landing operations in the Crimea. Significant Soviet naval forces were also employed on the navigable rivers of the Soviet Union and Eastern Europe, where their contribution to the Axis defeat did not make headlines, but was nonetheless meaningful. Even in the Baltic, towards the end of the war the Baltic Fleet was able to gain some freedom of movement in order to both support Red Army operations on land and interdict German seaborne communications between pockets in the Baltic region and the shrinking heartland of the Reich. Finally, in the Far East Soviet naval forces would have a role to play in the defeat of Japanese forces – and a key role in the acquisition of not only the southern part of Sakhalin but also the Kurile Islands that remain Russian to this day. The naval war in the Far East will be considered very briefly in Chapter 23, but this chapter will look at the role played by the Soviet navy in the war against Nazi Germany and her allies in the West.

(*Above*) Sputnik 952. Throughout the war Soviet light naval forces saw considerable action. In the interwar period these forces were developed before Stalin had ambitions to create an 'Ocean-Going' fleet during the 1930s – and before the subsequent need to divert productive resources to the Red Army curtailed such ambitions. In this photograph a G-5 torpedo boat is shown somewhere off Odessa in August 1941. Although Germany had few naval assets in the Black Sea – getting them there was a major problem – her ally Romania did have limited naval forces in the region. These G-5 boats were not a particularly good design, because torpedoes had to be released off the back of the vessel in what was a slightly bizarre quirk. Their streamlined form did, however, give them a high top speed in suitable water, and also made them rather photogenic! This particular vessel seems to have survived the war.

(*Opposite, above*) Sputnik 59526. Although Stalin had ambitious plans for the production of new Soviet battleships in the 1930s, none of those laid down was ever completed. This left the Soviet navy with three pre-revolutionary battleships inherited from the former Tsarist fleet. Limited modernisation of these vessels could not hide the fact that they were very much outdated by the Second World War, having a top speed of only 21.5 knots in the case of *Parizhskaia kommuna*. Nonetheless, these battleships were equipped with twelve 12-inch guns, making them useful platforms for the fire-support of ground forces if they could be protected from enemy air and naval threats. Here the battleship *Parizhskaia kommuna* (renamed *Sevastopol'* in 1943) fires her guns – in all likelihood in support of ground forces – on 15 September 1941 somewhere off the city after which she was initially named and would be named again from 1943.

(*Opposite, below*) Sputnik 932. Here is the battleship *Parizhskaia kommuna* again, this time during the summer of 1942. The photograph seems to have been taken from a heavy cruiser, probably *Molotov*. If the date given for the photograph of August 1942 is correct, then she is pictured at anchor at Poti in Georgia, with Sevastopol' having fallen by this time. Interestingly, this vessel was modified to carry tanks, as the Soviet high command considered using her to ferry twenty-five KV-1 heavy tanks to the besieged city of Sevastopol' at the end of May 1942. Probably because of the risk that she might be sunk by German air attack, this plan was not carried out.[12]

(*Above*) Sputnik 58773. The defence of Sevastopol' was a protracted affair lasting from the end of October 1941 through to the beginning of July 1942, when it was finally captured by German forces. Soviet naval forces played a role in the city's defence not only in providing fire-support for ground forces, but also in bringing in supplies and personnel – and evacuating the wounded, personnel and materiel, particularly when its fall was imminent. Here the aged Tsarist-era light cruiser *Krasnii Kavkaz* is shown loading Red Army personnel and equipment including an anti-tank gun in December 1941; according to the caption provided with the photograph she was bound for Sevastopol'. In December she indeed ferried men and materiel into Sevastopol' on a number of occasions, including troops and equipment of the 79th Special Rifle Brigade, but also ran missions to Novorossiisk.[13]

(*Opposite*) Sputnik 611112. The Soviet destroyer force was particularly heavily involved in supporting besieged Soviet forces in port cities in the Black Sea, where their speed gave them an advantage over larger vessels as supply runners and in hit-and-run attacks, and where they had greater firepower and lifting capacity than their lighter brethren. Here the Type 7U destroyer *Soobrazitel'nii* is shown somewhere off Sevastopol' on 23 April 1942. In the foreground are some of her anti-aircraft guns – two 37mm automatic and one outdated 45mm semi-automatic – soon to be replaced by an additional 37mm gun. In practice such warships never had enough anti-aircraft firepower, and were particularly vulnerable to air attack if caught in daylight. In one particularly unfortunate incident for Soviet naval forces in October 1943 the Flotilla Leader *Khar'kov* with the destroyers *Besposhchadnii* and *Sposobnii* were attacked by German dive-bombers as they were returning from shelling the ports of Feodosiia and Yalta in the Crimea at night. Caught in daylight without fighter cover on their way back to Tuapse in the Caucasus (just down the coast from Novorossiisk), all three warships were sunk with the loss of 780 lives. [GPW, p. 137]

(*Opposite, above*) Sputnik 1214. Here the flotilla leader *Tashkent* – which amounted to a very large destroyer or very light cruiser – is loading munitions in all likelihood bound for Sevastopol' sometime in the early summer of 1942 in the Black Sea. On 2 July 1942 she was sunk in a German air attack on Novorossiisk, having been badly damaged at sea on her return from Sevastopol' a few days earlier when she had to be towed back to port. On 24 June alone she had delivered 1,142 personnel and equipment of the 142nd Rifle Brigade along with 10 tons of concentrated foodstuffs to Sevastopol', and picked up 2,100 wounded to be taken back to Novorossiisk.[14]

(*Opposite, below*) Sputnik 127. Soviet naval vessels were particularly vulnerable to air attack if they were caught in their bases unable to take evasive action to try to avoid enemy bombs. This picture taken on 10 June 1942 shows the Type 7U destroyer *Svobodnii*, sunk at her mooring in Sevastopol'. Having been hit by nine bombs, her fate was sealed by an ammunition explosion. *Svobodnii* or *Tashkent* were not the highest profile victims of German air strikes against ports – the battleship *Marat*, for example, was effectively sunk by German aircraft off Kronstadt near Leningrad on 23 September when hits by two 1,000kg bombs led to an ammunition explosion. The remaining section of *Marat* would, however, continue to function as an artillery battery![15]

(*Above*) Sputnik 5990888. Safer at sea – and particularly in the mist – are a 'Kirov' Class cruiser – probably *Molotov* - and a Type 7U destroyer – shown here in the Black Sea off the Crimea on 15 July 1942. Such conditions did, however, bring their own problems, such as navigational issues. Note the substantial number of anti-aircraft guns on the cruiser – an anti-aircraft armament heavily augmented for this class as a result of wartime experience.

Sputnik 62639. Here naval 'reconnaissance' troops are boarding a dinghy on 24 September 1942 from a submarine, somewhere off the Ukraine. Soviet naval forces were used extensively for disembarking raiders and 'reconnaissance' forces along enemy-occupied coastline. Soviet reconnaissance forces all too often ended up as raiders – such was the culture regarding the activities of so-called 'reconnaissance' troops. The light machine gun carried by the sailor at the front of the dinghy is testimony to the very broad interpretation of 'reconnaissance' amongst Soviet forces.

Sputnik 59767. This picture, showing crew members racing to their torpedo boats on 2 September 1943 somewhere near Novorossiisk, highlights how as a result of German activity many Soviet naval resources were not based at the sort of permanent facilities at which they had been based before the German invasion. At this point Novorossiisk was still in German hands, despite the fact that the Red Army had advanced well to the west through the Ukraine. Novorossiisk had been captured by German forces back in September 1942 as they advanced into the Caucasus, and was finally liberated later in September 1943. Even when ports such as Novorossiisk were recaptured, it would be some time before they could be used as bases again after both the retreating Red Army and then retreating Axis forces had destroyed facilities in them.

(*Above*) Sputnik 667. The Soviet Northern Fleet saw considerable activity during the Great Patriotic War, with the region gaining increased importance over pre-war Soviet expectations because it was the principal conduit for the delivery of Allied Lend-Lease aid during the early part of the war. Soviet submarines had sustained access to German targets off Norway, with it being claimed that the Soviet submarine *K-21* had attacked the battleship *Tirpitz* in July 1942 with a spread of four torpedoes, although German forces were unaware that they had been attacked. Here a 'K' Class submarine is shown at its mooring in the principal naval base for the Northern Fleet at Poliarnoe near Murmansk. In the background to the right is a Type 7 destroyer.

(*Opposite*) Sputnik 230. Here a Type 7 destroyer is pictured at sea amongst the ice that typified the seas of the Soviet north beyond the reaches of the Gulf Stream. The visible crew members are clearly dressed for the cold. For much of the year the White Sea was completely frozen over, meaning that the port of Arkhangel'sk was not used as a destination for convoys for part of the year even where icebreakers were available. The waters off the port of Murmansk to the north-west, although further north, were warmed by the Gulf Stream. Icebreakers were certainly a necessity for transit along the Northern Sea route across the north of Russia even during the summer months.

(*Above*) Sputnik 1565. In somewhat more pleasant weather a Soviet 'S' Class submarine, *S-17*, is shown probably returning to its base at Poliarnoe. Construction of the submarine had begun deep inside Russia at Gorkii in 1939 (now Nizhnii Novgorod), but after she had been floated through inland waterways she was completed at Factory 402 at Molotovsk, now Severodvinsk, near Murmansk. The date provided for this photograph is June 1942, although *S-17* wasn't in service at that time, suggesting the photograph was taken much later, possibly at the end of the war. In the foreground is a pair of Large Submarine Hunter vessels, provided by the US under the Lend-Lease agreement. What appears to be *BO-215* on the left didn't enter service with the Northern Fleet until August 1944. The Northern Fleet was a recipient of significant Lend-Lease aid as well as receiving the US cruiser *Milwaukee* and the British battleship *Royal Sovereign* – in Soviet service *Murmansk* and *Arkhangel'sk* respectively – in lieu of Italian reparations after Italy left the war.

(*Opposite, above*) Sputnik 4718. Soviet riverine forces were active not only on major Soviet rivers but also the major navigable rivers of Eastern Europe. Here a pair of armoured cutters are pictured on the Danube near Belgrade by a destroyed bridge. The date for this picture is 19 October 1944. Note how the main armaments on the cutters are in fact in tank turrets as fitted to earlier versions of the legendary T-34 tank. Such cutters could provide useful fire-support during operations such as major river crossings, as well as ferrying troops. In order to get to the Danube these cutters often faced long journeys, with many of them manufactured well to the east at Astrakhan and shipped westwards by rail.

(*Opposite, below*) Sputnik 1561. Here Soviet infantrymen are shown disembarking from a similar cutter to that shown in Sputnik 4718 somewhere near Budapest in February 1945. Budapest is also on the Danube, on which the Soviet Navy had the Danube Flotilla of light naval vessels such as this. This particular cutter (*BK-433*) entered service with the flotilla in April 1944, and ultimately ended up as an exhibit outside the Central Museum of the Armed Forces in Moscow in 1979, where it can still be seen today. Naval light craft were even used on the river Spree in Berlin in April 1945 as shown in Sputnik 159 in Chapter 22.

Chapter 8

Counter-attack: the Soviet Winter Offensive of 1941–1942

This chapter brings us back to dry land and to late 1941, when despite numerous stunning defeats over huge concentrations of Soviet troops, German chances of a knockout blow against the Soviet Union were diminishing rapidly. Although in late November 1941 the German Wehrmacht was nominally at least still on the offensive near Moscow, analysis of actions on the ground clearly shows that German offensive operations had all but run out of steam by this point. Although a freezing of the mud that had slowed down movement in the autumn had brought a brief period of greater mobility to all vehicles in November, deep snow by the later part of December would soon once again make going difficult for most forms of transport. Local Red Army counter-attacks against weary German forces were increasingly frequent in late November and early December, even before the opening of a full counter-offensive near Moscow during the weekend of 5–7 December 1941 – one of the most pivotal weekends of the war. That weekend Japan would attack the United States at Pearl Harbor, soon followed by Hitler's misguided declaration of war on the United States. Soviet offensive operations near Moscow from that weekend onwards quickly gained back territory from German forces as Hitler ordered his troops to dig in and hold ground. Under the circumstances, this decision may have saved much of the German army near Moscow, because with German troops often tenaciously defending key settlements that tended to be on transport arteries, it proved difficult for Soviet forces that had broken through on their flanks to resupply or move artillery up to support breakthroughs in the German lines. Initial Soviet successes had, however, given Stalin a sense of optimism about Soviet chances of a decisive blow against German forces that winter that would prove counter-productive. Despite mounting losses, Stalin – apparently against his general's advice – ordered the Red Army to push forward in offensive operations not only around Moscow but across the whole of Germany's Eastern Front. Through-out the remainder of the winter and into the period of the spring thaw Soviet forces hammered away at German positions with only limited success, but at horrendous cost in men and materiel.

During the battles around Moscow as a whole (that is, from the beginning of October to late April 1942) one Russian author has recently put the cost for the

Red Army at a staggering 1.6–1.66 million 'irrecoverable losses' – that is, those killed, missing, captured or died of wounds during casualty evacuation. Not that the Wehrmacht got off lightly, suffering in the region of 1.09–1.19 million similar losses, but for the Red Army these losses were on top of the millions already lost in the previous summer across the whole front. Retrospectively we can suggest that as a proportion of forces committed to the fighting German losses were more severe – as high as 52 per cent compared to as high as 35 per cent for the Red Army – but this very cold comfort was not available to the Soviet population at the time.[16] Nonetheless, despite having a higher population, the Soviet Union could not afford to squander human resources at the rate it was doing so – having lost more than 3 million troops alone captured by German forces by the end of 1941.[17] Just as German forces had failed to defeat the Soviet Union in Operation 'Barbarossa' during the summer of 1941 as hoped, and indeed had failed to do so when the initial timetable was extended with Operation 'Typhoon', so the Red Army had failed to crush the Wehrmacht during the winter of 1941/1942 as Stalin had optimistically sought. The war could not be won quickly by either side, and would drag on for another three years.

Sputnik 391. The first picture of this chapter shows Soviet artillery in action at the very beginning of December 1941 near Kalinin (now Tver'), to the north-west of Moscow. Although it is not clear whether they are supporting troops on the offensive or defensive, it serves as a reminder that the offensive operations of 5 December onwards did not suddenly take place out of the blue, but on the ground will have seemed more of a part of what went before than might be seen to be the case with the value of hindsight. Local attacks and counter-attacks characterised the first few days of December near Moscow. This picture is of interest to the equipment buff because it shows troops using mountain guns – ageing 76.2mm Model 1909 mountain guns that were used during the First World War and the Russian Civil War. Soviet forces made good use of even older equipment in late 1941. Most examples of this gun type were lost during the war.

(*Above*) Sputnik 2565. Soviet troops pass through a liberated town during the early phases of the Moscow counter-offensive on 6 December 1941. The troops in the picture seem to be well provided for with winter equipment, although the Red Army was experiencing shortages of such equipment at this time due to a combination of demand and stocks lost to enemy action. Note the horse-drawn sled in the background, behind which is what appears to be a horse-drawn field kitchen.

(*Overleaf*) Sputnik 435. Back in Chapter 5 Sputnik 2549 (see p. 65) shows Soviet cavalry on the attack in deep snow prior to the weekend of 5–7 December 1941. Cavalry units would have a major role to play in Soviet offensive operations that were part of the wider counter-offensive near Moscow from that crucial weekend onwards. In this photograph cavalry identified as being part of General Belov's cavalry corps (see Sputnik 2517 back in Chapter 4 (see p. 50)) are shown on the attack on 5 December 1941. Whether posed or not – there is no evidence in this picture of enemy counter-action – this photo gives some idea of what a Soviet cavalry attack on a German-defended settlement in early December might have looked like, at least with the cavalry at some distance away from and not being cut down by the concentrated small arms fire that would have been characteristic of an organised defence. The mobility of such cavalry at least gave scope for such troops to work around enemy defences if they were not all-round, but increasingly they were as German forces defended 'islands' located in a 'sea' of Soviet-dominated snow and forest. A cavalry charge such as this would only have some chance of success if appropriately supported by other arms, including tanks and artillery. Support from the latter in particular would often not be as forthcoming, however, if cavalry pushed on deep into German lines across the fields of deep snow, through which it would have been difficult for the artillery to follow and be resupplied. On 5 December Belov's corps was engaged in fighting to the north-east of Tula, and would on 8 December receive the honour of a Guards designation. As of 4 December the corps – with two cavalry divisions and corps headquarters – was significantly understrength, with the two cavalry divisions having a combined strength of 11,650 instead of the 'list' strength of 16,198.[18] Losses from mid-November through to 7 December had been heavy: 1,639 killed, 3,863 wounded and 176 missing.[19]

(*Opposite, above*) Sputnik 2548. Once again this picture shows Soviet cavalry during the Moscow counter-offensive, this time slightly later, on 15 December 1941. This is one of my favourite pictures from the war, in part because it has such a Russian 'feel' with the Orthodox church and landscape, but also because it has such an early war feel with the cavalrymen still wearing *Budenovka* hats against the cold even if they have their helmets strapped to their saddles. You can almost hear the crows cawing from the trees! The cavalrymen here are once again from Belov's cavalry corps. By the second half of January 1942 Belov's force consisted of in the region of 28,000 men – five cavalry (three light) and two rifle divisions, along with five ski battalions. With only eight tanks – and limited artillery assets – the corps was manoeuvrable but lacking punch – and particularly if the infantry and artillery were trailing behind. Belov's force was tasked with taking the key town of Viaz'ma, but was unable to do so. [RASWW, pp. 313–15]

(*Opposite, below*) Sputnik 1161. As Soviet offensive operations were making progress near Moscow, they were also doing so closer to Leningrad and in the south on the approaches to the Caucasus. At this time a major landing in the Crimea was supposed also to relieve the city of Sevastopol', then under siege. Here Soviet naval infantry are shown fighting for the town of Feodosia on the south-eastern side of the Crimea after the landings. The Kerch'-Feodosia Landing Operation would quickly become a major débâcle for the Red Army, with the landings contained by Axis forces and the Soviet pocket on the eastern part of the Crimea destroyed in May 1942.

(*Above*) Sputnik 2516. During the winter Soviet ski troops became a major thorn in the side for German forces with their ability to rapidly penetrate between German strongpoints and encircle them. However, as with their cavalry counterparts, their lack of organic fire-support would hamper their ability to tackle well-entrenched opposition. Here ski troops are shown near Tikhvin east of Leningrad on 11 December 1941. The fighting near Tikhvin saw German attempts to link up with the Finns and widen the encirclement of Leningrad defeated. It is worthy of note that the ski troops here do not have the white camouflage smocks that are almost iconic of the winter offensives from 1941 onwards. Such troops would, one would hope, have been some of the first in line for such smocks, highlighting that they were not as widely available as Soviet newsreel footage of the time might sometimes appear to suggest.

(*Opposite, above*) Sputnik 572. In this photograph ski troops embark on a reconnaissance mission somewhere near Leningrad in February 1942. Such troops were ideally suited to reconnaissance – which for the Red Army in practice often meant raiding behind enemy lines. This unit is well-equipped with PPSh sub-machine guns that were starting to become available in large numbers, giving Soviet forces much more firepower at close quarters. They are also wearing suitable clothing for their mission.

(*Opposite, below*) Sputnik 621. In order to increase mobility in deep snow, Soviet forces would employ the novel *aerosan* or air sled during the winter of 1941/1942. Here an air sled 'Destruction Unit' is shown on the North-Western Front during February 1942 at a time when Soviet forces were on the offensive across most of Germany's Eastern Front. The limitations of such a unit are perhaps apparent in the picture. Although very mobile, the sleds are armed only with machine guns and lack armour – making them useful for at best hit-and-run attacks. Air sleds were also apparently used for resupply, although their payloads were clearly limited. By 1 January 1942 twelve air sled battalions had reportedly been sent to the front lines, each one consisting of 40–50 sleds and 90–100 personnel. [RASWW, p. 323] That their use was not notable during subsequent winters of the war suggests that they were not necessarily deemed worth the investment.

(*Above*) Sputnik 785. The cow lends this picture something of a domestic feel, and you might be excused for thinking that those pictured here are partisans. In fact a colonel of the 4th Airborne Corps is receiving reconnaissance information as his brigade commissar looks on, early in 1942. The Moscow counter-offensive was one instance where the Red Army used parachute forces as intended – that is, by dropping them ahead of forces on the offensive. At the beginning of the war the Red Army had three airborne corps in the Soviet Union's western military districts, although there would never be enough transport aircraft to use them on a large scale. Like the cavalry, the airborne forces lacked heavy equipment and there were problems in resupplying them behind enemy lines. The airborne forces dropped near Moscow in early 1942 were supposed to facilitate the advance of the 33rd and 43rd Armies and indeed of General Belov's cavalry corps. Eventually Belov's corps did link up with the 8th Airborne Brigade [RASWW, pp. 317–18], which increased the cavalry's numerical strength but did not bring the sort of firepower that would enable them to deal with either German armoured or well entrenched forces, since Belov's force of late January had left behind its infantry divisions, heavy equipment and baggage train as it tried to take advantage of the cavalry's mobility. Although lacking potency, Soviet airborne forces continued to operate in the German rear for some time, and were also committed near Demiansk below Leningrad. In neither instance did they have the impact hoped of them.

(*Opposite, above*) Sputnik 669433. Both sides in the Great Patriotic War were heavily reliant on the horse throughout the war, the Red Army particularly so during 1941–1942. Here a 76.2mm Model 1939 Divisional gun (USB) is being pulled by a horse team somewhere near Moscow in late December 1941. The beauty of the trees encased in snow and ice provides something of a contrast with the weapon of war passing by. Fortunately the snow here does not appear to be sufficiently deep to seriously hamper movement, and the gun and limber also have the advantage of having pneumatic tyres. In deep snow with wooden wheels progress would have been much more difficult. Much as was the case for the F-22 gun, stocks of the USB would be largely expended by the end of the war, as the USB was not produced from 1943 onwards. Once again, seeing such a weapon in a picture is one clue as to when the picture was probably taken.

(*Below*) Sputnik 1166. Artillery losses for the Red Army during 1941 were sufficiently high not only for the Red Army to draw on antiquated weapons but for there to be a continued need to take advantage of captured German weapons throughout the winter of 1941/1942. Here Soviet artillerymen fire a German 105mm gun against its previous owners somewhere in the Kaluga region during the winter of 1941/1942.

(*Above*) Sputnik 436. As the first picture in this chapter including a Soviet tank we have a KV-1 tank crossing over an iced-up river somewhere near Kalinin to the north-west of Moscow in February 1942. Not only was the KV-1 tank difficult for German forces to destroy with most of the anti-tank guns available at the time, but it also had good cross-country capabilities – including in deep snow – thanks to its wide tracks. Nonetheless, at more than 40 tons it would often not be possible to be confident that even the thickest ice would hold its weight. The large building in the background certainly shows signs of heavy fighting.

(*Opposite, above*) Sputnik 560. Somewhat later in this picture – probably at the tail end of the Moscow counter-offensive – we see a T-34 tank of the Kalinin Front in action in forest terrain. T-34 production had been significantly disrupted by the Axis invasion at a time when production was being ramped up, and it would be into the spring of 1942 before productive capacity would recover and be sufficient to make the T-34 truly ubiquitous. Total production of the T-34 tank had been just over 3,000 in 1941. During 1942 – despite the destruction of the key Stalingrad Tractor Factory – production would be 12,527 for 1942 as a whole. [GPW, p. 186] The destroyed vehicle on the right is a German StuG assault gun. Its short-barrelled gun intended for infantry support would be replaced in later models in order to give it a much better anti-tank capability to allow it to deal with the T-34 and KV-series tanks.

(*Opposite, below*) Sputnik 589. The final two photographs in this chapter show fighting in the same area at a similar time. This first picture shows troops of the Soviet Western Front fighting near the town of Iukhnov to the south-east of Viaz'ma in a picture dated 5 March 1942. On that day the town was liberated by Soviet forces, although heavy fighting in the area would continue into the following month as Soviet forces sought to press on to Viaz'ma to no avail and at terrible cost.

Sputnik 281. This second photograph seems to have been taken at a similar time as Sputnik 589, and shows Soviet troops in a heavily damaged part of Iukhnov. Note the fact that the soldier on the right of the picture is using a German MP 40 sub-machine gun. With the increasing availability of the Soviet PPSh this would be less likely as the war progressed, as in some ways the German weapon was inferior. In fact, in 1942 it would be increasingly likely that German troops would be seen using the PPSh with its larger magazine.

Chapter 9

In the Enemy Rear: the Soviet Partisan Movement

During the winter of 1941/1942 Soviet efforts to reach Viaz'ma and destroy the German forces maintaining a foothold close to Moscow involved protracted heavy fighting that only petered out with the spring thaw. Not only were cavalry and airborne units operating behind German lines as part of this effort, but also partisans. Russia already had a long history of partisan warfare by 1941, including peasant resistance to Napoleon's invasion of 1812 as well as of irregular warfare during the Russian Civil War. Just who exactly constituted a partisan can be unclear. Although partisans are often seen as being those who are not uniformed members of the armed forces who are fighting an enemy, in both 1812 and the Great Patriotic War partisan forces were often led and stiffened by regular forces. It certainly suited the Soviet government to present what became the Soviet partisan movement as a 'popular' movement that had sprung up as an expression of popular resistance to the German invasion, although most of the early partisans were Party and state officials or Red Army personnel. After confused early stages of the partisan war that saw the Red Army, Communist Party and NKVD all sponsor 'partisan' units in enemy-occupied territory, in 1942 the Partisan Movement was formally developed as a Party-led organisation that would increasingly serve the needs of the Red Army for disruption in the enemy rear and reconnaissance information. Alongside these partisans there were also Red Army units operating behind enemy lines – reconnaissance troops and what would now be described as special forces. By 1942 partisans would temporarily at least be able to control huge swathes of German-occupied territory before at a certain point German forces led anti-partisan operations against them. It was very difficult for German forces to eradicate the partisan threat in a particular region, where more often than not they could only disrupt partisan forces that would often re-emerge in the same areas sometime later. It would, however, be 1943 before partisan numbers really took off in the face of German forced-labour conscription, brutal anti-partisan policies and in areas with a Jewish population anti-Jewish activity under the auspices of the Final Solution. By this point of the war going over to the partisans was made easier by the fact that it was increasingly apparent that Germany was losing the war.

As of 15 February 1944 the Soviet Partisan Movement as a whole – excluding the Ukraine – had officially lost 30,047 killed and missing out of 208,206 officially accounted-for participants. The actual number of deaths and of *de facto* participants will have been significantly higher. [RASWW, p. 286] Alongside partisan deaths many tens of thousands of Soviet civilians were killed by Axis forces in occupied territory, often as retribution for partisan activity in a particular area. At the same time German forces – led by the *Einsatzgruppen* – sought to implement the Final Solution to the Jewish question, which by 1942 increasingly meant the mass extermination of the Jewish populations of Europe. This chapter primarily looks at the Soviet war behind German lines; the concentration camps and the Final Solution will rear their ugly heads in pictures later when Soviet troops liberated some of them towards the end of the war.

(*Below*) Sputnik 965. The first picture of this chapter shows a Red Army commander showing new recruits to a partisan unit one of the weapons that they might be fighting with somewhere in the Smolensk region at the end of August 1941. Although many of the men shown here will have had some sort of military training – either having served for a period in the Red Army or had some sort of pre-conscription military training – for some of them it could have been some time ago. He is probably showing them his own pistol – they will more likely be using rifles such as that being held by one of the recruits on the left. Lightly armed and clothed, many such units would head off into the forests that summer. Few of these units would still be in operation by the end of the year, as German activity or the hostile winter conditions they faced by then saw them either destroyed or seeking to make their way back to Soviet lines.

(*Opposite, above*) Sputnik 1534. Soviet partisans head off on an assignment somewhere in German-occupied Soviet territory during the late summer of 1941. Note how they are largely armed with rifles, although there is a light machine gun in the first cart. Such a unit may have been able to disrupt German activity in remote areas, but would have had little hope when facing a German unit with any sort of firepower.

(*Below*) Sputnik 217. Here young Soviet partisans in the Pskov region are shown in position with a captured light machine gun. Such young people ended up joining the partisans in large numbers, in part because they were left in German-occupied territory if they were too young to have been drafted into the Red Army. Such young people were often targeted by Germany for forced labour from 1942 onwards, and the alternative was to join the partisans. Soviet partisans were compelled by circumstances to make widespread use of captured weapons throughout the war to make up for shortages in available Soviet weapons that had either been carried, flown or dropped into occupied territory. Weapons caches had been prepared in the 1930s for partisan use in the event of foreign invasion, but those responsible for such preparations seem to have been killed off during the paranoia of the Great Purges, leaving such preparations undermined.

(*Opposite*) Sputnik 5816873. The survival of partisan units depended not only on them surviving German attempts to destroy them, but also simply surviving in terms of having the necessary food and shelter when required. Much of the food eaten by partisans came from the local population of the areas in which they were operating – sometimes willingly provided, sometimes not. In this picture partisans are being provided with food – at great risk to the woman pictured here – by a member of the local population in Belorussia in March 1942. Partisan encampments had to be in difficult-to-access areas in order to evade German counter-measures – the partisans in this instance are clearly in such an area.

(*Above*) Sputnik 61528. Particularly during the winter months it was important for the partisans to have shelter. Here a female partisan prepares food outside a makeshift shelter in a partisan encampment near Rovno in the Ukraine in the winter of 1943. Although such encampments provided shelter – and even allowed the partisans to protect some members of the local population in what sometimes became little villages – they were a liability when they tied partisans to a particular location that might be discovered and attacked by German forces. In such circumstances partisans often took heavy losses, and many non-combatant partisans were killed either during the fighting or afterwards.

(*Overleaf*) Sputnik 215. The local civilian population wasn't just important to the partisans as a source of food and new recruits, but also as a source of information. Here a member of the local civilian population is apparently showing a group of partisans the route to get to German forces nearby during the winter of 1942/1943, somewhere in the German-occupied territory of Russia. Once again, she will have been putting herself at great risk by associating with the partisans – German forces were often swift to take out their frustrations at local partisan activity on the

civilian population, and particularly if there was evidence of it providing assistance to them. If someone was hostile to Soviet power, choosing to throw their lot in with the Germans would also have been a dangerous strategy – particularly earlier in the occupation partisans killed many who collaborated with the Germans. Many of those who collaborated with German forces in rural areas were former 'Kulaks' who had lost most from the collectivisation of agriculture from the late 1920s. Some of these 'Kulaks' were provided with land in exchange for their collaboration. Note how the partisans here are all armed with sub-machine guns, by now widely available and a popular weapon with partisans.

(*Opposite, above*) Sputnik 608601. The costs of occupation were often high. The official caption for this photograph suggests that the civilians here are looking for the bodies of loved ones amongst those killed by the Germans, with a view to reburying them. This shot was taken in the recently liberated Dneprovskii District in the Ukraine in September 1943.

(*Opposite, below*) Sputnik 864064. One of the most important functions of the partisan movement was to disrupt German lines of communication to assist the Red Army at the front line. Here partisans in the Crimea prepare to destroy a section of railway line in March 1942. Although key railway lines were relatively well guarded by German forces and local collaborators, it was difficult to guarantee the security of all sections of the lines at all times. In the summer of 1943 partisans across the Soviet Union launched a major operation to destroy railways and disrupt the German rail network – an operation known as the 'War of the Rails'. Although German forces became adept at quickly replacing damaged sections of track, the 'War of the Rails' was a considerable drain on German personnel and resources, and also caused disruption to the resupply and reinforcement of the front line.

(*Opposite*) Sputnik 2451. Although the majority of partisans were young people who had been of pre-conscription age when the war began – with some partisans of conscription age having been brought into the German rear from Soviet lines – there were some who were older than either of these two groups. Here an older partisan is shown somewhere in Belorussia in April 1943. Just how useful he would have been in a dynamic combat situation with German forces is debatable, but such shots helped spread the notion that the partisan movement was one of 'all of the people' in occupied territory. The young people in the background are more typical in age for a partisan unit. This unit seems to be fairly well provided for in terms of clothing and equipment, to the extent that it even has a 76.2mm Model 1927 Regimental Gun (shown behind the older partisan). Whilst such a weapon would undoubtedly have been useful in action against German forces, moving it through the sort of terrain that partisans often moved through would have been challenging to say the least, as would keeping it supplied with ammunition. Some partisan units built makeshift airstrips in the forest for resupply, but such assets tied partisans to particular areas and made their discovery by German forces all the more likely.

(*Above*) Sputnik 61709. Mounted troops were used by both partisans and German forces in the partisan war. Here, in a scene reminiscent of a Wild West movie, young Ukrainian partisans on horseback prepare to move off on some sort of mission in June 1943. Mounted troops were particularly suited to the scouting role, where they could of course cover a lot of ground quickly and relatively quietly.

(*Opposite*) Sputnik 1165. Mounted troops also allowed some partisan units to launch deep penetrations into enemy-held territory, the most famous instance of which is probably the raid led by
Sidor Kovpak in the Ukraine to the west of the Dnepr as far as the Carpathian Mountains during
the second half of 1943. Kovpak was a locally well-known veteran of the Civil War in the Sumi
region of the Ukraine, who would once again engage in irregular warfare during the Great Patriotic
War. Here he is shown – bearded and wearing the black hat in the centre of the picture – with a
column of his forces sometime in 1943, and probably during a raid somewhere in the Sumi, Orlov,
Briansk and Kursk regions in the winter of 1942/1943. It is testimony to the sheer size of the
territories concerned that Kovpak's forces as pictured here were not located and destroyed by
German forces, especially since the long column including sleds pictured here was far from
manoeuvrable compared to mounted troops on their own.

(*Above*) Sputnik 494. Here is a slightly later picture of some of Kovpak's partisans, taken in the Kiev
region in March 1943. Of note is not only the youthfulness of the partisans pictured here, but that
they are well-equipped with automatic weapons, from the PPSh sub-machine gun to the DP light
machine gun first introduced in 1927 being carried by a number of the partisans in the foreground.
I am not convinced of the wisdom of wearing a German field blouse, as in the case of the third
partisan from the left in the front row!

(*Above*) Sputnik 851357. Some partisan units were sent from Soviet lines into the German rear, with many of their members either being military personnel or serving as partisans as an alternative to serving in the Red Army. Such units as the one shown here in February 1943 in German-occupied territory in front of the North-Western Front were usually very well equipped and militarily far more capable than those locally raised in German-occupied territory. Even in the case of the latter, qualified and specialised personnel were sent from Soviet lines to assist them, and as the war progressed such units were 'professionalised' and 'militarised', more and more taking on the form of military units operating in the German rear complete with a larger number of uniformed personnel. In this picture note that the personnel are clearly of conscription age, are wearing Red Army clothing, and are generally well provided for, including with the radio set in the foreground. A lack of radio sets early in the war meant that partisan units were often unable to provide timely intelligence to those on the Soviet side of the front line. By 1943 most partisan units of any size were provided with at least one radio set. The downside of having radio communications was that it gave German forces the possibility of intercepting communications and triangulating the location of a partisan unit from its radio transmissions.

(*Opposite*) Sputnik 2278743. Alongside partisans there were other Soviet troops operating on German and Axis-occupied territory. Some of those troops were Red Army scouts, such as Senior Sergeant Frolchenko pictured here in August 1943 after he had participated in the Battle of Kursk. Frolchenko fought from the Battle of Stalingrad through to the Battle of Berlin. He is wearing a camouflage coverall as frequently worn by Red Army scouts during the latter half of the war, has a pair of binoculars, and is armed with the by this point ubiquitous PPSh sub-machine gun. Although such reconnaissance troops were more likely to be found closer to the front line, they sometimes penetrated deep into enemy-held territory.

Sputnik 1230. The final picture in this chapter shows Leningrad region partisans meeting up with advancing forces of the Red Army at Luga in the Leningrad region in February 1944. Although the liberation of their operating areas was no doubt a joyous moment for partisan units, the war was for many of those in such units not over on liberation. By the later part of the war the Red Army was all too often desperately short of infantrymen, and many partisans would find themselves drafted into the Red Army as their partisan units were overrun by advancing Soviet forces.

Chapter 10

Soviet Women and the War Effort

Although the Soviet government had championed women's liberation during the 1920s, by the late 1930s it had backtracked on the notion of sexual equality. Even during the 1920s it had not gone as far as to allow women to undertake combat roles in the armed forces as there was little need for them to do so – in the early 1920s the financial exigencies of the period meant that the armed forces were being cut, not looking for an additional category of recruits. Consequently, when Nazi Germany invaded the Soviet Union on 22 June 1941 there were few women in the Red Army – the only area in which significant numbers of women were employed being the medical services, and even then the preference was to keep them as far from the fighting as possible. There were, however, significant numbers of women working in industry, where women would rapidly increase as a proportion of the workforce. Also, as men were conscripted into the armed forces, women had to make up for the shortfall in agricultural labour, where human effort also had to replace some that had been provided by horses drafted into the Red Army in huge numbers. Women of all ages were also employed when the situation demanded it in building defences in a desperate attempt to halt Axis forces before Moscow and Leningrad. Very quickly the manpower situation in the Red Army started to deteriorate as well, and there were significant numbers of young women available who were both keen to serve in uniform and often had meaningful pre-conscription training through organisations such as OSOAVIAKHIM (see Chapter 1) and the youth wing of the Party, the Komsomol. Such women were initially used in what were technically non-combat roles – as drivers, telecommunications operators and as nurses and *fel'dsher* (paramedics). Although these roles did not involve killing the enemy, they frequently put young women in the line of fire. A limited number of women did find themselves more directly involved in the killing of the enemy in militia units hastily organised to face the enemy advance or as partisans, although the numbers involved were proportionally small. By 1942, however, once the scale of manpower losses in 1941 had sunk in, far greater numbers of young women were sought for roles within the Red Army and indeed became involved in the partisan movement. By now it had been accepted that women would be employed in some 'combat' roles. Regarding anti-aircraft guns, for example, the Soviet Union did not have the sort of qualms about women being employed as anti-aircraft gunners as in the West, where even in Britain – where women did crew anti-aircraft guns –

a line was drawn over women actually firing the gun and hence being directly involved in killing. In the Soviet armed forces relatively small numbers of women were employed in what were clearly front-line combat roles – from the crews of light bombers employed at night to snipers – many of the women had shown their marksmanship skills before the war in the Komsomol. There was pressure from women for their employment at the front line within the ground forces to move beyond isolated instances to the employment of whole units of female combatants. Indeed, a 6,983-strong women's rifle brigade was formed but was not allowed to see action at the front line, instead being employed in rear-area security. [RASWW, p. 327] The Soviet-sponsored Polish armed forces did, however, cross the line in employing female combat units in what were clearly combat operations at the front, since for them manpower shortages were even more acute until they reached Polish territory. Although historians have disagreed on the exact number of women who saw service with the Red Army during the Great Patriotic War, it is likely that approaching a million women saw military service of some sort during the war, with at least a third of these seeing service with the Soviet fronts – that is, those formations making up the front-line forces. [RASWW, pp. 324–5] Be it in the rear, or close to or at the front line, Soviet women played a far more visible role in the Soviet war effort than women in the West, and this chapter highlights the many dimensions of that role.

Sputnik 348. Although the Soviet Union already had a significant number of women in the industrial workforce prior to the Great Patriotic War, that number would increase dramatically during the war with women taking on roles that had previously typically been undertaken by men. Here in early 1943 women are working in a Leningrad factory that had been mothballed during the worst period of the blockade, to be reinstated after the siege had been partially lifted. By this time the manpower shortage in the Red Army – and in particularly in front-line infantry units – was starting to become even more acute, meaning that men who had previously been in protected work were sent to the front and replaced by women.

Sputnik 892437. Large numbers of women in the Soviet Union were, even more so than was the case in Britain, for example, involved in munitions production. Here a young woman is engaged in the production of mortar bombs in a Moscow factory sometime during 1942. Even before the war the Soviet working week had been increased to six days, which when combined with long hours made such factory work gruelling.

(*Above*) Sputnik 835682. Women of all ages were employed in the construction of defensive positions during the war, although in this picture the women concerned are all younger women who have been mobilised by the Communist youth organisation, the Komsomol. They are shown constructing an anti-tank ditch somewhere in the Moscow region on 8 July 1941 as it became apparent that the capital was under threat.

(*Opposite, above*) Sputnik 732. From early in the war Soviet women were employed in the air defence network, initially in local roles that included what in Britain was known as Air Raid Precautions (ARP). Here a group of young women are being employed by the Local Air Defence organisation for Leningrad. This picture was taken in May 1942 from the roof of Building Number 4 on what is now Millionnaia Street in the centre of what is now St Petersburg.

(*Opposite, below*) Sputnik 90487. It did not take long for women to start replacing men in anti-aircraft defence roles as part of the Air Defence Forces of the Soviet Union, firstly in the defences of Soviet cities and other objectives. On 25 March 1942 the Soviet State Defence Committee ordered that 100,000 young women aged 19–25 be mobilised for service in the Air Defence Forces to replace men not only in such roles as radio and telephone operators and observers, but also in crews for searchlights and anti-aircraft guns. [RASWW, p. 326] Later in the war women would be employed in such roles as part of the advancing Red Army. Here Tatiana Shmorgunova and her colleagues are shown with an optical rangefinder as part of the defences for a Soviet crossing-point over the Oder river in the heart of Germany near Berlin in late April 1945.

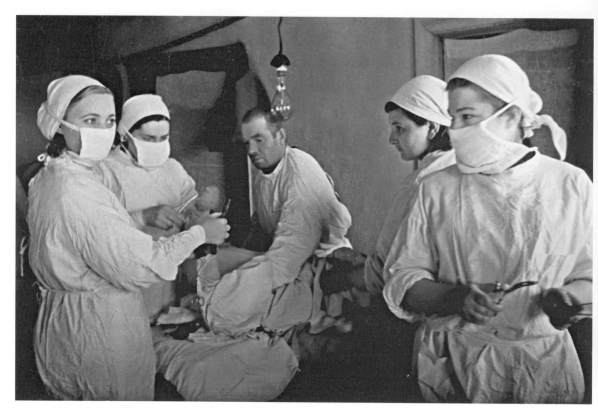

(*Above*) Sputnik 64114. Although the Red Army employed few women prior to the war, one area in which women were meaningfully represented was in military medicine, and in particular in a hospital setting. Women were not only employed as nurses and *fel'dsher* (paramedics), but as doctors: of 100,301 doctors liable for call-up in May 1941 only 36.8 per cent were men. [RASWW, p. 325] All but one of this surgical team at a medical battalion facility of the 2nd Ukrainian Front during the summer of 1943 are women. To have women serving in such units – behind the front line – was deemed appropriate even before the war. A total of 41,224 women would be conscripted into front-line military medical units during the war as a whole. [RASWW, p. 326]

(*Opposite, above left*) Sputnik 67355. Placing women in more dangerous medical roles closer to the front line was something Soviet authorities were reticent to do at the beginning of the war, but they soon changed their minds as there was a heavy demand for front-line medical personnel. Increasingly large numbers of young women volunteered for, or were conscripted into, a variety of front-line medical roles. Training to be a medic was one means by which women who were keen to join the Red Army and take a front-line role could do so during the early phases of the war. Here a female medic tends to a lightly wounded Red Army man sometime during September 1942.

(*Opposite, above right*) Sputnik 1416. Another area in which large numbers of women would be employed by the Red Army from early on in the war was in what might be described as 'house-keeping' duties, that is, undertaking such essential tasks as laundry, book-keeping and barbershop duties. Here a female barber shaves a Red Army man on the territory of the Baltic Republics during the summer of 1944.

(*Opposite, below*) Sputnik 457. One of the more dangerous non-combat roles carried out by Soviet women in the Red Army was as radio and telephone operators – a role that would frequently put them close to the fighting. Shown is a communications hub for the 138th Rifle Division during the fighting for Stalingrad in December 1942. Here men and women are operating the communications equipment from a basement of the Red October Factory. Some young women had received training for such roles in the Komsomol Communist youth organisation prior to the war.

Sputnik 42435. Perhaps one of the most famous roles for women in the Red Army – made so by footage and photographs of Maria Limanskaia at the Brandenburg Gate in Berlin at the end of the war – was as a traffic controller, that is, directing traffic at road junctions. I have chosen not to show one of the iconic images of Limanskaia since they are widely available, but of a different, unnamed, traffic controller also in Berlin at the end of the war. This image was taken on 4 May 1945.

Sputnik 68660. Soviet women were involved in combat early in the war within the Soviet partisan movement, in which typically younger women would play an increasing role as the war progressed. Here female partisans relax somewhere in Russia during September 1943. By January 1944 about 10 per cent of the officially accounted-for participants in the partisan movement seem to have been women, although it is likely that the actual proportion was significantly higher. [RASWW, p. 326]

Sputnik 2414. Perhaps the most iconic combat role for women in the Red Army was as a sniper. Many young women had become proficient markswomen in the Komsomol prior to the war, and were keen to carry their proficiency into a wartime role. Although Soviet military and political leaders were not willing to see combat units made up entirely of women engaged in the slaughter at the front line – and particularly given the potentially negative propaganda that could have resulted from pictures of the bodies of hundreds of young women killed in action – they were willing to employ women in front-line combat roles in isolated instances. Here two young female snipers of the 33rd Army of the 2nd Belorussian Front are shown in August 1944. The Central Women's School for the Preparation of Snipers created in May 1943 would send 1,061 female snipers to the front, as well as producing 407 female instructors in sniping. [RASWW, p. 327] The helmet on a stick is being used to try to lure enemy soldiers – particularly snipers – to reveal themselves.

(*Opposite*) Sputnik 825070. Before the war the Komsomol had given a select group of Soviet young people the opportunity to learn to fly. This in many ways set the scene for the activities of a limited number of female flyers during the Great Patriotic War. Perhaps the most famous female flying unit was the 588th Night Light Bomber Aviation Regiment, later becoming the 46th Guards Night Bomber Air Regiment. This unit was formed in 1941 and tasked with the harassment bombing of enemy units at night using the U-2 biplane aircraft. The unit – whose exploits were clearly used for propaganda purposes – gained something of a reputation with the enemy and earned them the nickname the 'Night Witches'. Here members of the unit are shown loading bombs on an aircraft in the summer of 1944.

(*Above*) Sputnik 63675. A limited number of Soviet women were allowed to serve as fighter pilots during the war. Hence, in the same order of the People's Commissar for Defence that had ordered the formation of the 588th Night Light Bomber Aviation Regiment on 8 October 1941, it was also ordered that a women's fighter air regiment be formed, the 586th Fighter Air Regiment.[20] Here female pilots Lidia Litviak, Katia Budanova and Masha Kuznetsova are shown with one of their Yak-1 fighter aircraft during the first half of the war – possibly by now as part of the 9th Guards Fighter Air Regiment. Even if units such as the 586th Fighter Air Regiment were in a sense tokenistic, the employment of women in such roles at all set the Soviet Union apart from the other major powers, and the combat and risks faced by such pilots was only too real. Guards Junior Lieutenant Lidia Litviak would not return from a combat mission with the 73rd Guards Fighter Air Regiment on 1 August 1943 – lost without trace alongside her male colleague Sergeant Nikolai Ugarov that same day.[21] That Lidia Litviak (along with Katia Budanova) was not kept in an all-female unit was undoubtedly testimony to her abilities as a pilot.

Sputnik 67371. The women of the Soviet-sponsored Polish Army that fought alongside the Red Army seem to have ended up being employed in unit strength in ground combat on the Eastern Front. Here female soldiers of the Women's Battalion of the 1st Polish Infantry Division 'Tadeusza Kościuszki' are shown in the division's camp near Riazan' to the south-east of Moscow in mid-July 1943. The division would receive its 'baptism by fire' at the Battle of Lenino in October 1943.

Chapter 11

'All for the Front!': the Soviet Rear

In the last chapter we had already started to look at what was going on behind the front lines of the Great Patriotic War when looking at the role of women in the Soviet war effort, and this chapter will further explore what was going in the Soviet rear to sustain the war effort. Although the Axis advance was halted and thrown back by the combat troops, they could of course not have done so without the millions of people either in uniform or otherwise toiling at various depths behind the front line. From the medical services of the armed forces to the peasantry working the fields, much of the Soviet population made some sort of contribution to victory over Germany and her allies. Food, equipment and munitions had to be produced and delivered to the front lines in a timely manner, just as the wounded had to receive medical treatment as quickly as possible and damaged equipment be repaired and thrown back into action.

Both Soviet agricultural and industrial production were severely dislocated during the early part of the war as enemy forces seized vast tracts of Soviet territory. Although the Soviet government started to evacuate factories to the East from the first days of the war, even if they were successfully loaded onto trains for their journey eastwards it would take some time to get production restarted in a new location. At least in the case of industrial concerns factories could be relocated – however, in the case of agricultural assets, animals and agricultural machinery could be evacuated but land lost to the enemy represented production lost. Production was also lost when the fighting ranged over agricultural areas, whether or not that territory was ultimately lost to the enemy for a meaningful period of time. Stalin chose suddenly to highlight the significance of loss of territory in his famous 'Not a Step Back!' order of 28 July 1942 – Order Number 227 of the People's Commissar for Defence for 1942. In the order, Stalin noted:

> Certain unintelligent people at the front comfort themselves with talk that we can retreat to the east even further, because we have a huge territory, vast quantities of land, a large population, and we will always have surplus bread ...
>
> Every commander, Red Army and political worker should understand that our resources are not without limits ... The territory of the Soviet Union, which has been seized and is in the process of being seized by the

enemy, is bread and other foodstuffs for the army and the rear; metals and fuel for industry; mills and factories, which are supplying the army with arms and munitions; and railway lines ...

... it is time to put an end to the retreat.

Not a step back! Such should now be our principal call. [GPW, p. 101]

The loss of agricultural land was particularly severe in 1942 and into 1943 as in the summer of 1942 the Axis swept across the agricultural lands of the Ukraine and southern Russia, when a second wave of industrial dislocation also took place. By this time, however, much of the plant evacuated in 1941 was up and running again as the Soviet economic effort was thrown behind the production of armaments and munitions. As the Soviet Union gained the upper hand in the war, considerable effort had to be expended to keep the Red Army advancing, as German forces destroyed thousands of kilometres of railway lines in their wake that had to be rebuilt. The final phase of the journey of troops and supplies to the front line took place by vehicle, horse-drawn transport or, in the case of the soldiers, often by foot. Making the situation easier in one sector of concern could often make it more difficult elsewhere. The Red Army's insatiable need for horses, for example, would deprive agriculture of motive power, just as the Red Army's manpower needs would denude the working population in the countryside in particular. That the Soviet war effort held together owes something to Allied material aid – a topic for a later chapter – but also to the often heroic efforts of the Soviet population not only on the battlefield but also in the rear.

(*Opposite*) Sputnik 643. We start this chapter with photographs taken closest to the front line with wounded personnel being evacuated to the rear. Getting the wounded from the front line to hospital facilities was often very challenging in a pre-helicopter era – and particularly where there was a shortage of suitable motor vehicles. Here a dog team pulls a wounded soldier towards a hospital of the 1st Ukrainian Front, sometime in June 1944. According to Svetlana Gladish, author of *Dogs of the Fronts of the Great Patriotic War*, 4,500 dog teams were employed in casualty evacuation during the Great Patriotic War, which evacuated in the region of 600,000 wounded Red Army personnel.[22] Sadly, dogs were also used to a limited extent in a tank destruction role, although their success in this (in the process of which they were killed) seems to have been limited.

(*Above*) Sputnik 1272. Sometimes it was possible to evacuate wounded deeper into the rear by aircraft, although rank-and-file personnel would not typically have had that luxury. Certainly such aircraft were more likely to be used for figures in leadership positions. For example, on 3 December 1941 the headquarters of what would soon become the 1st Guards Cavalry Corps sent an urgent request to Nikolai Bulganin – member of the Military Soviet for the Western Front – that an ambulance aircraft be sent for the evacuation of the political commissar for the unit, Brigade Commissar Shchelakovskii, who had fallen 'seriously ill'.[23] These ambulance variants of the legendary Po-2 aircraft allowed the patient to be accompanied by a member of the medical personnel, who in the confines of the enclosed rear compartment could at least access the patient's upper body during flight. This photograph was taken in August 1943 on the Kalinin Front. Clearly casualty evacuation by aircraft required suitable terrain. On occasion it proved possible to evacuate even wounded partisans by air from makeshift landing strips – sometimes cut out of forested terrain.

(*Opposite, above*) Sputnik 662769. Here a wounded soldier has reached a field hospital of the Volkhov Front near Leningrad in December 1941. According to one set of figures provided for the Red Army's field forces, up to 1 January 1942 there were 1,532,367 wounded and shell-shocked personnel requiring treatment, along with 5,570 burns cases, 29,625 cases of frostbite and 374,298 cases of sickness, giving a staggering total of 1,941,860 cases.[24] Given such figures, it is understandable how the military-medical services struggled to deal with such numbers, in particular where there were shortages of key personnel.

(*Opposite, below*) Sputnik 662771. Here an operation is taking place in a field hospital – also of the Volkhov Front – in January 1943. There continued to be shortages in the number of surgeons available throughout the Great Patriotic War; for example, up to the end of 1942 the number of general surgeons did not reach 50 per cent of the number required according to list strengths for medical units. Nonetheless, during this first turbulent period of the war to the end of 1942, of a total of nearly 7 million casualties 4,780,815 were recorded as either returning to their units or being sent to units for those 'recovering' from wounds. By the end of 1943 there were 588 200-bed mobile surgical field hospitals alone with the Red Army's field forces.[25]

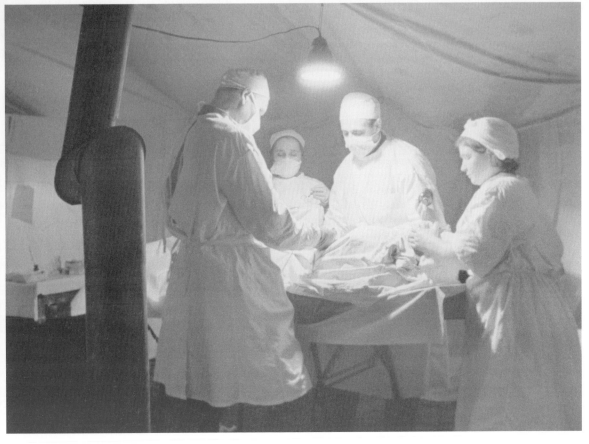

(*Above*) Sputnik 5632. Not only wounded people but damaged equipment had to be transported to the rear, and in the case of vehicles repaired. Here BA-6/10 armoured cars are undergoing repairs in a factory in Leningrad sometime during September 1941. The logistical issues surrounding returning vehicles to factories for repair should not be underestimated. As the war progressed the Red Army sought to undertake more repairs in the field, but sometimes there was no choice but to send damaged vehicles to factories in the rear.

(*Opposite, above*) Sputnik 865643. In addition to military vehicles requiring repair in the Soviet rear, another significant category for repair was railway locomotives and rolling stock. The railways were a crucial element in the Soviet war effort, be that for moving raw materials to factories, or taking finished goods and personnel to the front line. Railway locomotives were not only in need of repair through wear and tear, but also through enemy action, as trains were frequently subject to air attack. By the time this photograph was taken – in February 1945 – the German Luftwaffe's capacity to attack trains from the air had significantly diminished, but the Soviet railways had vast distances to contend with when moving and supplying the Red Army on German territory and all the way from the Arctic Circle down through to Bulgaria. The locomotive pictured here seems to be an early Soviet Eg or Esh model of the early 1920s that were produced in Germany and Sweden respectively, here being repaired at the Dzerzhinskii Factory in Voronezh. The Soviet Union produced few locomotives during the war, and although it would receive large numbers of locomotives from the United States under Lend-Lease, particularly earlier in the war those that it had on hand were not a resource to be squandered after the heavy losses of the first months of the war.

(*Opposite, below*) Sputnik 2466476. This photo – also including a railway locomotive – is of the famous Red October metallurgical factory in Stalingrad, shown as reconstructed by the time this photograph was taken in February 1944. The factory had been destroyed during fighting for the city in late 1942 and early 1943. Not only did the dislocation of industrial production by the war have a significant impact on Soviet production during late 1941 and early 1942 in particular, but the reconstruction of industry destroyed during the fighting or by the retreating Axis forces was also a drain on resources. After the defeat of Nazi Germany the Soviet Union would strip Germany of much of its surviving industrial plant as reparations for damage caused on Soviet territory.

(*Above*) Sputnik 611734. Some of the most unsung contributors to the Soviet war effort were Kolkhoz or collective farm peasants, who in far from conducive circumstances continued to produce food for the Soviet Union. With millions of men, horses and vehicles mobilised for the war, female and older collective farm peasants managed to provide the Soviet Union with some food from communal land and private plots. Much of the Soviet Union's prime agricultural land was under German occupation during the first half of the war, severely curtailing what the Soviet Union could produce, and military activity often severely disrupted the harvest in those areas over which fighting took place. Where in 1940 Soviet agriculture had produced 95.5 million tons of grains, during 1942 and 1943 production stood at only 29.7 and 29.4 million tons respectively. By the time this photograph was taken in the spring of 1944 in the Ukraine, Soviet agricultural production was on the road to a degree of recovery thanks to the liberation of agricultural lands by the Red Army, although production of grains for 1944 would still only amount to 49.1 million tons [GPW, p. 190]. Note how in this photograph ploughing is taking place with the help of cows rather than horses. Lend-Lease aid would make up for some of the shortfall in Soviet agricultural production.

(*Opposite, above*) Sputnik 5645971. That the Soviet economy was able to produce the armaments it did during the first half of the war – after the loss of sizeable territory in the more industrialised European part of the Soviet Union – constitutes something of an economic miracle. Here we see a production line for T-34 tanks at Tank Factory Number 183 in the Urals at Nizhnii Tagil in October 1942. By this point T-34 production had ramped up dramatically after industry relocated eastwards from the west of the country was back in operation. Factory Number 183 had started its life in Khar'kov, where it began producing T-34 tanks in 1940, during which the first 117 T-34 tanks were produced. After the Axis invasion, having produced more than 1,500 tanks to date in 1941, it was moved to the Urals where meaningful production restarted in 1942, by the end of which it had produced 5,684 T-34 tanks. This was just as well given that production at the Stalingrad Tractor Factory was knocked out by the fighting for the city in late 1942. During 1943 Factory Number 183 would go on to produce a further 7,466 T-34 tanks [GPW, p. 186].

(*Opposite, below*) Sputnik 634312. Here a batch of much-needed KV-1 Model 1941 tanks arrive near Moscow (Dubosekovo) in what according to the date provided with the photograph is late October 1941. During this period the Red Army was particularly short of tanks on the Moscow axis, especially heavy and medium tanks. The contribution that the tanks in this picture alone might have made to the defence of Moscow should not be underestimated. Tanks were shipped by rail from the factories, ideally not being driven for long distances before reaching the front line. The KV-1 tanks shown here are a variant with a cast turret. There was also a simplified variant of this tank with a welded turret that gave the tank a much more angular appearance.

(*Above*) Sputnik 62729. Having railway lines as close to the front line as possible was a perpetual challenge for Soviet railway troops, since as the Red Army advanced German forces destroyed what they could as they retreated. Particularly vulnerable to being destroyed were bridges, either by retreating German forces or in some instances by the Soviet air forces or partisans seeking to limit German reinforcement of, or retreat from, a particular sector of the front line. Here Soviet troops are rebuilding a bridge somewhere in Russia in March 1943. Due in part to language barriers, the non-Slavic nationalities of the Soviet Union were often disproportionately represented amongst troops carrying out such laborious rear-area functions. The speed with which such bridges and the railways could be rebuilt could play a significant role in the extent to which Soviet offensive operations could be sustained after their start dates.

(*Opposite, above*) Sputnik 978. Thousands of kilometres of railway line had to be rebuilt in the wake of the German retreat. German forces became efficient at destroying not only bridges, but also long sections of the track itself, using giant claws pulled by locomotives to tear apart the sleepers to which the track was attached. Here Soviet troops are shown rebuilding a section of track near Novorzhev in what was by 1944 the Pskov region. In addition to rebuilding sections of track, sometimes Soviet forces would add additional track to stretches of railway line in order to increase capacity.

(*Opposite, below*) Sputnik 1833. Often the Soviet advance was not along the route of railway lines, and this was certainly the case in the far north. Even where the advance could be supported by railway lines nearby, troops and supplies had to be moved from railheads to the front line, often through terrain where there were not even rudimentary roads. Here Soviet troops lay a corduroy road through the *taiga* in the Murmansk region in the far north in April 1942 that would allow wheeled vehicles to access this area even when the ground was waterlogged. As you can imagine, such roads demanded a significant amount of wood.

(*Above*) Sputnik 60230. Enemy mines were a hazard not only in battle, but for those troops following on behind the front-line troops. Millions of mines were laid by both sides during the war, and had to be cleared from key lines of communication. Here Soviet sappers clear mines on the edge of a road in late August 1943 in the aftermath of the fighting in the Kursk region. The soldier in the foreground on the left is using an electrical mine detector. As will be apparent in the final chapter of this book, the problem of mines was one that extended well into the post-war period, claiming many lives even after the war was over.

(*Opposite*) Sputnik 65896. The final photograph of this chapter puts us somewhere back near the front line where we began the chapter, and indeed at the very end of the war. Here Soviet troops are shown on a busy German road on the Berlin axis on 20 April 1945. Clearly evident is the Red Army's use of both horse-drawn and motorised transport, with both Soviet-manufactured and Allied-supplied motor vehicles in view. As will be noted later in Chapter 16, Allied-supplied motor vehicles played an important part in keeping up the Red Army's advance beyond the railheads, with what were by the end of the war ubiquitous Dodge trucks and a jeep both appearing in this shot alongside very traditional horse-drawn carts.

Chapter 12

'Not a Step Back!': Stalingrad and the Caucasus

In late 1941 the Red Army had gone from crisis on the approaches to Moscow in October to dramatic battlefield successes during the early phases of the Soviet counter-offensive near Moscow. This recovery did not, however, mean a complete transformation of Soviet fortunes. The subsequent overambitious Soviet winter counter-offensive of 1941–1942 would drag on far too long for increasingly limited gains, thanks certainly to a considerable extent to Stalin's insistence that the enemy was on the verge of being beaten and that a swift Soviet victory was possible. Although German forces had been halted before Moscow, on the approaches to the Caucasus and near Leningrad, the German armed forces and their allies not only survived the Soviet winter counter-offensives, but inflicted considerable losses on the Red Army in doing so. Certainly by the spring of 1942 conditions for ultimate German victory were far less favourable than they had been the previous year, in particular given that US industrial might was now being mobilised in earnest behind the Allied war effort. Soviet industry was also recovering from the dislocation of 1941, with at least some of the industrial plant from the west now in situ in the Urals and Central Asia. Nazi Germany was, however, far from being a spent force. Although the Soviet leadership expected that German forces would have a second attempt at capturing Moscow in the summer of 1942, Hitler's attention had shifted southwards towards the Caucasus, reflecting an acceptance of the need for resources in the inevitably more protracted war that Germany was now embroiled in. If Germany could capture the Caucasus and its oil – along with Soviet raw materials in the Donbass and the Black Earth agricultural regions of the Soviet Union on the way – then not only would what would become known as Fortress Europe be in a stronger position, but those resources would be denied to the Soviet Union.

As both sides made plans for the summer campaigning season of 1942, it was the Soviet Union that would get in the first major blow in a misguided attack in the Khar'kov region in the south in May. The failure of this attack – resulting in the destruction of a large Red Army mechanised force – set Germany and her allies up for initial success in the south as they pushed on across the Ukraine and southern Russia into the Caucasus. For Stalin, the speed of the Axis advance and the territory that their forces were acquiring were of grave concern – a concern that Stalin was for once willing to pass on to the Red Army rather than keeping up a pretence that everything was under control. Stalin's famous 'Not A Step

Back!' order of 28 July 1942 – issued in his role as People's Commissar for Defence – certainly marked a change in tone in such orders in that it was blunt in presenting the danger of the situation for the Soviet Union. Subsequently many Red Army personnel would recall how Order Number 227 was something of a 'wake-up call' for them in bringing home the urgency of the situation. [GPW, p. 100–2; RASWW, p. 354] New repressive measures to keep the Red Army fighting accompanied the order, with Stalin giving Nazi Germany praise in the order itself for its use of penal units as a disciplinary tool. That the epicentre of the fighting in the south became Stalingrad is well known, as both sides poured troops into the fighting for the city from the late summer into the autumn. Despite German forces capturing as much as 90 per cent of the city, Soviet defenders clung on to a small island of resistance in the city as on the periphery Soviet forces were massed for a counter-offensive. In the Caucasus as well the advance of German forces was halted before they had reached the principal oilfields in the far south. Hitler's gamble – to throw sizeable German forces into a headlong charge across southern European Soviet territory – had already failed as the winter set in, and even before the Soviet offensive of 19 November near Stalingrad – Operation 'Uranus' – turned failure into a débâcle.

(*Opposite, above*) Sputnik 491038. The first two photographs in this chapter capture something of the intensity and horror of combat. Here a British-supplied 'Matilda' tank – with accompanying infantry of the South-Western Front –is shown on the attack near Zmiev, south of Khar'kov, during the summer of 1942. This is certainly not a staged photograph, with a casualty certainly evident on the right-hand side of the tank, and possibly also the left. Although the Soviet practice of having infantrymen ride on tanks into battle meant that tanks were more likely to have close infantry support – and to some extent made up for shortages in armoured fighting and other vehicles to carry infantry into battle – it also resulted in heavy casualties. There is, as is clear from this photograph, little protection for infantrymen on the back of a tank, and their desperation to get off the tank into some sort of cover is very much evident.

(*Opposite, below*) Sputnik 666554. This second photograph, taken moments after 491038, shows the body of one of the infantrymen on the ground in the front-centre part of the picture, with what is quite possibly a second casualty on the far left. None of the infantrymen here has a PPSh sub-machine gun, a weapon that would become synonymous with tank-riding infantry as the war progressed. Consequently the infantrymen here would be very much dependent on the firepower of the accompanying tank when engaging enemy positions at close range.

ОТСТОИМ КАВКАЗ!

(*Opposite, above*) Sputnik 185. Here Soviet troops are shown dug-in defending the approaches to the Caucasus region sometime during the summer of 1942. Scenes from the 1975 Soviet movie 'They Fought for the Motherland' directed by Sergei Bondarchuk and based on a novel by Mikhail Sholokhov are certainly reminiscent of this photograph, which gives some idea of the terrain as the Steppe became the foothills of the Caucasus Mountains. During the Axis advance towards the Caucasus and Stalingrad relatively few Soviet units were encircled compared to the fighting in 1941 on most axes, where many Soviet units fell back onto either Stalingrad or into the Caucasus.

(*Opposite, below*) Sputnik 5823662. Here troops of the North Caucasus Front are engaged in combat in late July 1942 not long after German forces had taken Rostov-on-Don. In this instance the attacking Soviet forces at least have some cover to work with on the approaches to what is, one assumes, an enemy-held settlement. The use of 45mm anti-tank guns in an infantry support role with high-explosive ammunition was frequent, and each infantry battalion had in theory an anti-tank platoon with three such guns. [RASWW, p. 399]

(*Above*) Sputnik 136641. Although subsequently overshadowed by the defence of Stalingrad, the defence of the Caucasus was crucial for the Soviet Union's oil supply and indeed in order to secure what was the best route for Allied aid to the Soviet Union coming in through Iran. By the second half of 1942 the proportion of aid reaching the Soviet Union through the region was on the increase, with the fighting for the region meaning that aid had to be shipped across the Caspian Sea rather than reaching the Soviet heartland through the Caucasus. This 1942 poster shows a sailor of the Black Sea Fleet and a cavalryman standing in defence of the Caucasus, the slogan for the poster simply being 'We will defend the Caucasus!' In the original colour version of the poster, the cavalryman's scarf is red, along with any red stars in the picture and the text, but otherwise the original is also black and white.

(*Above*) Sputnik 6056082. Included as much as anything to show something of the striking land-scape of the Caucasus Mountains, in this photograph an anti-aircraft gun and its crew are shown in the region of the town of Ordzhonikidze in the northern part of the Caucasus. The mountains provided a natural defensive barrier protecting the principal oilfields further south, where only along the coastlines was there room for vehicles to manoeuvre.

(*Opposite, above*) Sputnik 59099. Although the fighting for the city of Stalingrad has captured the imagination of many authors, much of the fighting in the Stalingrad region from September onwards was taking place outside the city where Soviet forces launched numerous attacks on the German flanks even before the launch of Operation 'Uranus' on 19 November 1942. Here Soviet infantry are shown on the attack somewhere in the Stalingrad region in September 1942. Once again, this is clearly not a posed photograph, as the casualty in the centre of the picture testifies.

(*Opposite, below*) Sputnik 59601. The Axis advance towards Stalingrad and into the Caucasus during the summer of 1942 saw the Red Army in the region throw in almost any equipment it could get its hands on in order to try to stop the enemy. Here both later and mid-1930s variants of the T-26 tank that had survived 1941 thanks to being deployed away from the fighting in the western part of the Soviet Union are shown in the Stalingrad region in the summer of 1942, part of the forces of the 64th Army. Such tanks would be used again in the war against Japan, but the Stalingrad fighting saw their last use in meaningful numbers in the war against Nazi Germany and her allies in the western part of the Soviet Union.

(*Above*) Sputnik 2209. The Stalingrad Tractor Factory was a significant producer of the T-34 in early 1942, manufacturing 2,520 tanks during 1942 before production was shut down as a result of fighting for the city and indeed over the site of the factory itself. [GPW, p. 186] Here a batch of T-34 tanks is being readied for dispatch to the Red Army sometime in August 1942. Tanks rolled off the production lines of the factory until the very last moments when enemy activity made continued production impossible. You can tell if a T-34 tank was produced by this factory by the spoked wheel design on their variant of the tank.

(*Opposite*) Sputnik 2361. Taken on 28 August 1942, this photograph shows the crew of a DShK 12.7mm heavy machine gun engaging enemy aircraft from the territory of the Red October Factory in Stalingrad during a period of heavy German bombing of the city in late August. Large numbers of Soviet civilians were killed during these air attacks, as much of the civilian population had not been evacuated from the city. Soviet resistance and fuel shortages had temporarily stalled the advance of the German mechanised spearheads on the city, but as the intense German air activity over the city continued these spearheads renewed their advance.

(*Above*) Sputnik 5479000. In this picture, also taken in the late summer of 1942 somewhere in the Stalingrad region, the crew of a ZiS-3 76mm Model 1942 divisional gun are shown in combat, engaging the enemy in a direct-fire role. The ZiS-3 gun rapidly became the standard Soviet divisional field gun from late 1942 as stocks of other earlier weapons in this category were lost. Such weapons were very versatile in that they could be used not only in a direct- and indirect-fire role as artillery, but also had excellent anti-tank capabilities, as well as a relatively light carriage for an artillery piece.

(*Opposite*) Sputnik 2514. This is the sort of picture that you might be expecting in a chapter to a large part dedicated to the Soviet defence of the Stalingrad region in the late summer of 1942. Here Soviet infantry are shown making their way through some sort of communications trench amongst ruined buildings of the city. The soldier in the foreground is armed with the increasingly ubiquitous PPSh sub-machine gun, which is perhaps seen by many as the iconic weapon in fighting for the city. Certainly its large 71-round drum magazine made it a popular weapon not only for Red Army troops, but also for their German opponents, for whom the smaller 32-round box magazine of the MP-40 was liable to run out at inopportune moments against Soviet troops armed with the PPSh. Another reason for German troops to acquire the PPSh was the fact that a greater proportion of Red Army troops were often armed with this weapon than German troops with the MP-40, with whole units of troops being provided solely with the PPSh. Whilst only being armed with the limited-range PPSh could be a major drawback in open terrain, this was less likely to be the case in urban fighting such as that taking place within Stalingrad.

(*Above*) Sputnik 819. Given the significance of the Volga river that bounded Stalingrad to the east as an internal waterway, it is unsurprising that Soviet naval personnel were involved in the defence of the city. The Soviet Navy not only provided naval infantry, but also shipped troops and supplies into the city and evacuated the wounded. Here Soviet naval personnel seem to be restoring a communications cable on the banks of the Volga near the city. Although vulnerable to damage from shelling and air attacks, such cables were more secure than radio communications.

(*Opposite, above*) Sputnik 141. The fighting in the southern regions of the USSR and growing manpower shortages in the Red Army prompted renewed mobilisation of non-Slavic peoples of the Crimea, Caucasus and Central Asia into Red Army combat units during 1942. This photograph clearly shows an ethnically diverse group of Red Army soldiers somewhere in the southern regions of the Soviet Union, apparently in 1942. Reticence about the use of such personnel stemmed in part from language issues, but a lack of enthusiasm for using them in ethnically distinct units also stemmed from questions over their loyalties to Stalin's Soviet Union. During the fighting in the southern regions of the Soviet Union the German armed forces did attempt to turn some of the peoples of the Caucasus, for example, against the Soviet regime and to employ them in units of collaborators within the Wehrmacht.

(*Opposite, below*) Sputnik 5823660. Whilst the battle for Stalingrad ground on during the later summer and autumn of 1942, fighting also raged in the Caucasus region. Here Red Army soldiers of a mountain rifle division defend a mountain pass somewhere in the Caucasus in December 1942. Many of the Soviet Union's 'mountain' troops had been thrown into combat in regions without mountains, and the quality of their mountain training was often poor. In theory their equipment was better suited to mountain warfare than was that of a standard rifle division, but even so the mountain troops in action early in the fighting for the Caucasus were poorly provided for. Soviet attempts to improve their capabilities during the fighting led to some improvements, but those German mountain units committed to the region remained far superior. Fortunately for the Red Army the German mountain forces committed were few in number, and could not make up for the fact that elsewhere the Red Army was gaining the upper hand. Alexander Statiev's *At War's Summit: The Red Army and the Struggle for the Caucasus Mountains in World War II* (Cambridge University Press, 2018) is very much recommended for further reading.

Chapter 13

The Turning Tide: German Defeat in the South

The Soviet November 1942 counter-offensive in the south – Operation 'Uranus' – and subsequent widening of the offensive – Operation 'Little Saturn' – are two Soviet offensive operations that were clearly major strides on the road to the defeat of Nazi Germany. The Stalingrad and Don River counter-offensives have, with good reason, been described as the 'turning point' in the war in the East, and indeed for the war against Nazi Germany as a whole. On 19 November 1942 Soviet forces advanced quickly across the steppe on the flanks of the Stalingrad battle to enact the most significant Soviet encirclement of Axis forces to date. In previous instances where German forces had been encircled during the winter of 1941/1942, such as for example at Demiansk and further south at Kholm in north-west Russia, German forces had held out until relieved and received supplies by air. These were, however, very small encirclements in comparison to the full German army (6th Army), elements of the 4th Panzer Army and Romanian divisions trapped in the Stalingrad pocket. Looking to repeat what had happened on a smaller scale during the winter of 1941/1942, Hitler ordered that the 6th Army should not seek to break out, but to hold the city until relieved. That relief would not come, as the troops that were supposed to relieve them ran into Soviet forces that were attempting to turn the encirclement of a German army into the encirclement of a German army group (at this point in fact two, Army Groups A and B). The German Luftwaffe would have struggled to supply these beleaguered forces in the Stalingrad pocket even in summer conditions as the Soviet air forces were an increasingly potent threat, and proved incapable of doing so when faced with enemy air activity and winter weather. Whilst Soviet forces did not achieve the wider encirclement that would trap Army Groups A and B, they did tear through Hitler's allies on the German flanks and all but destroy Italian, Hungarian and to a lesser extent Romanian forces on the Eastern Front. At the same time the Red Army forced the German armed forces to pull back from the Caucasus lest they be caught in a larger encirclement in one of the few instances where Hitler had the sense to authorise a withdrawal. Nonetheless, by the spring of 1943 the Red Army had not only destroyed the German 6th Army and the Romanian forces in the Stalingrad pocket – a force that had been more than 250,000-strong – but had also ripped the heart out of Axis forces on the southern part of Germany's Eastern Front. Mounting Soviet casualties and extended supply lines eventually allowed German forces to counter-attack and regain some territory, setting the scene for the fighting at Kursk in the summer of 1943. Nonetheless, after the German defeat at Stalingrad and in the wider south we can see with the value of hindsight that the chances of German victory in the East had significantly diminished and the tide of the war on the Eastern Front had turned. Even at the time it was apparent that the Red Army was clearly on the ascendancy, at a time when British and Commonwealth forces had finally and conclusively gained the upper hand in North Africa and were being joined by US forces, and where in the Far East after their defeat at Midway the Japanese had been forced onto the defensive.

The tide turns, 19 November 1942 to the end of 1943.

Sputnik 5646055. To open this chapter, which deals with a period starting with the Soviet counter-offensive near Stalingrad – Operation 'Uranus' – we have a picture taken on 20 November 1942, a day after the official start of the operation. Taken somewhere near Stalingrad, this picture is unusual in that it was taken at night, where achieving a good photograph without flash would have been far from easy. Fortunately in this instance the photographer has caught this T-34 at just the right moment to have the flash from the gun firing illuminate the tank. Tank buffs and those with a keen eye for such details will have noticed that this tank differs from those in earlier photos of T-34 tanks in this book and indeed from the tanks in Sputnik 882842 in this chapter (see p. 162), where the turret shape is significantly different. The tank pictured here is the 1942 variant of the T-34 tank. When comparing this variant to its predecessor, particularly important to note is the addition of a commander's cupola on the turret. This gave the commander much better vision from within the tank through vision blocks in the cupola than in the previous version of the tank.

Sputnik 2373. This picture from late 1942 also shows Model 1942 T-34 tanks outside Stalingrad, this time with tank riders in snow smocks and armed with PPSh sub-machine guns. This picture gives some idea of how the Soviet spearheads that conducted the initial encirclement of Axis forces at Stalingrad would have looked.

(*Opposite, above*) Sputnik 882842. As Soviet forces outside Stalingrad encircled Axis forces in a large pocket including the city itself, Soviet forces within the city continued to engage in fighting for the city at a horrendous cost to both sides, but with the balance of capabilities and casualties moving increasingly in favour of the Red Army. In this picture as well T-34 tanks are shown in action, this time supported by infantry in an attack on German positions somewhere within the city. Although elements of the German 4th Panzer Army were trapped within the Stalingrad pocket, severe shortages of fuel and ammunition would soon hamper their activities as much as enemy action.

(*Opposite, below*) Sputnik 2245. Fighting for the factory districts of the city of Stalingrad continued after the November encirclement of the city. Here a Soviet gun crew – once again as in the previous chapter with the new ZiS-3 divisional gun – is shown in action within the confines of the Red October Factory. Also, the gun is similarly being used in a direct-fire role, as indicated by the fact that the barrel is nearly on the horizontal. As noted earlier, the Red Army was particularly likely to use divisional artillery in such a manner, where relatively manoeuvrable guns (if you compare this to the German divisional artillery pieces in Sputnik 1166 in Chapter 8 (see p. 101, Sputnik 1166) their relative manoeuvrability becomes apparent) were easier to train to hit a target when used in such a manner. This picture was apparently taken on 10 December 1942.

(*Above*) Sputnik 2249. Here, once again around the Red October Factory, Soviet soldiers are shown after the start of the 19 November counter-offensive that would lead to the encirclement of Axis forces in and around the city. Although this may have been posed, I chose this picture largely because it gives something of a first-person view of the Red October Factory in ruins as seen by the two Red Army soldiers in cover in the foreground. Note the grenade in the hand of the Red Army soldier on the left.

(*Above*) Sputnik 450. A chapter on the fighting for Stalingrad during the winter period of 1942/1943 would not be complete without at least one picture of Soviet snipers operating within the city. The Soviet sniper Vasilii Zaitsev has become synonymous with the fighting for the city even in the West, but he was one of many Soviet snipers operating during the fighting. Prior to the war the Red Army had encouraged 'sniping' skills, but typically for those operating within the confines of rifle sections and platoons, not as free-ranging individuals or typically pairs operating on their own. The war in Finland and Finnish snipers had started to change things, so that by the time of the winter of 1942/1943 it was increasingly accepted that snipers were more effective if not tied too closely to standard rifle units – a component of a significant cultural shift towards tolerating elements of decentralisation. By this time the so-called 'sniper movement' had caught hold in the Red Army and in particular within Stalingrad, to the point where whole companies of snipers were organised – even if there were not necessarily enough specialist sniping rifles to go round. [RASWW, pp. 385–9] German forces too employed numerous snipers within the city.

(*Opposite, below*) Sputnik 451. Most Soviet troops were far better equipped for the winter weather in the Stalingrad region than their German counterparts, who often had to resort to stripping the bodies of Soviet dead of their clothing. Here a group of Soviet troops pass a corpse in Stalingrad in late 1942 as Soviet forces applied increasing pressure on the beleaguered Axis defenders.

(*Left*) Sputnik 62751. Although Vasilii Zaitsev is perhaps the most renowned Soviet sniper of the battle for Stalingrad, here we will profile another famous sniper at the time Maksim Passar, a member of the Nanaitsi people, a small ethnic group from the banks of the Amur river and its tributaries the Ussuri and Sungari in the Soviet Far East. Passar – a member of the Komsomol – volunteered for Red Army service in 1942, soon became a sniper and ended up in Stalingrad. On 17 September 1942 he was put forward for the Order of the Red Banner by the commander and commissar of his regiment, the 117th Rifle Regiment of the 23rd Rifle Division, by which time he was credited with having killed fifty-six German soldiers. He was killed in action on 22 January 1943, by which point he was credited, as the official caption to the photograph notes, with 236 'kills'.[26] In this November 1942 picture, Passar is shown with a German MP 40 machine-gun – perhaps a trophy from one of his 'kills'.

Sputnik 2392. Here a Soviet Model 1938 120mm mortar prepares to fire somewhere near Stalingrad in late 1942. The sheer size of the 120mm mortar round is clear in this picture. Although developed much earlier, mortars were adopted with enthusiasm by the Red Army only after the war in Finland highlighted their value, they are simple and easy to maintain, and relatively cheap to manufacture. The Soviet 120mm mortar was essentially copied by Germany during the war.

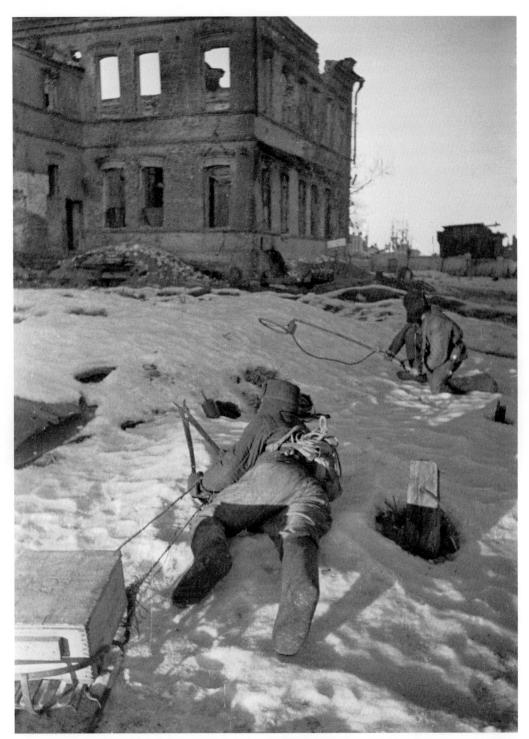

Sputnik 2247. Both sides employed large numbers of mines when on the defensive. Here Soviet sappers seek mines in Stalingrad in December 1942. Both are wearing traditional Russian felt winter boots called *valenki*, that were much sought after by German troops seeking some protection for their feet from the extreme cold. They are also wearing *vatniki*, padded jackets that were widely used and often worn with similar padded trousers by Soviet troops in colder conditions.

(*Above*) Sputnik 61643. This photograph from within Stalingrad is perhaps the most unusual of those published in this book. I have tried to select a number of photographs for this book illustrating aspects of soldiers' day-to-day life beyond the fighting, and what could be more important than food. Getting food to front-line positions was a dangerous task in itself, as is highlighted by this Red Army man carrying hot food on his back through the rubble and armed with a PPSh sub-machine gun. The importance of getting food to the troops – and the value of a hot meal of some sort to front-line soldiers in winter – should not be downplayed.

(*Opposite, above*) Sputnik 602161. This final picture from within the city of Stalingrad shows a group of Red Army soldiers moving through the ghostly ruins of the city on 2 February 1943 – the day that Axis forces in the pocket surrendered on the orders of their commander, the recently promoted Field Marshal Paulus. When reporting to Stalin in the early evening of 2 February after the surrender, the commander of the Don Front, Colonel General Rokossovskii could report with some satisfaction that 'operations in the city and regions surrounding Stalingrad' had ceased, by which point 'more than 91,000' prisoners had been taken, including more than 2,500 officers and 24 generals' – and of course one field marshal. [GPW, p. 108] A force of more than 250,000 enemy troops had been destroyed in the Stalingrad region. Many of the German troops captured at Stalingrad – like their Soviet equivalents captured in major encirclements by German forces of 1941 – would die in captivity.

(*Opposite, below*) Sputnik 411726. Although Soviet forces were unable to trap the German Army Group A in the Caucasus as hoped, the destruction of much of Army Group B further north – including the 6th Army in Stalingrad – meant that continued German operations in the Caucasus

were unsustainable and for once Hitler authorised withdrawal in early 1943. In this picture Soviet troops are shown fighting German rearguard forces for the key city of Rostov-on-Don on 14 February 1943 – the day it was liberated for a second time by the Red Army. As is apparent in this picture, Rostov-on-Don fortunately did not suffer the wholesale destruction meted out on Stalingrad.

Sputnik 60907. In the aftermath of the destruction of the Stalingrad pocket and the withdrawal of the German Army Group A from the Caucasus, the Red Army was able to push on a considerable distance westwards through Ukrainian territory. Soon, however, attrition and supply issues were hampering the Soviet advance, and German counter-attacks were able to regain some ground. The much fought-over city of Khar'kov changed hands twice within a short space of time as it was liberated by the Red Army in mid-February before being recaptured after intense fighting within the city by German Waffen SS forces in mid-March 1943. In this photograph a *tachanka* or cart-mounted machine gun of the 4th Guards Cavalry Corps is shown in position on 18 March 1943. The 4th Guards Cavalry Corps was at the time part of the Southern Front, and had been pursuing the retreating Axis forces in the lead-up to when this photograph was taken. On 12 March the formation crossed the river Don not far from Rostov-on-Don, giving some idea where this photograph was taken.[27]

Chapter 14

The Bitter Road back to Smolensk and Beyond

Although events in the Stalingrad region in late 1942 and 1943 have tended to overshadow those taking place further north, it would be wrong to assume that means little was going on elsewhere at the same time. We have already looked at the Leningrad region in Chapter 6, where the siege of the city was partially lifted in January 1943. We have not, however, looked at events on the approaches to Moscow in 1942 and early 1943, where although German forces were pushed back from the city during the winter of 1941/1942, they nonetheless retained a foothold in the Rzhev region in the spring of 1942. Stalin and the Soviet military leaders had clearly assumed that during the campaigning season of 1942 Germany would for a second time attempt to seize Moscow, meaning that potential routes of advance to the capital were well defended. German disinformation that sought to convince Soviet leaders that Germany did indeed plan to try to capture Moscow during 1942 was apparently successful because it fell on fertile ground – Soviet leaders could be reassured that German intentions were as they already assumed. With a considerable proportion of Soviet strength positioned to defend Moscow, Soviet forces were also positioned to undertake offensive operations against the German Rzhev salient – a crooked finger that if cut off would not only reduce any threat to Moscow, but also mean the destruction of a sizeable German force.

Although Soviet forces had launched an ill-informed offensive in the Khar'kov region to the south in May 1942, they also continued throughout the summer of 1942 to hammer away at German defences on the Rzhev salient. Although the Stalingrad counter-offensive, Operation 'Uranus', and its associated wider offensive Operation 'Little Saturn' have been portrayed as the key Soviet offensive operations of late 1942, they were not necessarily the sole focus of attention even in November 1942. It is clear from archival sources that Operation 'Mars' – a major operation planned against the Rzhev salient that would overlap with 'Uranus' – was the subject of considerable Soviet attention and resources. This operation was sufficiently important for the later legendary Soviet general Zhukov to take principal responsibility for 'Mars' rather than 'Uranus'. 'Mars' would, however, turn into a débâcle, with Soviet forces losing tens of thousands of troops for little gain, even if the offensive did limit the scope for Germany to transfer resources southwards. In March 1943 German forces would evacuate the salient of their own accord – another rare instance of Hitler sanctioning

withdrawal in the aftermath of the Stalingrad disaster. With their lines significantly shortened, the German capacity for putting up stiff resistance in central European Russia was renewed. Through the spring and early summer of 1943 Soviet offensive operations on what was now the Smolensk axis would continue to cost the Red Army dearly for often only limited gains prior to the aftermath of 'Citadel', when the rapid Soviet advance to the Dnepr would to some extent undermine German resistance further north. Nonetheless, even from the late summer of 1943 through to the end of the year, the Soviet advance in the centre over terrain far less suited to the advance than the steppe to the south would be particularly bloody and far from rapid. This chapter deals with Soviet operations in central European Russia from the spring of 1942 to the end of 1943.

(*Opposite*) Sputnik 212. The first picture of this chapter was taken on the southern side of what might be seen as the northern sector of the front in European Russia in the region south of Lake Il'men near Staraia Russa – a considerable distance from either Moscow or Leningrad. Although there is a tendency in all but the most specialised histories to focus on the principal Leningrad, Moscow and what we might term Stalingrad axes, it is important to remember that fighting and dying was taking place across the whole front. Here in the summer of 1942 Red Army troops struggle to push a 45mm anti-tank gun with antiquated spoked wooden wheels up a rather boggy slope in conditions very much typical of much of north-western and central-western European Russia and Belorussia.

(*Below*) Sputnik 1033. The sort of terrain over which the soldiers in the previous photo were fighting would have also included many water obstacles, from larger lakes such as Lake Il'men to small rivers and streams, all to varying degrees hindering movement. Often soldiers made do with locally available resources to cross such obstacles, such as the traditional Russian boat in the foreground of this picture being used in this water crossing somewhere on the North-Western Front during the summer of 1942. Dinghies such as that behind the wooden boat were also used in such crossings, having the advantage of being easily transportable to where they were needed.

БЕЙ, КОЛИ, ГОНИ, БЕРИ В ПОЛОН!

А. СУВОРОВ

(*Left*) Sputnik 136707. This 1942 propaganda poster reflects a trend in Soviet propaganda of the early war period towards rehabilitation of pre-Soviet Russian heroes to be mobilised in support of the Motherland – something that had started shortly before the war with, for example, the 1938 movie 'Alexander Nevsky'. Alexander Nevsky's defeat of the Teutonic Knights in the thirteenth century had obvious potential contemporary parallels, and he appears in a number of Soviet posters of the period. In this poster – produced in a more traditional style than some wartime posters that continued the revolutionary avant-garde tradition – Tsarist-era general and hero of the Patriotic War of 1812 Alexander Suvorov is shown in the background of fighting in the current war. Such suggestion that the contemporary invader should and would suffer the same fate as their predecessors was a recurring theme in Soviet propaganda of this period, whether the past enemy be the Teutonic Knights or Napoleon's Grand Army.

(*Opposite, above*) Sputnik 595790. Here are two more pictures taken on the North-Western Front during the summer of 1942 that show two moments in the fighting near the settlement of Gridino on the western bank of the river Lovat'. This area saw sustained fighting throughout much of the period with which this chapter is concerned and indeed during the Soviet winter counter-offensive of 1941–1942. In this region the Soviet forces sought to destroy the German forces encircled at Demiansk. It is unclear exactly where this photograph was taken and on which day. As an example of the intensity of the fighting in and around Gridino, on 17 June 1942 the 914th Rifle Regiment of the 246th Rifle Division launched an assault on Gridino that began with an air strike followed by an attack by a company of tanks supported by tank-riding infantry. Although two of the tanks made it to the settlement, the remainder got stuck in a ditch approximately half a kilometre from Gridino. With insufficient fire-support, the infantry of the 914th Rifle Regiment were forced to go to ground, and after engaging the defenders returned to their start positions having suffered heavy casualties.[28]

(*Opposite, below*) Sputnik 663473. According to the war diary for the 246th Rifle Division, the 914th Rifle Regiment suffered 128 killed, 336 wounded and 25 missing in the attack on Gridino on 17 June alone.[29] Something of the horror of assaulting enemy positions is certainly captured in this and the preceding photograph taken only seconds apart.

(*Opposite, above*) Sputnik 637051. In this picture Soviet artillerymen are shown with their 152mm Model 1937 gun-howitzer (ML-20) somewhere in the Rzhev region during the early summer of 1942. The static nature of much of the fighting in this region over a protracted period of time lent itself to the amassing of artillery resources. This weapon was produced throughout the war in a single factory, and even equipped the SU- and ISU-152 assault guns. A total of 6,884 examples of this weapon were manufactured between 1937 and 1946. German industry even produced munitions for this gun, since nearly 1,000 examples were captured by the Wehrmacht.[30]

(*Above*) Sputnik 637033. The static nature of much of the fighting in the Rzhev region also meant that there was time for the development of extensive minefields as part of defences. Here Soviet sappers with mine detectors are at work on the North-Western Front in late June 1942. Lifting mines under fire was clearly a nerve-wracking task.

Sputnik 297. Here, by now in the autumn, elements of the 167th Rifle Regiment of the 1st Guards Rifle Division move forward somewhere near Sukhinichi to the west of Tula in October 1942. You may recall the mud of the autumn of 1941 from earlier chapters, with the period of the *rasputitsa* or 'time without roads' of the spring thaw and autumn rains making movement difficult for both sides. Some attempt has been made here to provide a makeshift corduroy path across the marshy ground. Just how static the front line was in this area is highlighted by the fact that Sukhinichi itself was liberated by the Red Army back in January 1942.

Sputnik 597. Another winter in the Rzhev salient. Here tanks with tank-riding infantrymen are ready to move off to the start line for an attack, somewhere on the Kalinin Front in February 1943. The tanks here are still the earlier variant of the T-34 without the commander's cupola. The effectiveness of the infantry's snow camouflage is apparent in this picture.

Sputnik 60565. Here Soviet artillery advances north-west of Viaz'ma near Moscow in mid-March 1943. Soon, German forces would abandon the Rzhev salient in order to shorten their lines, moving much of the fighting further west where Soviet forces would once again get bogged down. This artillery piece is being pulled by a tracked tractor that is also pulling a sledge behind the gun. I chose to include this picture in part because it is very Russian, with the Orthodox church building adding further character to the birch trees and crows' nests that are so typical of the Russian landscape. This peaceful scene of course contrasts strongly with many others in this book.

Sputnik 2540. Here, also in March 1943, Red Army soldiers are shown digging in. Many infantry-men spent a lot of time digging trenches or foxholes, but there are relatively few photographs of them doing so. Infantrymen would spend more time digging in when they were advancing, when they would have to repeatedly dig in to provide protection in the event of enemy counter-attacks.

Sputnik 493. Here some young Red Army soldiers of the Western Front pay their last respects to their fallen commander, somewhere near Gzhatsk in the Smolensk region during April 1943. Many fallen soldiers – even commanders – did not get anything like such elaborate memorials constructed for them in the field.

Sputnik 882839. Here, the Polish general Zygmunt Berling is shown with troops of the 1st Communist Polish Infantry Division at their camp near Riazan' (south-east of Moscow) sometime in early July 1943, prior to their blooding on the battlefield alongside the Red Army at Lenino on the Smolensk axis in October that same year. What in July 1943 was merely a division would grow by the end of the war into a Communist Polish force consisting of multiple armies. The baptism of fire for the 1st Polish Infantry Division at Lenino was in an engagement typical of many Soviet attacks made at high cost with limited success on the central sector of the front during 1942 and 1943.

Sputnik 59101. The names of the Soviet fronts would change as the Red Army made its painstaking progress across central European Russia in 1943, where by the time this picture was taken in October 1943 these troops advancing in the region were part of the 1st Belorussian Front. Note once again the corduroy road laid in an attempt to keep vehicles from bogging down on the muddy autumn roads. The gun here is the by now ubiquitous ZiS-3, being pulled, however, by US-manufactured vehicles provided under Lend-Lease. The crews here have gone to some effort to provide camouflage for their guns.

Sputnik 2446. Given the importance of food, comfort and relaxation in a soldier's life (or indeed anyone's for that matter), it is perhaps a shame that more pictures of soldiers in a setting such as this are not reproduced in books on the Great Patriotic War. Although their faces suggest that the atmosphere here is far from relaxed – and where some sort of political meeting is perhaps being held – the rest and warmth of the fire were no doubt most welcome to these soldiers pictured sometime during November 1943 in rather dreary autumn weather.

Chapter 15

From Kursk to the Dnepr

In the aftermath of the destruction of the German 6th Army at Stalingrad the Red Army's advance in the south had been halted by the spring of 1943, and German forces had even recaptured some lost ground. Nonetheless, the Red Army was clearly becoming relatively stronger as the German armed forces struggled to find the means for offensive operations that would have more than local significance. Germany was under pressure not only on the Eastern Front, but also from the Allies in the West where the successful conclusion of the North Africa campaign meant that Germany's ally in the Mediterranean – Italy – was clearly under threat, and Allied strategic bombing was becoming an increasingly serious drain on German resources. As both sides made plans for the summer campaigning season of 1943, the best that Germany could plan for in the East was to destroy a Soviet salient centred on the city of Kursk that had been formed in the line when German forces recaptured territory in the Khar'kov region in March. Although the German fantasy scenario was that the destruction of the Kursk salient and forces within it might lead to more, realistically all that could be hoped for was the destruction of a sizeable Soviet force, a simplification of the front line and the buying of time. The Soviet Union had more options, with Stalin's initial preference being for the Red Army to go onto the offensive again as soon as possible. However, as the Soviet side gained a better intelligence picture of German intentions, Stalin would ultimately be convinced that the Red Army would be better off receiving and absorbing a German attack in the Kursk region before itself launching major offensive operations. In the light of what had happened in 1941, Stalin's unease at the concept is understandable, but the situation in 1943 was very different. For one, Germany would not benefit from a meaningful element of surprise, and the Red Army had also gained significant experience in absorbing German armoured blows that included the blunting of the German relief effort at Stalingrad. Although Soviet leaders were concerned when the attack at Kursk did not happen in May and June, waiting until it finally did in July would reap dividends. Although German armoured thrusts from the north and south sides of the Kursk salient penetrated deeply into Soviet defences, the Kursk salient had been so heavily fortified and such large Soviet forces amassed that even elite units of the Wehrmacht and Waffen SS could not complete the planned encirclement. That German forces penetrated as far as they did was testimony to the enduring quality of elements of the Wehrmacht, and the Red Army was compelled to throw in some of the forces held back for the counter-attack phase of its plans in order to halt the German offensive.

Nonetheless, the Red Army could afford to do so given the resources amassed over the preceding months.

With their plans thwarted at Kursk, German forces soon fell back under heavy Soviet pressure towards what was hoped would be a solid defensive line on the Dnepr river. Such a defensive line had not been pre-prepared – that would have been defeatist and unacceptable to Hitler. Soviet forces were, at many points, able to force the Dnepr river and in the far south advanced deep into German-held territory further west. Further north Kiev had been liberated before the year was out, at which point even the most delusional Nazi leader must have been starting to have doubts in ultimate German victory. Stalin of course grew in confidence, to the extent that he was increasingly willing to be seen as being at the helm of a Red Army that was now meting out rather than being on the receiving end of defeat.

(*Opposite, above*) Sputnik 851334. Soviet defences in the Kursk salient designed to absorb the blow of a German attack were multi-layered and in depth. Soviet forces in the salient had plenty of time to prepare for a German attack, including digging trenches such as the one shown here, constructing other defensive positions and laying mines. In this picture a lieutenant of the artillery observes the scene in front of his position through binoculars, his telephone operator behind him, on 5 July 1943, the day on which German forces launched Operation 'Citadel' against the Kursk salient. Some effort has been put into concealing this position. Future Major General F.W. von Mellenthin with the German XLVIII Panzer Corps at Kursk later suggested that such Soviet *maskirovka* of troops and positions meant that Soviet strength on the salient 'was considerably underestimated'. [RASWW, p. 444]

(*Opposite, below*) Sputnik 793. This photograph of a Red Army anti-tank rifle team lying beside a knocked-out tank is also recorded as having been taken on 5 July in the Kursk salient. Although by this stage of the war other armies were discarding their anti-tank rifles as ineffective against most tanks, and even the powerful Soviet rifle shown here was of little value against the German tanks being fielded at Kursk, this weapon still had utility. The Red Army continued to use such anti-tank rifles as a useful weapon against the multitude of lighter armoured vehicles in use with German forces, such as the Sd.Kfz.250 and 251 half-tracked armoured personnel carriers used by the German Panzergrenadiers, armoured reconnaissance units and others. As noted earlier, on occasion this weapon was also used for sniping and against aircraft by virtue of its high muzzle velocity and range.

(*Above*) Sputnik 607854. A key reason for the German delay in attacking the Kursk salient during the spring and early summer of 1943 was that Hitler was waiting for new German tanks to be available for the offensive. The Tiger and Panther tanks fielded in significant numbers at Kursk were indeed potent weapons, with heavy armour and powerful guns – on a one-to-one basis they were more than a match for the T-34. The new heavily armoured German tanks were also difficult to destroy with the lighter anti-tank guns in the Soviet arsenal. As new Soviet assault guns and a new variant of the T-34 with an 85mm rather than 76mm gun were being developed and rushed into service, as a stopgap measure the Red Army would employ 85mm anti-aircraft guns in an anti-tank role, as shown here somewhere in the Kursk salient. Unlike German forces with their 88mm anti-aircraft gun, these Soviet guns were not consistently used in an anti-tank role.

(*Opposite, above*) Sputnik 65872. This photograph, taken after the fighting in the Kursk salient during the summer of 1943, shows renowned Soviet poet, writer and journalist Konstantin Simonov sitting on the barrel of a German 'Ferdinand' tank destroyer. The 'Ferdinand' was one of the most powerful mobile anti-tank weapons of the war, although in its early incarnation shown here it was seriously flawed in not having a machine gun for close defence from infantry. Simonov's 1941 wartime poem 'Wait for me' is undoubtedly one of the most famous pieces of artistic work to come out of the Great Patriotic War (see p. xiii).

(*Opposite, below*) Sputnik 3427. With the German attack on the Kursk salient blunted, the Red Army launched major offensives both north and south of the salient. Soviet reconnaissance of enemy positions before an attack often took the form of 'reconnaissance-by-battle' – something undertaken by Soviet forces far more frequently than their opponents or allies. 'Reconnaissance-by-battle' was, as the term suggests, the process of finding out about enemy positions and strength by launching an attack of limited scale. According to the official caption, that is what is taking place in this picture taken on 15 July near Mtsensk to the north of the Kursk salient. As you can imagine, troops engaged in 'reconnaissance-by-battle' often took heavy casualties. In the foreground one of the soldiers has a light mortar – a weapon like the anti-tank rifle more typically associated with the early period of the war and increasingly sidelined in favour of heavier mortars with better range and high-explosive capabilities as the war progressed.

СТАЛИН ВЕДЁТ НАС К ПОБЕДЕ!

(*Left*) Sputnik 136658. By 1943 Stalin was willing to be portrayed in Soviet propaganda as leader of the Soviet Union, where his absence had been conspicuous in 1941–1942. Clearly Stalin did not want to be visibly associated with the defeats of the early period of the war, but all that had changed by the time this poster was published. The text reads 'Stalin will lead us to victory!' This poster is by the Soviet Georgian artist Iralklii Moiseevich Toidze (1902–1985), whose 'The Motherland-Mother Calls!' of the beginning of the war is perhaps his most famous wartime work. In the colour version of this poster the text, flag and red star on Stalin's cap are all red, the remainder black and white.

(*Opposite, above*) Sputnik 889. This dramatic photograph – worthy no doubt of a prize if one was to have been available – shows Red Army soldiers on the attack in August 1943, breaching a barbed wire obstacle whilst under fire. Notice once again, as in many other photographs in this book, the absence of helmets – something that if worn would have saved many lives and prevented many serious injuries. Many Red Army soldiers continued to choose not to wear helmets even when they were available. The photographer, Max Alpert, did receive the Order of the Red Star (1943) and the Order of the Patriotic War 2nd Class (1945) for his wartime work. Max Alpert's most famous photograph is undoubtedly the often reproduced iconic photograph entitled '*Kombat*' or 'Battalion Commander' of 1942, which shows a Soviet commander encouraging his troops forward only minutes before he was subsequently killed.

(*Opposite, below*) Sputnik 603769. German and British forces saw reconnaissance slightly differently from Soviet practice, where observation and the avoidance of combat was typically more important than engaging in probing attacks on enemy territory. In this role, British and German forces made considerable use of armoured cars, a vehicle type that the Red Army too had invested in prior to the war but ended up using as light tanks or even armoured personnel carriers rather than for reconnaissance. During the war, as the Red Army sought to develop mechanised reconnaissance forces somewhat more akin to those of their opponent, the BA-64 armoured car was produced in limited numbers for such a role. Just how small these armoured cars were is highlighted in this picture! These vehicles were based on the chassis of the GAZ-64 – the Soviet equivalent of the jeep – and it is therefore unsurprising that with the addition of light armour they were underpowered. These vehicles did, however, continue to serve throughout the war in the absence of anything better, often serving alongside US-manufactured light armoured personnel carriers such as the M3 'White' Scout Car. This platoon of armoured cars is pictured operating on the South-Western Front during the advance on Krasnoarmeisk in the Donbass in mid-July 1943.

(*Above*) Sputnik 2711. The Soviet Union continued to employ large cavalry formations throughout the war, which over time were provided with far greater mobile firepower than their early-war equivalents. Such formations were in many ways ideally suited to the pursuit of the enemy, as was the case in the aftermath of the fighting at Kursk. Here Cossack cavalry in traditional attire ford a river somewhere on Russian territory in September 1943. The Cossacks were allowed to serve in the Red Army from 1936, having previously been seen with some justification as staunch defenders of Tsarism at the time of the Revolution. At times when the Soviet regime was trying to incorporate disparate national groups into regular rather than 'national' Red Army units, the Cossacks were still allowed to serve in the so-called 'Cossack' divisions formed from 1936 onwards [RASWW, p. 28]. During the war the German army was able to form a number of 'Cossack' units from those would-be Cossacks apparently hostile to the Soviet regime, including émigrés who had left Russia during the Russian Civil War.

(*Opposite, above*) Sputnik 67381. Here Soviet forward elements – dressed in the camouflaged overalls increasingly issued to reconnaissance troops by this stage of the war – pass a German Marder III Ausf. H tank destroyer somewhere near Poltava to the south-west of Khar'kov in the Ukraine. Although there were camouflaged overalls in use in limited numbers earlier in the war, seeing such overalls in any numbers in a picture typically dates it to the second half of the Great Patriotic War.

(*Opposite, below*) Sputnik 5823667. In this picture advancing Soviet troops are shown further north on Russian territory in the recently liberated town of Sevsk, situated to the north-west of Kursk just outside the northern boundary of the Ukrainian Soviet Socialist Republic. The troops at centre-left are carrying the baseplates for 82mm mortars, the barrel of one of which is being carried by the soldier in the foreground on the far left. Other soldiers are carrying spades to facilitate the entrenching of the unit.

Sputnik 60651. The initial Soviet crossings of the Dnepr river often started off as impromptu affairs by advance elements of the Red Army, with soldiers using whatever means they could lay their hands on to facilitate getting across to the other side. Here on 21 September 1943 troops are using makeshift buoyancy aids in order to help get themselves across with hopefully largely dry weapons. In order to encourage enthusiasm for crossing the river the regime offered the prospect of the Hero of the Soviet Union award for in particular officers whose units were in the vanguard. For the forcing of the Dnepr river 47 generals, 1,123 other officers and 1,268 NCOs and other soldiers became Heroes of the Soviet Union. [RASWW, pp. 465–7]

Sputnik 4458. Here the Dnepr is being crossed on something of a makeshift bridge in October 1943, somewhere near Kakhovka, a town not far from Kherson and the Crimea in the far south of the Ukraine. It was in the south that the Red Army made the most rapid progress in crossing and advancing beyond the Dnepr river during the autumn of 1943.

Sputnik 1209. Crossings of the Dnepr were also made much further north than Kakhovka during the autumn of 1943. Here, in this evocative photograph, Soviet troops are shown near a destroyed bridge on the banks of the Dnepr in the much fought over and symbolically important city of Smolensk at the end of September 1943. Smolensk is about two-thirds of the way along the key Warsaw–Moscow highway. What had taken German forces a matter of weeks to reach back in 1941 had taken the Red Army approaching two years to liberate in the aftermath of the Moscow counter-offensive of 1941–1942. The next key marker on the advance to the West on this axis would be the capital of the Belorussian SSR, Minsk – another third of the way to Warsaw.

Sputnik 828. Here Soviet tankers relax beside their T-34 tanks somewhere near Kiev in November 1943. Kiev, on the western bank of the Dnepr, fell to Soviet forces on 6 November. The recapture of the city was of considerable political significance for Soviet forces, since it was the capital of the Ukrainian SSR. During the process of liberating Kiev in an operation that involved the bold use of tank forces such as these in operations sweeping around the city, counter-attacking German forces were badly mauled. The city itself was liberated not only by Soviet forces, but with the participation of the 1st Independent Czech Rifle Brigade. [RASWW, pp. 468–70] Although the Communist Czech armed forces were not as large as those of their neighbour, Poland, the Soviet Union was careful to note their role in the defeat of Nazi Germany on the Eastern Front with a view to fostering Communist influence in a post-war Eastern Europe. It would only be a matter of weeks from this point until the Red Army reached the 1939 Soviet border in the West.

Chapter 16

Allied Aid and the Soviet War Effort

One of the greatest Soviet wartime achievements was in keeping the war economy going despite the loss of vast tracts of territory and resources, along with the dislocation of much of its industry and agriculture. There can be little doubt that the Soviet Union halted the Axis advance largely with domestically produced weapons and equipment, and with an army and population clothed and fed largely from domestic supplies. That the Soviet Union did so constituted an economic miracle of sorts given how much territory, resources and industrial plant were lost during the period of the Axis advance in 1941–1942. The evacuation of much of the Soviet Union's industrial defence capacity from the western regions to the Urals and Central Asia from the first weeks of the war was an enormous undertaking, and a considerable achievement. Although Soviet factories weren't up and running again in a meaningful way further east quite as quickly as Soviet propaganda suggested, by the spring of 1942 that capacity was coming online again just before the loss of further capacity during the Axis advance in the south. The defence sector was nonetheless able to increase production of many items thanks to the system being capable of switching civilian production to military production as planned prior to the war. As damaging as the dislocation of industrial production was, the loss of agricultural land, and particularly of the 'Black Earth' region in the summer of 1942, was perhaps even more significant in a situation where Soviet agriculture was suffering from a shortage of labour and motive power thanks to mobilisations into the Red Army. The year 1943 proved to be a bleak one for Soviet food supply. The Soviet Union had nonetheless survived to halt the Wehrmacht and its allies, but it was hungry and starting to require some of the goods that had been produced by factories switched to military production or lost to the enemy, goods that were now needed to keep the wartime Soviet Union going.

The Soviet Union had survived with a little help from its new friends – Britain and the United States – although it is difficult to argue that without that help it wouldn't have done so. Britain and its Commonwealth had started to ship war materials to the Soviet Union via its northern ports only weeks after the German invasion. This war material was soon being shipped on a Lend-Lease basis, whereby materials needed for the prosecution of the war against Germany were provided without charge, with any items surviving the war to be either returned (often in practice disposed of) or paid for. By November 1941 the Soviet Union had formally been incorporated into the US Lend-Lease system, even if it would be well into 1942 before US aid reached significant levels, thanks to the fact that much early production was diverted to the US armed forces after the Japanese attack on Pearl Harbor and Hitler's declaration of war against the United States in December 1941. Nonetheless, materials provided by Britain at the end of 1941 and in early 1942 arrived at a critical juncture for the Soviet Union, when even modest additional inputs of equipment could make a meaningful contribution to Red Army capabilities. For the Soviet Union in late 1941 and early 1942 figures for equipment losses and new production were a little too close for comfort. British-supplied tanks and aircraft contributed to the defence of Moscow in November and early December 1941, for example, and the failed Khar'kov offensive of May 1942 was launched with a considerable number of British-supplied tanks.

It would be late 1942 before US production could start to meet Soviet needs in a meaningful way, but what had started as a trickle soon became a stream that flowed increasingly through the Middle East into the Soviet Union via Iran. Not only was the Soviet Union sent military equipment that it either lacked or was short of – a good example being medium bombers – but it also started to receive other deficit items within the Soviet economy and armed forces. The Soviet Union received not only aircraft and tanks, but other key items such as motor vehicles, railway locomotives, clothing, and foodstuffs not only in large quantities by weight, but dried, concentrated and tinned foodstuffs ideal for a Red Army on the move. Without these items the Soviet advance would undoubtedly have been slower and more costly. Although the Soviet people were doing most of the Allies' dying on the Eastern Front, to some extent the material effort there was an Allied one, as it was in the British Isles as the Western Allies prepared for D-Day and beyond. This chapter looks at Lend-Lease supplies and the Soviet Union during the war, and should be of particular interest to modellers and wargamers.

(*Opposite, above*) Sputnik 611114. Some of the first pieces of military equipment to reach the Soviet Union from Britain in late 1941 were tanks, and more specifically British infantry tanks. Slow and under-gunned, but well- armoured, British infantry tanks first saw action on the Eastern Front in late November 1941. By the end of 1941 the Soviet Union had received 446 such tanks from Britain. [GPW, p. 173] British-supplied 'Matilda' tanks appear in photographs in Chapter 12. The other tank provided to the Soviet Union from late 1941 was the 'Valentine', a slightly lighter tank with the same weak 2-pounder main gun armament as the 'Matilda', but nonetheless reliable and well-armoured for its day, and later provided in an up-gunned version. Many 'Valentine' tanks were manufactured in Canada, from which almost the entire production was shipped to the USSR. Here a 2-pounder gun-armed 'Valentine' is shown well after it was delivered to the Soviet Union in action in the Crimea in early May 1944, somewhere near Sevastopol'.

(*Opposite, below*) Sputnik 697702. Less popular with Soviet tank crews than the 'Valentine' was the M3 'Lee', provided by the United States along with the lighter M3 'Stuart'. A total of 711 light and 676 medium US tanks had reached the Soviet Union by 1 November 1942, with a further 522 light and 456 medium tanks en route as of that date. Some Soviet sources claim that because the M3 had a petrol engine it was more likely to 'brew-up' than diesel-powered tanks, and its very high profile made it an easy target. Consequently the tank was nicknamed 'Guaranteed Death for Seven' or 'Shared Grave for Seven'.[31] Nonetheless, these tanks saw action across the Soviet Union, many soldiering on for several years. Here a knocked-out M3 'Lee' is shown beside the grave of its crew in the Smolensk region in August 1943.

(*Above*) Sputnik 600789. More popular among Soviet crews than the earlier M3 'Lee' was the US-supplied M3 'Sherman' tank, later models of which armed with a 76mm gun are shown here on the streets of Vienna at the very end of the war in Europe. The United States supplied Sherman tanks to the Soviet Union from the mid-war period until the end of the war, moving from supplying the 75mm gun variant, of which 2,007 were sent, to the 76mm gun variant later in the war, of which 2,095 were sent. The 'Sherman' would see action in all theatres of the war.

(*Opposite, above*) Sputnik 884552. One area in which the Red Army was conspicuously lacking from the very beginning of the war was in armoured personnel carriers that would allow infantrymen to accompany the tanks with a degree of safety, at least from small arms fire and shell fragments, and that could also be used as reconnaissance vehicles. Armoured personnel carriers didn't really exist in the Soviet inventory at all at the beginning of the war, with the only Soviet-manufactured armoured personnel carriers of consequence being BA-10 armoured cars converted for the purpose, an example of which is shown in Sputnik 389 in Chapter 20 (see p. 252, Sputnik 389). The British made considerable use of the Lloyd and Bren 'Carriers' throughout the war, and a small number of such vehicles were supplied to the Soviet Union. As a specific example, fifty-three such carriers arrived with convoy PQ-12 to the Soviet Union in March 1942, with these vehicles being allocated to tank brigades. [GPW, p. 177] This photograph, taken in September 1944 in Poland, shows a number of such vehicles in use with the Red Army.

(*Opposite, below*) Sputnik 64991. From the mid-war period the United States supplied the Soviet Union with more meaningful numbers of M3 'White' Scout Cars, a vehicle that saw widespread use with Soviet reconnaissance forces through to the end of the war. The Soviet authorities reported having received 3,068 M3A1 scout cars during the war – of 3,340 reported as sent by the United States – the bulk of which were received after November 1942.[32] Here Soviet infantrymen and a 'White' Scout Car are shown at the end of the war in Vienna. On the right of the picture is a later-war variant of the successful German Sd.Kfz.251 armoured personnel carrier. The Soviet Union also received smaller numbers of the larger, half-tracked US M2, M3 and M5 armoured personnel carriers – essentially the US equivalent of the German Sd.Kfz.251 – including more significant numbers of specialised anti-aircraft and anti-tank variants.

(*Above*) Sputnik 611512. Given the large number of water obstacles to be crossed by the Red Army, it is perhaps unsurprising that it had some enthusiasm for amphibious vehicles. Prior to the war the Soviet Union had developed its own amphibious light tanks, and was keen to receive amphibious vehicles from the United States. Here Ford GPA amphibians are shown in Poland during 1944. Such vehicles functioned best in very calm waters, although the Red Army tended to push their capabilities. In one incident in the far north in 1944, when they were being used in a fjord, a number of these vehicles ended up being washed out to sea! The gun perched slightly precariously on the vehicle in the foreground is a DShK heavy machine gun, a variant of the weapon being used in an anti-aircraft role in Sputnik 2361 in Chapter 12 (see p. 153). The variant for sustained ground fire tends to date a photograph as being from the second part of the war.

(*Opposite, above*) Sputnik 1085. Particularly valuable for the Soviet war effort were the hundreds of thousands of US-supplied lorries or trucks. The Soviet Union drastically curtailed production of 'trucks' during the war to focus industrial attention on armoured vehicles, producing only 32,409 lorries and buses in 1942 (compared to 139,879 for 1940). [GPW, p. 188] With heavy losses of motor vehicles in 1941–1942, the Red Army would have been left far less mobile during the periods of advance of late 1943 onwards if it hadn't been for the huge number of vehicles supplied by the United States. This photograph, apparently taken at Mozhaisk not far from Moscow in the summer of 1944, shows Studebaker trucks of the Reserve of the Headquarters of the Supreme High Command awaiting transfer to the front lines. Not only were hundreds of thousands of trucks provided by the US, but many of them had far superior cross-country capabilities and could carry greater payloads than available Soviet trucks. The US supplied the Soviet Union with 362,825 trucks of more than ¼-ton size from October 1941 to June 1945. By 1945 as many as 30 per cent of the vehicles in the Red Army's 'vehicle park' were US-supplied vehicles.[33]

(*Opposite, below*) Sputnik 59807. Studebaker trucks became almost synonymous with the famous Soviet 'Katiusha' rocket system during the second half of the war, with Allied-supplied lorries and trucks being allocated for use with the system by the State Defence Committee – the Soviet equivalent of a war cabinet – from early in the war. Here 'Katiusha' rocket launchers mounted on Studebaker trucks are shown in action in Hungary at the end of 1944.

Sputnik 1916. Also popular with the Red Army were what have tended to be known simply as 'Jeeps' regardless of who manufactured them. Such light 4 × 4 vehicles were provided to the Soviet Union, as to other US allies, in large numbers – 48,956 'Jeeps' were received by the Soviet Union during the war. They were frequently used by officers as staff vehicles. Soviet poet, writer and journalist Konstantin Simonov – who appears in Sputnik 65872 in the previous chapter (see p. 187, Sputnik 3427) – mentions making use of 'Jeeps' on a number of occasions in his wartime memoirs.[34] In this picture Soviet troops are pictured with their 'Jeep' in Prague at the very end of the war in Europe.

Sputnik 5584217. I chose this picture not because it is typical, but for its novelty. The Soviet Union was not particularly short on small arms for most of the war, although early in the war it could clearly have done with more sub-machine guns as production of the PPSh was ramped up. During that period a significant proportion of production of the US Thompson sub-machine gun was shipped to the USSR. There is certainly evidence that some ended up in the hands of tank crews, although in this case it looks like an infantryman has acquired one, pictured here in January 1943 near Stalingrad.

Sputnik 62416. The principal conduit for Lend-Lease aid to the Soviet Union during the early phases of the war was via the Soviet Arctic, on the so-called 'Arctic Convoys'. This dangerous route – liable to interdiction from German air and naval forces based in Norway – gave many Allied sailors the opportunity to set foot in Russia, albeit with very little freedom and few opportunities for fraternisation with the local population or Soviet forces thanks to strict controls placed on such matters by the Soviet authorities. This picture, taken in August 1942, shows a relatively rare and no doubt orchestrated instance of such fraternisation between sailors of the Royal Navy and the Soviet Northern Fleet. In the background is a Soviet Type 7 destroyer.

Sputnik 60653. To a large extent because of the role of the Northern Fleet in the defence of the 'Arctic Convoys', the Allies provided the Soviet Navy with considerable material support under Lend-Lease. This support included providing surface vessels with a view to them enhancing the anti-submarine capabilities of the Northern Fleet. The Soviet Northern Fleet also received Allied vessels in lieu of reparations from the Italian Navy after Italy's surrender. In this picture, taken in September 1944, the Soviet battleship *Arkhangel'sk* – the former HMS *Royal Sovereign* – seems to be leading a group of 'Town' Class destroyers – transferred from the US to the UK in 1940 and then to the Soviet Union in 1944 – in northern waters. Although the 'Town' Class vessels were of First World War-vintage, they were equipped with ASDIC and modern anti-submarine weapons.

Sputnik 578. In a few instances military equipment was transferred by the Western Allies to Soviet forces after having being used by their Commonwealth crews on Russian territory. One such instance was the case of two squadrons of Handley-Page Hampden torpedo-bombers with British and Australian aircrew that were deployed to the Soviet north in defence of convoy PQ-18 in September 1942 and then, rather than attempting to make the hazardous journey back to the UK, were left to the Soviet Northern Fleet. Here one of those aircraft is shown loading a torpedo in October 1942. The writing on the torpedo in Cyrillic reads 'For Kiselev', a reference to one of the pilots of the Soviet unit that would take over the aircraft and operate them into 1943.

Sputnik 3488. Far more aircraft were transferred to the Soviet armed forces either after having been shipped into the Soviet Union by sea via the Arctic or flown in from Iran, Iraq or via Canada and Alaska. Some of the earliest aircraft provided to the Soviet Air Forces or VVS were Bell P-39 Airacobra aircraft, but a wide range of other Allied fighter aircraft were also provided, including P-40s, Hurricanes and later Spitfires. Here we have an example of an Airacobra piloted by Soviet 'ace' and Hero of the Soviet Union Nikolai Guliaev. This picture was apparently taken during 1944, at a time when as is indicated on his aircraft Guliaev had fifty-three aerial 'kills' to his credit.

Sputnik 585233. The final photograph in this chapter relates to the provision of food by Lend-Lease, with Lend-Lease supplies here being made available to children in Moscow. This picture was taken shortly after the end of the war in Europe in July 1945, at which time the Soviet Union was still receiving Lend-Lease aid due to its promise of participation in the war against Japan. During the war in Europe much of the food delivered via Lend-Lease ended up being used by the Soviet armed forces by virtue of it being in a form – tinned, dried or otherwise preserved – suited to military use. Lend-Lease food supplies played an important role in not only feeding the advancing Red Army, but also increasing the overall food supply within the Soviet Union at a time when it was critically low as a result of enemy action and dislocation of production relating to the war. Just how serious the situation was by the end of 1942 is highlighted by production figures for that year, at the end of which the potato harvest was, for example, only 23.8 million tons compared to 75.9 in 1940; of grains only 29.7 million tons compared to 95.5 in 1940; of eggs only 4.5 billion compared to 12.2 billion in 1940; and of milk only 15.8 million tons compared to 33.6 in 1940. The United States alone shipped more than 4.5 million tons of food to the USSR during the war, much of it in concentrated (often dried) form. [GPW, pp. 187, 190]

Chapter 17

The Axis Undermined: from the Ukraine to Romania and Hungary

In the aftermath of the German Kursk offensive in early July 1943 the Red Army launched major counter-offensive operations in the south that by the end of the year would see German forces pushed beyond the Dnepr – first in the far south and then further north near Kiev. The peak of winter was not, however, going to stop the Soviet advance continuing, as after pausing for breath and allowing supply lines to catch up with the front-line forces, the Red Army renewed its advance in the south before 1943 was out. The Dnepr-Carpathian Offensive would see the Red Army not only liberate most of the Ukraine west of the Dnepr, but push on beyond the Soviet 1939 border into Eastern Europe. By the spring of 1944 the Crimea was once again in Soviet hands with the exception of Sevastopol', and Soviet forces had pushed into Romania and also reached the extremities of the Carpathian mountains. Although extended supply lines, attrition and the inevitable German counter-attacks forced a temporary halt, by this stage of the war Soviet back-to-back offensives across the Eastern Front were like a tide inexorably coming in. Although it would be July 1944 before Soviet forces pushed deep into the Carpathian mountains and August before Soviet forces finally pushed convincingly into Romania, on the back of these operations and before the winter of 1944/1945 the Red Army had pushed deep into Hungary and linked up with Communist partisan forces in Yugoslavia.

In the process of Soviet offensive operations in southern Europe, Romania and Bulgaria switched sides in the war, with only German intervention preventing Hungary doing the same. At the same time the Red Army soon controlled huge swathes of southern Eastern Europe as Stalin looked towards finally securing revolution in Eastern Europe that had eluded the forces of international communism at the end of the First World War. Although Stalin was clearly intent on securing influence across as much of Eastern Europe as possible, it was, however, Hitler who chose to make Hungary one of the most intensive battlegrounds of late 1944 and early 1945 in what was not only a desperate gesture to keep an ally in the war, but more importantly a futile attempt to regain access to the all-important oilfields. Consequently it would be into 1945, after the fall of Budapest in February and the blunting of the desperate German counter-attack Operation 'Spring Awakening' in early March 1945, before fighting in the region would die down, only weeks before the fall of the Reich itself. This chapter looks at Soviet offensive operations in southern Eastern Europe all the way through from the autumn of 1943 to the spring of 1945.

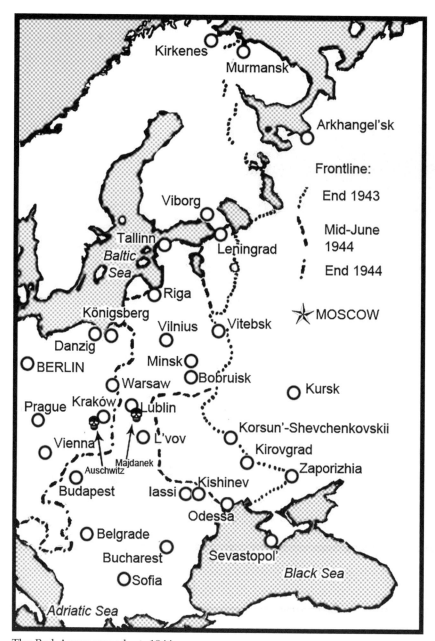

The Red Army ascendant, 1944.

(*Opposite*) Sputnik 911. Our first photograph in this chapter overlaps with the previous chapter, and shows Red Army troops of the Southern Front in fighting for the coal-producing and industrial Donbass region in September 1943. At the time of writing of this book, the region is perhaps best known for its Russian-backed movement for separation from Ukraine, although during the Great Patriotic War the region would probably have been seen increasingly more as simply Soviet than Russian or Ukrainian. The recapture of the region by Soviet forces did not mean that its resources could be quickly put to use by the Soviet Union, since the German 'scorched earth' policy during the retreat meant it would take some time to make good the damage to facilities there.

(*Opposite, above*) Sputnik 59091. The vast open steppe of the Ukraine had proven eminently suited to German mechanised warfare during 1941 and 1942, but by late 1943 the Red Army could also exploit its relative lack of inhibitors to movement to sweep across it. The Red Army's cavalry forces provided an important means for what were essentially mounted infantrymen to keep pace with the tanks. Here cavalry of the 3rd Ukrainian Front heads towards Odessa in April 1944.

(*Opposite, below*) Sputnik 489. Some time ago I had wondered how Soviet cavalrymen carried PTRD anti-tank rifles without always having horses and carts for them, and this photograph suggests an answer: with some difficulty. This photograph certainly reinforces the idea of Soviet cavalry by this stage of the war as mounted infantrymen. These Cossack cavalrymen of General Pliev's 4th Guards Cossack Cavalry Corps of the 3rd Ukrainian Front are also pictured somewhere near Odessa in April 1944.

(*Above*) Sputnik 60527. Soviet spearheads often took the form of tanks with tank-riding infantry, with whatever other vehicles could be found to accompany them. In this instance the tanks are being accompanied by motorcycles with sidecars. Motorcycles – be they of Soviet production or provided under Lend-Lease – continued to be used by the Red Army in relatively small numbers in such a role until the end of the war. Clearly neither the motorcyclists nor the tank riders have much protection against even small arms fire, one reason why German forces had all but abandoned the motorcycle combination in their reconnaissance forces by the latter part of the war. This picture was taken in early April 1944.

(*Overleaf*) Sputnik 53555. Although the Dnepr is the most famous of the river obstacles crossed under fire by the Red Army on Soviet territory, the Dnestr – the interwar boundary between Romania and the Soviet Union – was also one of many significant water obstacles to be crossed. Although after reaching the Dnestr there was a pause in Soviet offensive operations on that sector of the front, it was nonetheless a river line on which German and Romanian forces were unable to conduct a sustained defence once the Red Army had regrouped and even after sizeable Romanian and German forces in the far south of the Soviet Union had fallen back across it early in the spring of 1944. Here Soviet troops are shown on the eastern bank of the Dnestr after having just reached it in mid-April 1944. When the Red Army restarted offensive operations against it that summer and

pushed deep into the country, Romania changed sides and Romanian units subsequently fought alongside Soviet troops against German and Hungarian forces. This act of changing sides certainly had an opportunistic component – Romania and Hungary had longstanding territorial disputes, and siding with the Soviet Union against Axis Hungary gave Romania an opportunity to decide these disputes in its favour.

Sputnik 603807. Although the steppe across which Soviet forces fought in the south during late 1943 and into 1944 was often flat and featureless – terrain ideally suited to armoured operations – German defensive positions of course still typically required the 'poor bloody infantry' to capture them. Soviet infantry often had to assault them, with varying degrees of support. Here infantry of an undisclosed rifle regiment are seen on the attack, with the regimental command point in the foreground directing the troops sometime during July 1944. Note that many of the infantrymen have made some attempt at camouflaging themselves to fit in with the terrain – a practice that was increasingly typical for the mid-war period onwards compared to the early phases of the war.

Sputnik 61805. In September 1944 Soviet troops reached Hungary on the back of operations against Romania, and during October launched a major attempt to knock Hungary out of the war as had been done with Romania. Heavy German and Hungarian resistance under a newly instated Hungarian puppet government prevented Hungary from falling quickly to Soviet forces as had been hoped, turning Hungary into a major battleground during the closing phases of the war in Europe. Here Soviet ISU-122 assault guns – often used in an anti-tank role thanks to their high-velocity 122mm guns – await orders to head into Hungary at the beginning of October 1944. Soviet assault guns played a major role in blunting German attacks in the region.

Sputnik 59420. Somewhat less imposing than the ISU-122 in the previous picture was the SU-76 assault gun used by Soviet forces, often in an infantry support role. This photograph – giving something of a first-person perspective – shows one such gun in action sometime during October 1944 in Hungary. As is apparent in this picture, the fact that this gun was open-topped and had relatively low armoured shielding meant that the crew had very little protection from shrapnel, grenades, artillery rounds and hand-held Panzerfaust anti-tank rounds, nor indeed from the elements. It is easy to see how the weapon was often not popular with its crews, although it would have been welcomed by the infantry that it often came to support.

Sputnik 4808. When Soviet troops entered Yugoslav territory in September they found a well-organised and ideologically sympathetic ally in Josip Bros Tito's Yugoslav communist 'partisans'. Soviet troops and Yugoslav partisans – along with Bulgarian forces – would operate alongside each other in the Soviet Belgrade offensive of September–November 1944. Here Yugoslav 'partisans' – all impeccably turned out in uniforms – confer with a Red Army officer in October 1944.

Sputnik 1359. In this picture a battalion-level observation post, apparently of the 3rd Ukrainian Front, is shown in December 1944, probably therefore putting it somewhere on Yugoslav territory. That this post has a radio set is in itself indicative that this is a late-war photograph, as towards the end of the war the availability of radio sets was far greater than early in the war, thanks to a large extent to Lend-Lease deliveries of such equipment.

(*Opposite, above*) Sputnik 57717. Further north in late 1944 Red Army forces were at the same time fighting their way through the Carpathian mountains, where initial fighting for the Dukla Pass area not far from Košice in Slovakia in September–October was followed by continued and heavy fighting on eastern Slovak territory. Red Army forces were ostensibly attempting to fight their way through to make contact with Slovak insurgents, who had rebelled against the Nazi-sponsored puppet government in Slovakia. Here Red Army artillery of the 4th Ukrainian Front is shown in fighting in the Carpathian mountains sometime during late 1944. Note that the artillery in this picture consists of both captured German artillery in the foreground and Soviet guns in the background. Even at this stage of the war the Red Army continued to use captured enemy equipment. Communist Czechoslovak forces would fight alongside the Red Army during the liberation of Czechoslovak territory. After the war the Soviet Union annexed some eastern Carpathian territory to the Ukraine.

(*Opposite, below*) Sputnik 3057901. Some of the heaviest street fighting of the later part of the war took place during the protracted Soviet siege of Budapest. Following the pro-German coup of mid-October, Soviet forces sought to take the city as quickly as possible, albeit with under-strength forces. In the end the city wasn't encircled until Christmas, and the siege then dragged on until an attempted breakout effectively ended it in mid-February 1945. Here Soviet troops of the 3rd Ukrainian Front are shown in fighting for the city at the beginning of February 1945.

(*Above*) Sputnik 58231. A meaningful proportion of available German armoured strength was thrown into the fighting in Hungary in late 1944 and early 1945, along with precious fuel. Here Soviet troops are shown with captured German armour somewhere in Hungary in November 1944. The German Army Group South as of 4 September had only 66 operational German and 231 Hungarian tanks or equivalents, but this number had increased to 475 German and 53 Hungarian tanks by the end of the year – highlighting the significance of the region for Hitler back in Berlin. [RASWW, p. 531]

(*Above*) Sputnik 2651. An even more impressive haul of German armour is shown in this picture of tank wrecks on the approaches to Budapest in January 1945. Visible are a number of 'Panthers' and a 'Jagdpanther'. The last major German offensive of the war, Operation 'Spring Awakening' in the Lake Balaton region in March, would see Army Group South with 742 German and 48 Hungarian operational tanks and their equivalents as of 15 March 1945, even if fuel shortages would hamper their mobility. Nonetheless, by this stage of the war the Red Army could still maintain a significant numerical superiority in both tanks and even personnel, as was the case for the 2nd Ukrainian Front in the region at the beginning of December 1944, where the Soviet front had an approximate superiority of 4:1 over the enemy. This was just as well given the intensity of the fighting, much of it taking place in built-up areas. [RASWW, p. 531]

(*Opposite, above*) Sputnik 1558. Here Soviet sub-machine gunners – in Russian *avtomatchiki* – are shown in Budapest towards the end of the siege in February 1945. Between 29 October 1944 and 13 February 1945 Soviet forces of the 2nd and 3rd Ukrainian Fronts had lost at least 80,000 troops as 'irrecoverable losses' – largely killed – along with at least 240,000 sick and wounded in the fighting around and in Budapest. Hitler's choice to make Hungary a major battleground at the end of the war was not something that Soviet leaders were disappointed with, since it diverted resources from the key Berlin axis further north. [RASWW, p. 532] The headwear on these soldiers suggests that they are possibly Cossack troops.

(*Opposite, below*) Sputnik 5643057. This final picture from Budapest in early 1945 was taken on 15 February 1945 after the siege was over. It is perhaps of particular interest to the military modeller or wargamer in showing an Italian M13/40 tank amidst the rubble of the city. Desperation would see a wide range of captured and outdated equipment being used by Axis forces in the fighting towards the end of the war. In this case the tank may have been used by German forces for 'internal security' before one assumes it was knocked out by Soviet forces.

Chapter 18

'Bagration': from Minsk to Warsaw

Soviet military successes in the south during late 1943 and into 1944 were not mirrored on the key central axis of the Soviet-German front during this period, although the dramatic gains that had eluded the Red Army on this axis of advance were soon to come. Although significant territory had been liberated in the centre, with Smolensk for example back in Soviet hands before the winter, the advance had been relatively ponderous, and at a heavy cost compared to gains. Certainly the terrain on the central axis was more of a hindrance than in the south, where further north forest and marsh were far more likely to be encountered than on the steppe. German forces had continued all too often to be able to rush reserves to those areas in which Soviet forces threatened to break through in circumstances where freedom to manoeuvre was often limited. The relative stability of the central axis compared to that in the south certainly lulled the German high command into a sense of false security about the prospects of major Soviet offensive operations there during the summer of 1944. Continued Soviet offensive operations to the north and south in the spring and early summer undoubtedly fed into this false sense of security, despite the fact that Army Group Centre was stuck on a so-called 'balcony' that jutted out well east of German forces in the south and on a map offered a very tempting target. What Berlin was particularly unwilling to come to terms with was the fact that the materials balance was shifting so much in Soviet favour that the Red Army had already launched overlapping offensive operations on different parts of the front, and could do so again – launching major operations in the centre although significant German armoured resources had been deployed to the south in expectation that the advance would be renewed there. The German Army Group Centre was a formidable force on paper, but it was far from mobile and stuck in part defending fortified urban areas that were supposed to slow down the Soviet advance by allowing German forces to control key points on any lines of communication in a region. Army Group Centre had the misfortune of having what on paper was a Panzer Army, but in reality it was without Panzer divisions! By this point, although the Red Army was feeling the cost of the millions of troops lost earlier in the war, it did have plenty of tanks and other weapons systems, along with an increasingly capable logistical and supporting tail. Nonetheless, the Red Army committed more than 2 million personnel to Operation 'Bagration' against Army Group Centre that summer.

When Operation 'Bagration' struck against Army Group Centre in late June 1944, Soviet forces were able to make rapid progress despite at times difficult terrain. During 'Bagration' the Red Army was able not only to destroy significant German forces but also before the summer was out to advance all the way to the Vistula river and the gates of Warsaw well to the west. During 'Bagration' or the Belorussian Operation Soviet forces were able to advance as much as 600km over a 68-day period, for some of the time slowed more by the need to bridge rivers and establish supply lines than by enemy resistance. Certainly the cost to the German armed forces of Operation 'Bagration' was on a par with the costs of Operations 'Uranus' and 'Little Saturn' during the winter of 1942/1943, but with what by 1944 amounted to an army group being destroyed during the latter. To add insult to injury, 'Bagration' was then followed by the L'vov-Sandomierz Operation to the south – just what the German high command had been expecting – but now taking place after German tanks had been sent northwards! The L'vov-Sandomierz Operation would see the Red Army advance as much as 350km over 48 days. [RASWW, p. 511] If there could be any reasonable doubts about the inevitability of German defeat before 'Bagration', there could not be any afterwards – and particularly since 'Bagration' was launched at the same time as the Western Allies were establishing a foothold in 'Fortress Europe' in France after D-Day, and during a period in which the Red Army was making gains elsewhere as well. This chapter looks at Operation 'Bagration' from its beginning in late June 1944 through to events at the gates of Warsaw in August and September, when the Warsaw Uprising led by Poles loyal to the Polish government-in-exile in London was launched with the expectation of imminent liberation by the Red Army, but was crushed despite the presence of Soviet forces only a short distance away across the Vistula river.

(*Opposite, above*) Sputnik 60510. In this first photograph for this chapter Red Army men load rockets onto the rails of a truck-mounted 'Katiusha' rocket system in June 1944. Soviet forces were able to amass considerable firepower for the breakthrough phase of major operations such as at the beginning of 'Bagration', in which the 'Katiusha' rocket system was a core component.

(*Opposite, below*) Sputnik 604050. The Bobruisk Offensive component of Operation 'Bagration' by the 1st Belorussian Front took place on the southern side of the operation as a whole, on the northern fringes of the Pripiat' Marshes and the marshy land northwards along the Berezina river. The nature of much of the land in the area is evident in this photograph of Red Army troops advancing near Bobruisk on 27 June 1944 – the day before the town was liberated.

Sputnik 61675. There was heavy fighting near and within the Belorussian capital Minsk before it was liberated by the Red Army on 3 July 1944. By the time it was liberated it had only a fraction of its pre-war population. Here outside Minsk Red Army soldiers are being greeted by peasants at the end of June. To both the south and the east of the city there were sizeable encirclements of German forces that would have to be reduced by the infantry.

Sputnik 604055. Here troops of the 1st Belorussian Front push on towards the key railway town of Baranovichi in the Brest region in what must have been early July 1944. Although pictures of lorries and other motor vehicles are typical when portraying the advance of the Red Army in 1944–1945, most rifle divisions continued to be reliant on the horse for motive power even during the later phases of the war. Here in the foreground a 45mm anti-tank gun and limber are being pulled by a team of two horses.

Sputnik 67351. In this picture – the first of two taken moments apart – Red Army troops are shown on the attack west of Minsk in mid-July 1944. Of particular interest is the man on the left who is shown releasing the smoke from the 'smoke pot' to provide the soldiers with a degree of concealment from the enemy. The use of smoke in such circumstances was increasingly frequent as the war progressed, with 'smoke pots' being provided in large numbers by the US under Lend-Lease.

Sputnik 4477. Also evident in these two pictures taken in mid-July west of Minsk is the camouflage that the soldiers have applied to themselves. The Russian term *maskirovka* covers all aspects of concealment, from camouflage at the level of the individual soldier all the way up to strategic deception where coordinated efforts were made to convince the enemy that large Soviet formations were or were not in a particular location. Such deception utilised physical means such as dummy vehicles or a small number of vehicles being driven round-and-round in an attempt to suggest that there were more of them, and non-physical means such as radio deception whereby radio traffic was generated to portray the presence of a formation that wasn't in fact there.

Sputnik 611866. Very quickly Operation 'Bagration' took the Red Army beyond the Soviet Union's 1939 borders and into Polish territory. Here Soviet artillery is shown in fighting for the city of Lublin in eastern Poland in July 1944. The city would be in Soviet hands by 24 July. The Soviet Union made Lublin the seat of government for its communist rival government to the Polish government-in-exile in London until Warsaw was finally liberated in January 1945. Fortunately Lublin would not be reduced to rubble as was the case for Warsaw.

Sputnik 921. In this picture Polish communist troops parade through Lublin on 24 July 1944. Those in the picture are all armed with light machine guns, a weapon that in practice was distributed within rifle units. That the Polish communist forces – at the start of 'Bagration' numbering close to 80,000 and making up the 1st Polish Army – participated in the liberation of Polish territory gave the Polish communist government established in Lublin a certain legitimacy that it would otherwise have lacked.

Sputnik 1222. Soviet heavy artillery moves past the bodies of dead horses along a road in Belorussia as the Red Army advances during the summer of 1944. Very little attention is paid in the literature to deaths amongst non-humans relating to war. Hundreds of thousands of horses were killed at the front lines and in the pre-frontal areas during the Soviet-German War. The increasing mechanisation of the Red Army's front-line forces, even if far from complete, at least meant that some horses that would otherwise have died were probably spared.

(*Opposite, above*) Sputnik 615436. Crawling with parts of a mortar on your back cannot have been easy at the best of times, and certainly not under enemy fire. Here a mortar team of the 1st Belorussian Front changes position in mid-August 1944 during Operation 'Bagration'.

(*Opposite, below*) Sputnik 5646054. One indicator that the Red Army was on Polish territory during 'Bagration' beyond the ethnic composition of the population was the changing nature of both architecture and the enclosure of land. Here a Red Army heavy machine gun team pulls their gun across a field near a damaged Polish church somewhere near Warsaw in August 1944.

(*Above*) Sputnik 628214. By early August 1944 the Red Army had reached Praga, a suburb of Warsaw on the eastern (Soviet) bank of the Vistula river. By this time Soviet units that had fought through much of Belorussia and into Poland were not only tired and had extended supply lines, but also often at low strength as cumulative casualties took their toll. Certainly successfully forcing the Vistula river in order to create meaningful and defensible bridgeheads after such an extended period of advancing was beyond the Red Army. Soviet attempts to seize Praga off the march were beaten back by German forces. Here what we can reasonably assume are reconnaissance or spearhead troops thanks to their camouflage smocks are shown in fighting for Praga during August 1944. The depreciation in Soviet strength at the tail end of Operation 'Bagration' is illustrated by the statistics that as of 8 August the three tank corps of the 2nd Tank Army – one of the principal Soviet formations in the drive on Warsaw, arriving on the outskirts of the city having driven towards it from the south-east along the Vistula river – had only 322 operable 'tanks', having a month earlier on 8 July had 809 operable vehicles![35]

(*Opposite*) Sputnik 627452. Here, slightly later, a Red Army gun team is also shown in fighting for the Praga suburb of Warsaw in August 1944. The outline of a tall building can be made out in the background. With the Warsaw Uprising in full swing, Polish communist forces seem to have genuinely attempted to link up with the rebels across the Vistula but were unable to enlarge or even sustain a bridgehead. For example, on 16 September the 1st Belorussian Front reported that reconnaissance troops, followed by an infantry battalion, had made it across the river into southern Warsaw, but this bridgehead was only short-lived. [GPW, p. 236] The Warsaw Uprising would be finally crushed by German forces by the beginning of October 1944.

(*Above*) Sputnik 534830. Soviet leader Iosif Stalin is shown here in Moscow in 1944. In the background are prominent Marshals of the Soviet Union Georgii Zhukov and Konstantin Rokossovskii. During the Warsaw Uprising it was clear that Stalin was unwilling to see the Red Army expend considerable resources on relieving the besieged insurgents, and he was undoubtedly only too pleased for German forces to destroy much of any future potential Polish opposition to Soviet authority in Eastern Europe.

(*Overleaf*) Sputnik 708. As Soviet forces advanced into Poland they uncovered the first of the German concentration camps to be liberated by Allied forces. Majdanek was liberated by Red Army forces on 23 July 1944, the day this photograph of the crematoria was apparently taken. The Majdanek camp had started its life in July 1941 as a Soviet PoW camp, and ended up being 'a hybrid concentration, labour and extermination camp'.[36] Red Army soldier M.N. Pentegov recalled during a debriefing in August 1944 that, after he'd arrived at the camp in late 1943, 'from the field, where the ovens were located, screams and fire from automatic weapons could be heard every day, meaning that every day people were being slaughtered'.[37] The camp's personnel clearly evacuated the camp in a hurry as the Red Army approached, the last executions in the camp apparently taking place on 21 July 1944. The next day the last German personnel left the camp, with soldiers of the Red Army arriving soon afterwards.[38] What awaited the Red Army on its arrival was described in eloquent detail by Soviet journalist Konstantin Simonov (see p. 187, Sputnik 65872) in a booklet that ended up being translated into multiple languages, including into English as *The Lublin Extermination Camp* (1944). At least 80,000 people had been killed in the main camp, of whom at least 60,000 were Jews.[39]

Chapter 19

The Air War: The Soviet Air Forces Ascendant

By 1944 we have certainly reached a point where it is worth highlighting the contribution of the Soviet air forces or VVS (*Voenno-Vozdushnie Sili*) to the defeat of Axis forces on Soviet territory and in Eastern Europe. Although the VVS had started the war as a huge force with thousands of aircraft in the western border districts alone, and many of these aircraft such as the I-16 had been state-of-the-art in the mid-1930s, they were by 1941 looking somewhat long in the tooth compared to the latest versions of their German equivalents, in this case of the Me 109. By this time newer Soviet aircraft than the I-16 were available in increasing numbers, with 1,289 MiG-3 alone having been manufactured by 22 June 1941, but many of these aircraft were suffering teething troubles and performance issues due to inadequate engine performance. Considerable aircraft losses during the first days and weeks of the war – more than 1,100 in the western military districts alone on 22 June 1941 – meant the loss of much of this inventory, although since many aircraft were destroyed on the ground the number of available pilots did not drop to the same extent. [RASWW, pp. 186, 208]

Although during 1941 and well into 1942 the German Luftwaffe could obtain air superiority over the battlefield essentially when required, in the vast expanses of the East there was always room for the VVS, which even during the dramatic German advances of 1941 and 1942 was often there to harry German forces on the ground. During the German attempt to supply the Stalingrad pocket from the air in late 1942 and early 1943 the VVS was able to increasingly interdict German resupply efforts as large numbers of the next generation of Soviet fighter aircraft became available. In the Kuban in 1943 – once again at the extremities of the front – the VVS was able to challenge the Luftwaffe for local air superiority. Although at Kursk the Luftwaffe continued to be able to assert temporary air superiority for its own operations, it was not able to hold back the increasing strength of the VVS and in particular its considerable ground-attack capability focused on the Il-2 Sturmovik ground-attack aircraft. By 1944 in many ways the tables had turned on the Luftwaffe, in part thanks to the drain on its resources in the West that had begun with the transfer of air resources from the East to the Mediterranean in late 1941. Although the Luftwaffe was never completely absent from the skies in the East, it was increasingly limited in its activities to the fringes of the principal axes of the Soviet advance that were flooded with air resources doled out in huge packets from the centre. Although medium and particularly long-range bombing were areas neglected by the VVS by 1941, by 1944 the Soviet VVS was increasingly able to interdict German lines of communication deep in the rear thanks to large numbers of medium bombers supplied under Lend-Lease. As the war headed towards its conclusion, better ground-to-air communications enabled the VVS to provide its own equivalent of the taxi ranks of fighter-bombers deployed so successfully by the Western Allies. By now its fighter aircraft were superior to those being fielded by Germany, with the exception of the Me 262 jet aircraft deployed in the West, although there was a period later in the war when the Luftwaffe was able to gain a little ground when it was operating from home bases on German territory. Nonetheless, as the war headed towards its conclusion, the VVS remained master of the skies in the East, and provided a significant boost to the capabilities of Soviet ground forces pressing in on the Reich.

(*Below*) Sputnik 413431. In addition to the MiG-3 mentioned above, one of the newer aircraft that the Soviet VVS would start the war with was the LaGG-3 fighter aircraft, an early example of which is shown here, quite probably during the winter of 1940/1941. Only 322 examples of this aircraft had been produced by the time of the Axis invasion, with 158 having formally been handed over to the VVS at the end of May 1941. Although looking sleek, modern and purposeful, this aircraft was not a success. The desire to get new aircraft into production seems to have meant that LaGG-3s entered series production despite having known defects![RASWW, pp. 186–7]

(*Opposite, above*) Sputnik 1193. This photograph also shows LaGG-3 aircraft, in this case of the 3rd Guards Fighter Air Regiment as it was receiving the prestigious Guards designation awarded for outstanding combat performance. This was at a time when the unit was part of Soviet high command or Stavka reserves at Dmitrov near Moscow in February 1942. Being a Guards regiment often meant getting better equipment, and this unit would soon upgrade its LaGG-3s for the far superior wartime La-5 aircraft. Note that the aircraft have skis rather than wheels.

(*Opposite, below*) Sputnik 1231. These medical evacuation aircraft are also on skis, and pictured sometime during February 1942. Light aircraft such as these do not appear all that frequently in collections of photographs, and their representation is certainly not proportional to their numbers. Despite its antiquated appearance, the U-2 or Po-2 continued in production in the Soviet Union until late in the war, with many variants built; these aircraft were used not only for casualty evacuation (shown also in Chapter 11), but also as trainers, liaison aircraft, light night bombers (see Chapter 10) and artillery spotters, in addition to having many civilian applications.

(*Above*) Sputnik 2315. Many aircraft designed and constructed during the early to mid-1930s remained in service with the VVS in sizeable numbers at the beginning of the war. Here an I-153 biplane aircraft is shown in service with what appears to be naval aviation somewhere near Odessa in August 1941. In fact, of 763 such aircraft in service at the beginning of the war, one Russian author suggests that 687 I-15 and I-15bis were in service with naval aviation.[40] Slow and poorly armed by 1941 standards, one of the few saving graces of such aircraft was their tight turning radius and the very limited runway required for them to operate. A small number were reportedly used as night bombers near Moscow later in 1941.

(*Opposite, above*) Sputnik 603666. Also in the south, and in service with the Black Sea Fleet, were these two I-16 monoplane fighters shown flying over the transport vessel *Kursk* in the Black Sea while it was en route to Sevastopol' during the summer of 1941. Whilst still inferior to the marks of the Me 109 being used by the Luftwaffe, the I-16 remained better than some of the fighters being employed by Hitler's allies in the south, such as the PZL P.24 still in use by Romania at the beginning of the war. The highly manoeuvrable I-16 would continue in service in small numbers into 1943, by which time the VVS was receiving far superior aircraft in increasing numbers to allow the type to be retired.

(*Opposite, below*) Sputnik 5479038. Keeping an element of geographical continuity, the next photograph shifts to 1944 but still shows fighter aircraft of the Black Sea Fleet, in this case Yak-9Ds of the 6th Guards Fighter Air Regiment taken in the spring of 1944 near Sevastopol'. The Yak-9 was the most widespread Soviet fighter aircraft of the later war years. According to Russian aviation historians Yefim Gordon and Dmitri Khazanov, by the summer of 1944 the number of Yak-9s in the Soviet inventory was greater than all of the other types combined – testimony to the success of the design.[41] Aircraft 22 is being piloted by Mikhail Ivanovich Grib, awarded the title Hero of the Soviet Union in October 1942.[42]

(*Above*) Sputnik 5515385. Perhaps the most famous Soviet aircraft of the Second World War period in the West is the Il-2 Sturmovik: the principal Soviet ground-attack aircraft of the war. Pictured here are some early Il-2 aircraft at the end of October 1941. There were few of these aircraft available at the very beginning of the war – the first production aircraft was only flown on 10 March 1941, with a total of 249 manufactured by the start of hostilities in June 1941. [RASWW, p. 182] Production soon ramped up, which was just as well since the early version shown here took heavy losses against enemy fighters in part because it lacked the rear gunner added in later versions. Its basic armament of two 20mm cannon and two machine guns gave it a heavy basic firepower in addition to any bombs or rockets it carried.

(*Opposite, above*) Sputnik 2381. Here a later model of the Il-2 is shown somewhere near Stalingrad, probably during the winter of 1942/1943. Note the addition of the self-defence machine gun to the rear of the cockpit, giving the aircraft a greater chance of survival than in its earlier incarnation. Nonetheless, ground-attack remained a very dangerous undertaking not only because of enemy fighters, but because of the increasing anti-aircraft firepower available to German forces as the war progressed. One source suggests that more than 3,500 of these aircraft were lost during 1943 alone. [RASWW, p. 494] Such aircraft were often allocated en masse to support offensive operations.

(*Opposite, below*) Sputnik 65922. In addition to having the Il-2 'Sturmovik' for ground-attack, at the outbreak of war with the Axis the VVS had the Pe-2 light bomber. Based on the PB-100 high-altitude fighter under development in 1940, the Pe-2 was developed to a large extent after the Soviet Union had received a number of German aircraft including the Ju 88 during the period of the Nazi-Soviet Pact. At the time the VVS lacked a similar aircraft capable of dive-bombing, and it was decided that it needed one. Soon in 1941 Pe-2s were rolling off the production lines. Although they ended up doing little dive-bombing, and a fighter variant was soon dropped as it became apparent that twin-engined fighters were no match for the latest single-engined monoplanes, it was a successful light bomber and reconnaissance aircraft. Here bombs are being loaded aboard aircraft in September 1941. A very similar aircraft, the Tu-2, was also in production during the war, with by Soviet standards relatively modest numbers being produced, although that still meant just over a thousand aircraft![43]

(*Opposite, above*) Sputnik 601126. The same aircraft type as in the previous photograph is shown in flight somewhere over what is probably Russian terrain in November 1942. This photograph is of particular interest for giving such a good view of what was very typical terrain in the European part of Russia. Not only did such terrain hamper movement, but it also gave ground forces plenty of places to hide from aircraft. When these factors are combined with the large territory being fought over – in which ground forces could more easily be 'lost' than in the West – it is perhaps easier to see why air power had less of an impact on ground operations across much of the Eastern Front than in the West.

(*Opposite, below*) Sputnik 232. The Soviet Union also started the war with more than one medium bomber type. The SB (an abbreviation of Fast Bomber in Russian) was then available in significant numbers with stocks having been built up from 1936 until the beginning of 1941, by which time more than 6,500 aircraft of all variants had been produced.[44] Such aircraft were – in terms of speed and defensive armament – increasingly vulnerable by the summer of 1941, and losses of this type were heavy during the first weeks and months of the war, both on the ground and in the air. This example is shown soldiering on in July 1943 in what are very much field conditions!

(*Above*) Sputnik 6050116. Some of the SBs were used for towing transport gliders, one of which is shown at centre-left in this picture alongside two U-2/Po-2 liaison aircraft in the Kiev region in November 1943. Such gliders were not only used by the airborne forces, but were sometimes used to supply partisans operating in the Axis rear areas. Soviet airborne forces were used in operations to bridge the Dnepr river during the period at the end of which this picture was taken.

(*Above*) Sputnik 601119. One of the larger bombers available in significant numbers in the Soviet inventory was the DB-3 (or later Il-4), a pre-war design that made up the backbone of the Soviet Union's long-range bomber force during the war. The abbreviation DB in Russian means Long-range Bomber. Although long-range and larger than the SB, these bombers were significantly smaller and carried smaller payloads than the heavy bombers being fielded by the Western Allies, although they were used in attacks on Berlin from Soviet territory early in the war. In that sense the DB-3 is perhaps best considered as an equivalent to German bombers such as the Heinkel 111. Typically DB-3s were used to support the ground forces, with for example DB-3s being allocated as part of a Shock Air Group for the suppression of the Demiansk Pocket in early 1942. [RASWW, p. 321] This is undoubtedly an impressive photograph of this bomber, taken in September 1942 as bombs were being loaded. Only very small numbers of the TB-3 bomber were available to the Soviet Union during the Great Patriotic War – a bomber that was more akin to the Allied heavy bombers of the period and indeed the TB designation means Heavy Bomber!

(*Opposite, above*) Sputnik 613653. In chronological terms now heading towards the end of the war, in this picture we see Yak-3 fighter aircraft of the Normandie-Niemen Squadron somewhere in East Prussia in January 1945. The Yak-3 was another successful Soviet fighter design of the later war period, in this instance being flown by French volunteer pilots of the 'Free French' or 'Fighting French' forces. This group of French pilots had asked to be allowed to fight against Nazi Germany on the Eastern Front in early 1942, and the squadron was officially formed on 4 December 1942 as part of the VVS. [RASWW, pp. 334–5]

(*Opposite, below*) Sputnik 1882. As will be briefly chronicled through pictures in Chapter 23, after the war in Europe was concluded Soviet forces were committed against the Japanese in August 1945. In this picture pilots of the 7th Fighter Air Division of the Soviet Pacific Fleet run to their aircraft somewhere in the theatre, apparently on 16 August 1945. Their fighter aircraft – distinct from the Yak aircraft shown earlier because of their radial engines – are LaGG-7s, yet another very successful Soviet fighter design of the late war period that also saw service in the closing period of the war in Europe.

Chapter 20

The War in the North: from the Barents Sea to the Baltic

In Chapter 16 it was noted that it was through the Arctic that the Soviet Union received much of the Lend-Lease aid provided during the earlier phases of the war against the Axis. This situation gave the far north much more significance during the Great Patriotic War than it might otherwise have had, although in some ways repeated a situation that belatedly existed during the First World War, when Britain and France ended up sending supplies to Russia through northern ports, even if most of that material support arrived too late to be used as intended. In the Great Patriotic War, however, supplies from Britain and the Western Allies would start to arrive in the Soviet Union within weeks of the onset of hostilities. German offensive action in this region, and to a lesser extent along the Baltic coastline, was therefore in part about denying the Soviet Union access to the sea, which in the far north soon meant severing its communications with its new Western Allies. Whilst the northern sectors of the Eastern Front of the war in Europe remained relatively static during much of 1942 and 1943, during 1944 these areas also saw the Red Army make significant military progress.

The most important Soviet city in the region with which this chapter is concerned was Leningrad. We have already looked at the situation immediately below Leningrad in Chapter 6, but not at the continuation of those offensive operations into the Baltic republics that finally ended the siege of the city. From the summer of 1944 the Red Army would push into the Baltic region, cutting off from the Reich significant German forces that would remain bottled up in the case of those in Kurland until the end of the war. During the summer of 1944 the Red Army would also go over to the offensive on what had been one of the quietest and most static parts of the front line for much of the war – that primarily north and north-east of Leningrad where Soviet forces were opposed by Finnish forces. In 1941 Finnish forces had retaken territory lost to the Soviet Union in late 1939 and early 1940 and then dug in. In the summer of 1944 Finland would soon buckle under Soviet pressure and seek to leave the war, removing yet another German ally, even if not one that was a fully fledged member of the Axis. Finally, in the autumn of 1944 the Red Army would go on the offensive in the far north within the Arctic circle, and not only liberate Soviet territory lost along the coastline towards Murmansk during 1941, but push on into Norwegian territory. By this stage of the war whether the Red Army would gain ground was no longer in question, but what the Soviet advance in these three regions shared was that the Red Army achieved much over terrain that was considerably more challenging for the attacker than most of that in the far south, and in the far north arguably even more challenging than much of the terrain encountered on the key Smolensk-Brest-Warsaw-Berlin axis. This chapter looks at the war in these northern regions for the whole of the war but with particular emphasis on Soviet offensive operations in 1944–1945.

(*Below, left*) Sputnik 603956. The first few photographs in this chapter show something of Soviet operations in the far north during the period prior to the Petsamo-Kirkenes Operation in October 1944. In this first picture T-26 tanks are shown on the bleak tundra of the Ribachii peninsula to the west of Murmansk in December 1941, as members of their crews are shown reconnoitring over a rise in the ground. Relatively little use of tanks was made in the far north, with early-war vehicles soldiering on in the theatre until later in the war. Some of the difficulties of operating over terrain such as this – be that on the defensive or offensive – are evident in this picture, where cover from both the elements and the enemy is somewhat limited.

(*Below, right*) Sputnik 1090. The coastline and coastal belt over which the bulk of the opposing forces operated in the far north was very craggy, as is highlighted in this picture of communications troops laying a cable over some sort of outcrop on the Ribachii peninsula, also in December 1941. The official caption suggests that the personnel shown are naval, but it is difficult to tell in a black and white photograph where winter outerwear was often the same for naval and army personnel.

Sputnik 1506. In this picture communications troops are also laying cable but from a sled being pulled by a dog team somewhere to the west of Murmansk during February 1942. As will be seen in subsequent photographs, a variety of animals adapted to the conditions were made use of in this very specific terrain north of the Arctic Circle.

Sputnik 60548. Here dogs are about to be used to pull a sled, but in this case by reconnaissance troops, also somewhere in the Murmansk region but in early January 1943. The trees here are a welcome addition over the previous two scenes. It is of some interest that by this stage of the war none of those in the picture is carrying a sub-machine gun, indicative of the nature of the terrain over which a surprise encounter at close range would be far less likely than one over some distance.

(*Opposite, above*) Sputnik 1301. In addition to dogs, reindeer were also used by Soviet forces in the region as draft animals. In this photograph British Royal Air Force ground personnel are shown enjoying the novelty of being with reindeer and their keeper on an airfield in the far north sometime – according to the date provided with the photograph – in June 1942. Such fraternisation was generally discouraged by the Soviet authorities except for public relations photographs.

(*Above*) Sputnik 42461. The nature of the terrain in the north and poor overland communications were reasons why Soviet forces made considerable use of the seaborne flank when attacking German forces in the region. Here Soviet troops are being landed from a Soviet-built MO-4 submarine chaser of the Northern Fleet in early April 1942. That the Soviet Northern Fleet's main base was at Poliarnoe near Murmansk and close to the areas being fought over would help Soviet naval forces to secure local naval superiority as the war progressed. Although a variety of German capital and other surface ships did operate at times in the region, they were based further south along the Norwegian coastline and had either been sunk or in the case of the *Tirpitz* neutralised by the British before the Petsamo-Kirkenes Operation in late 1944. Regardless, the German Kriegsmarine didn't have the fighter cover available by 1944 for operations to threaten Soviet naval activity in the region with surface vessels.

(*Opposite, below*) Sputnik 611174. The most significant Soviet offensive operation in the far north was what came to be known as the Petsamo-Kirkenes Operation of October 1944, which would ultimately see Soviet forces push into German-occupied northern Norway. This operation had a considerable amphibious component, with Soviet troops being shown here en route to Petsamo in US-supplied submarine chasers (SC-497) during that operation.

Sputnik 739. In this photograph Soviet troops are shown actually landing from the same type of vessel during the Petsamo-Kirkenes Operation, in this case near the small previously Finnish port of Liinakhamari that was subsequently incorporated into Soviet territory, probably on or close to 12 October 1944. Once again, in something far more typical of the later war period, Soviet troops are advancing under the cover of a smoke screen.

Sputnik 307. Turning our attention to events further south, in June 1944 the Red Army launched another of its major offensive operations of 1944, in this instance against the Finns north of Leningrad. Here, at the beginning of the offensive that would see the Red Army advance through Karelia towards Viborg, a Soviet IS-2 tank is shown on a rough road through the forest. The IS-2 tank was an excellent heavily armoured tank for breaking through enemy defensive positions.

Sputnik 399. In this picture Red Army personnel are readying pontoons for the construction of a bridge across one of the many water obstacles in Karelia during the summer of 1944. It is perhaps interesting to compare this photograph with the bridging operation shown back in late 1939 in the same region in Chapter 3. Not only is there much more suitable equipment available for rapid bridging operations in this later photograph, but the two photographs have a very different feel thanks to a large extent to the more modern uniforms in this latter picture, where those in the former are very much of the era of the Russian Civil War.

Sputnik 893873. Here Soviet sappers in camouflage overalls are shown removing mines from a road along which Soviet forces were advancing in June 1944 towards the town of Medvezh'egorsk, well to the north-east of the Karelian Isthmus. In this region, as in Karelia, Soviet forces proved far more capable in 1944 than they had been back in 1939–1940.

Sputnik 389. Here Soviet mechanised forces are shown on the streets of the town of Viborg in the north-west of Karelia. Once again there is an IS-2 heavy tank in the picture, but of particular interest is the BA-10 armoured car that has had its turret removed and has been converted to serve as an armoured personnel carrier. As noted in Chapter 16, even with Lend-Lease vehicles the Red Army was relatively short of armoured personnel carriers compared to its Allies in the West. Such vehicles were important in allowing infantry to keep pace with the tanks in far more safety and comfort than if they were simply riding on them! That there are more tanks shown in this chapter than some others should not be taken to suggest that more tanks were involved in these operations than others: far from it. It may very well have been because fewer tanks were used in proportion to the overall force in Finland and the far north in particular that there are some excellent pictures involving those tanks that did participate!

Sputnik 611326. Still further south, here T-34/85s – the later-war up-gunned version of the iconic and ubiquitous T-34 tank – are shown with Red Army forces on Lithuanian territory in the spring of 1944 on the approaches to Alytus, a town to the south-west of Vilnius. The heavy fighting that took place in the Baltic Republics in 1944–1945 is often not given much space in books on the war for the obvious reason that operations here were far from being as decisive as those further south, even if the trapping of sizeable German forces in the region prevented them from being used to reinforce German positions on the key Berlin axis.

Sputnik 202. Here, in early 1945, Soviet 'Katiusha' rocket systems on US-supplied trucks of the 2nd Pribaltic Front are shown advancing along a track. By this point the bulk of the territory of the Baltic Republics had been 'liberated' by Soviet forces even if German forces would hold out in the region until the end of the war. Significant numbers of Estonians, Latvians and Lithuanians fought alongside German forces in 'defence' of the region from the Red Army, including the armed-wing of the SS, the Waffen SS.

Sputnik 894. This last picture in this chapter shows some of the German equipment captured by the Red Army within the Kurland Pocket west of Riga at the end of the war in Europe. More than 200,000 German troops and a large numbers of tanks, tank destroyers and other armoured vehicles were captured within the pocket, many of which had been unable to function effectively owing to a shortage of fuel. [GPW, pp. 240–1] In this picture we see not only motorcycles in the foreground, but also armoured and un-armoured half-tracked vehicles and even a couple of Kettenkrad half-tracked motorcycles. Of particular interest is perhaps the Soviet BA-10 armoured car that had been pressed into German service, visible in the top right-hand corner of this picture. It is quite possible that it had been used for 'internal security' duties in occupied territory.

Chapter 21

From the Vistula to the Oder

It took the Red Army nine months to get from Warsaw to Berlin and bring the war to a conclusion. With the value of hindsight, it is quite possible to argue that Stalin could have directed the Red Army to finish off Nazi Germany considerably earlier than May 1945, and that Warsaw could have been liberated in 1944, not 1945. When Soviet forces reached the Vistula river and Warsaw in the summer of 1944 at the end of Operation 'Bagration' they were operating at the end of extended supply lines and were in need of rest, recuperation and reinforcement, but they need not have waited until January 1945 to resume their offensive operations towards the heart of the Third Reich. As we saw in Chapter 17, considerable resources were being expended on operations to the south in late 1944 and early 1945, some of which might have been used on the key Berlin axis. Whilst some of this effort could be justified on the grounds of securing the flanks of any advance into the heart of the Reich, and increasingly it was Hitler, not Stalin, who selected Hungary as a major battleground, there is plenty of evidence that Stalin was keen to take his time on the Berlin axis as the Red Army consolidated the Soviet hold over the remainder of Eastern Europe. By late 1944, however, Allied progress to the West made a resumption of the advance on the key Berlin axis politically sensible if the Red Army was going to ultimately take the German capital, where the Western Allies were themselves closing in on Germany.

This chapter deals with the Soviet advances into Poland, eastern Germany and Prussia in late 1944 and early 1945, and in particular the Vistula-Oder Operation of January 1945 that would take the Red Army from the heart of Poland deep into Germany and put it within striking distance of Berlin along the Oder and Neisse river line. At the same time as the Vistula-Oder Operation there was heavy fighting on the flanks in Prussia and Silesia, where still considerable German forces fought stubbornly, with shortening German supply lines going some way to compensate for heavy losses. Germany by this point was throwing the increasingly young and old into the fray through the *Volkssturm* militia, and could still field large numbers of tanks and other armoured fighting vehicles, even if with increasingly meagre fuel resources to provide them with any mobility. German troops might have been increasingly poorly trained, but they were often provided with significant firepower in the form of machine guns and infantry anti-tank weapons suited to the increasingly built-up environment through which the fighting was taking place. The Red Army by this time was extremely well equipped, but front-line manpower was an issue, where Red

Army units were at times obliged to mobilise recently liberated Soviet PoWs and foreign workers in Germany (*Ostarbeiter*) directly into their ranks to keep their infantry numbers in particular at a sustainable level. Sadly, with ultimate victory in sight, many tens of thousands of Red Army soldiers would lose their lives to achieve not only the defeat of Nazi Germany, but also Stalin's revolutionary and territorial ambitions.

(**Below**) Sputnik 2648. Although in the autumn of 1944 the Red Army was not advancing on the key Berlin axis, Soviet forces did penetrate German territory further north in East Prussia. German resistance in the region was stoked by claims in Nazi propaganda of what Soviet forces would unleash on the local population should German territory be captured. Here Soviet troops are shown near fortifications in the region sometime in October 1944. The ferocity of the firepower to which the Red Army subjected these positions is very much evident in this picture.

(**Opposite, above**) Sputnik 611500. Possibly the first German town of any meaning to be captured by the Red Army was what at the time was the East Prussian town of Ebenrode, formerly Stallupönen until 1938 and later becoming Nesterov from 1946 when the region became part of the Soviet Kaliningrad region. Here Soviet troops of the 3rd Belorussian Front are moving into Ebenrode on 24 October 1944, about halfway between Vilnius and their ultimate goal, Königsberg.

(**Opposite, below**) Sputnik 3059084. Relative quiet further south did give those troops and units that would launch the Vistula-Oder Operation in January time to recoup, refit and train, as well as to meticulously plan their next move. Here Marshal Georgii Zhukov, who would command the 1st Belorussian Front during the Vistula-Oder Operation, is shown with the commander of the 2nd Belorussian Front, Marshal Konstantin Rokossovskii, at a command post near the village of Modlin not far from Warsaw in November 1944. Also shown is Colonel General Pavel Batov of the 2nd Belorussian Front speaking on the telephone in the centre of the picture.

(*Above*) Sputnik 61708. At the same time as the Vistula-Oder Operation was being launched to the south in January 1945, the Red Army pushed deep into East Prussia with the East Prussian Operation by the 2nd and 3rd Belorussian Fronts. Although not receiving the publicity of the Vistula-Oder Operation, this operation involved far from trivial resources and heavy fighting. More than 1,222,000 troops and more than 2,000 tanks were committed to this operation. [GPW, p. 251] Here Soviet cavalry of the 3rd Guards Cavalry Corps is shown on the approaches to Allenstein (Olsztyn), due south of Königsberg, on 22 January 1945. The corps would record in its war diary for that day that the town had been prepared for defence and was garrisoned by 'more than a regiment of infantry', including *Volkssturm* and police units. Nonetheless, according to the war diary, 'a large part of the garrison, demoralised by the surprise night attack, fled to the forest north of Allenstein'. Although these forces soon rallied, and apparently counter-attacked with the help of reserves, the town remained in Soviet hands. The war diary would go on to state that losses in this one episode had been 'relatively minor', but that still meant 'up to 250 people killed and wounded', and the loss of three guns and four tanks.[45]

(*Opposite*) Sputnik 1667. Further south, here Red Army soldiers are shown on the front line somewhere on the outskirts of Warsaw a couple of days before the Vistula-Oder Operation would begin in earnest on 12 January 1945. They are still using a PTRD anti-tank rifle, and also have an array of grenades at their disposal. Behind them Soviet forces were massing and readying themselves for their major leap forward to the Oder river.

(*Above*) Sputnik 884553. The Red Army launched the multi-front Vistula-Oder Operation with not only overwhelming force but considerable stockpiles of supplies and ammunition. The 1st Belorussian Front alone had amassed a force including 3,220 tanks and self-propelled guns at the beginning of the operation, with the 1st Ukrainian Front deploying a similar 3,244. [GPW, p. 250] During the first phase of the operation forces of the 4th Tank Army of the 1st Ukrainian Front to the south were able to advance as much as 220km by 19 January, [RASWW, p. 522] meaning that many population centres in the path of the Red Army were not subjected to heavy fighting during this period. A good example of such a centre was the major Polish city of Łódź, south-west of Warsaw, through which Soviet ISU-122 assault guns of the 1st Belorussian Front are shown moving in this picture of 19 January 1945.

(*Opposite, above*) Sputnik 1348. Also spared the destruction meted out to Warsaw was the city of Kraków. In this photograph Red Army reconnaissance troops on horseback are shown fraternising with members of the local population on 19 January 1945. Although their welcome might not have been as warm as it had been on pre-1939 Soviet territory, for those who had not experienced Soviet rule in 1939–1941 the Red Army still came to liberate them from a brutal Nazi regime that had looked down upon the dominant Polish population as racially inferior. Even worse off, however, were the Jews of Poland, with the Kraków Ghetto having been one of a number of major urban Jewish ghettos established by the Nazi regime for the containment of Jews. The situation for the Jews of Kraków was undoubtedly made worse by the fact that Kraków was the administrative centre for the General Government, that is, the part of Poland incorporated into Germany after the German-Soviet invasion of September 1939. According to the German Governor-General Hans Frank on 12 April 1940, Kraków was to be the city in the German General Government that was 'the most cleansed of Jews'.[46] Most of Kraków's Jews who had not already left the city were subsequently sent to concentration or slave labour camps.

(*Opposite, below*) Sputnik 219. This is another photograph showing Red Army troops in Kraków on the same day as Sputnik 1348, 19 January 1945. The Red Army soldiers are marching past the Kraków Barbican, a fortification of the late fifteenth century that served as an outpost of the old city. Behind the barbican is St Florian's Gate on the city walls, to which the barbican was once connected.

(*Above*) Sputnik 2569269. Some of Kraków's Jews ended up in the Auschwitz concentration camp, liberated by elements of the 60th Army on 27 January 1945. Shown here are some of the lucky survivors of the camp as they pass through the gates of the facility with the seemingly innocuous slogan 'Work makes one free' above them. That Auschwitz was a concentration camp was not immediately apparent to the advanced elements of the Red Army, which included troops of the 100th and 322nd Rifle Divisions, wary of what might be behind the barbed wire after the former in particular had seen heavy fighting in recent days. It would not, however, take long for the horrors of what had taken place inside to become apparent as they were greeted by some of the survivors of the camp who had not been evacuated by the Germans. Subsequently, 27 January would become the international day for commemoration of victims of the Holocaust.

(*Opposite*) Sputnik 2544. East and West Prussian urban areas such as Elbing (Elbląg), a town to the south-east of Danzig, were not as fortunate as some of their counterparts immediately west of the Vistula. Here the intensity of the urban fighting that took place in Elbing is very much evident in this photograph taken on 10 February 1945, as is the vulnerability of in particular open-topped armoured vehicles in such an environment. Both grenades and *Panzerfaust* projectiles were frequently thrown or fired down from upper floor windows on armoured vehicles below, either straight into crew compartments or against weaker top armour. The knocked-out SU-76 self-propelled gun shown here was a far from ideal vehicle for urban warfare, with both weak armour and an open-topped crew compartment.

Sputnik 3058240. Although the fighting for and capture of territory in East Prussia that dragged on until the end of the war facilitated the claim of the Soviet Union to the territory, in military terms the protracted fighting served little purpose. Here a Soviet T-34/85 tank is shown alongside an assault gun in a small town on the approaches to the city of Königsberg in late February 1945.

Sputnik 2619. Here, a month later than in Sputnik 3058240, Soviet infantry are shown on the attack in East Prussia as the Red Army slogged its way towards the local 'prize': the city of Königsberg. Königsberg would become the Soviet city of Kaliningrad after the war, and to this day remains part of a Russian enclave well to the west of the rest of Russia.

Sputnik 863751. The interwar 'free city' of Danzig had symbolic significance for Germany's breaking away from the constraints of the Treaty of Versailles, and was the site of the opening moves of the Second World War in Europe on 1 September 1939. By late March 1945 it had largely been reduced to rubble, finally being taken by the Red Army by the end of the month. Here Soviet heavy artillery is shown in action during fighting for the city on 25 March 1945.

Sputnik 45016. Going was better for the Red Army on the key Berlin axis during the Vistula-Oder Operation than it was in East Prussia, and Soviet forces were not only able to liberate huge swathes of Polish territory but also at the end of the operation to bridge the Oder river. Here US-supplied Ford GPA amphibians are being used along with a pontoon to cross the river on 10 February 1945. Although the final push on Berlin would not take place until April, the Red Army was now within a single bound of Berlin.

Sputnik 62724. Much further south, by this time the Red Army was also making rapid progress after having been bogged down in Hungary for so long in late 1944 and early 1945. Here Soviet troops are shown on the attack on the approaches to Vienna in Austria on 7 April 1945. With the Western Allies having crossed the Rhine and broken into the Ruhr, the island that was Nazi German territory was rapidly becoming smaller.

Chapter 22

The Prize: the Battle for Berlin

It had been a long slog for the Red Army to reach the Oder-Neisse river line in February 1945, but at this point the end of the war in Europe was undoubtedly in sight. The Red Army had reached the last major water obstacle before Berlin. Although sizeable German forces still existed in numerous pockets to the north and south, their increasingly limited mobility in the face of fuel shortages and Allied control of the air meant that they had little chance of influencing events elsewhere. Germany's last significant counter-attacks – near Stargard on the northern flank of the Vistula-Oder operation in February and in Hungary in the Lake Balaton region in March – had been relatively straightforward to contain. It is questionable whether the Soviet high command and Stalin saw a genuine threat to their flanks when they chose not to move on Berlin in late February or March – and it is unlikely that saving lives was on their minds given their willingness to squander them in the ongoing slogging match that was the fighting in East Prussia. During the East Prussian Operation, which ran from 13 January all the way through to 25 April 1945, the Red Army would in fact lose more than 126,000 men as 'irrecoverable' losses – largely killed – nearly triple the number lost in the Vistula-Oder Operation on the Berlin axis from 12 January to 3 February 1945. [GPW, p. 261] It is quite possible that holding back from Berlin was a political decision to allow Stalin and the Red Army to extract the most politically from the Western Allies and to consolidate the Red Army's hold over most of Eastern Europe. By early April, however, it was clear that the Western Allies were making rapid progress in the West, and Stalin was concerned about the possibility of collusion between the Germans and the Western Allies and the chance that it would be the British and Americans who would take Berlin. Consequently, in early April 1945 Stalin pushed Zhukov to take Berlin in an offensive operation that was, compared to the Vistula-Oder Operation, hurriedly organised and that would see Zhukov's 1st Belorussian Front struggle to break through German defences behind the Oder river on the Seelow Heights in mid-April. Having broken through these German defences the race for the German capital was on between Zhukov's 1st Belorussian and Konev's 1st Ukrainian Fronts – a race undoubtedly cynically fostered between two ambitious sub-ordinates by Stalin to get the job done quickly. More than 1.5 million front-line troops, nearly 4,000 tanks and assault guns and more than 15,000 pieces of field artillery of 76mm calibre and above, all supported in the air by nearly 7,000 aircraft, would be committed to the final *coup de grâce* for the Third Reich. [GPW, p. 267] That with decreasing chances of escape from the beleaguered capital

Hitler chose to stay in his bunker and ultimately commit suicide is well known, with the garrison of the city finally surrendering on 2 May 1945 after intense, and at times fanatical, German resistance. This resistance had inflicted almost a further 80,000 'irrecoverable' losses on the Red Army, along with nearly 275,000 sick and wounded, according to conservative counts. [RASWW, p. 559]

By this time the Western Allied and Soviet forces had met up on the Elbe river and Admiral Karl Dönitz's residual National Socialist government had only days left to govern increasing little. The death throes of the Nazi regime were played out not in some sort of Alpine redoubt as the Western Allies had feared, but in fighting in and around Prague that continued after both the Western Allies and the Soviet Union had accepted the German surrender on 8 and 9 May respectively.

The fall of Berlin.

Sputnik 2040. In the first photographs of this chapter we look at the end of the drawn-out fighting for East Prussia. The protracted siege of Königsberg finally came to an end on 9 April 1945 when the remnants of the German defenders surrendered. In this picture taken on that day Soviet troops take a well-earned rest after the fighting. In the background are some of the ruins of this medieval city turned into a modern-day fortress on Hitler's orders and reduced to rubble on Stalin's.

Sputnik 1706. A second shot taken in Königsberg on 9 April 1945 showing the devastated city for which the Red Army had fought for so many weeks. Not only thousands of Red Army soldiers and German defenders had died, but also much of the city's population in fighting that was testimony to both Hitler's nihilism and Stalin's ambitions.

Sputnik 2183. The Soviet Berlin Operation involved not only the capture of the city but also its encirclement to prevent the escape of any of those within it – and the possibility of reinforcement for the defenders. Here in this undated photograph apparently taken sometime in early May, Soviet troops are shown in action in Brandenburg, a town to the immediate west of Berlin. Of particular interest in this picture are the small arms being used by the Red Army soldiers: captured Sturmgewehr 44 assault rifles. These weapons deployed by the German armed forces at the end of the war – and from which the legendary Soviet Kalashnikov (AK-47) was clearly developed – represented a major advance in small arms design in allowing a higher rate of fire than a rifle, but longer range, greater accuracy and more penetrative power than a sub-machine gun.

Sputnik 1590. As the fighting for Berlin raged, Soviet forces were also advancing west towards the Elbe river. Here, on 24 April Cossack troops of the 1st Ukrainian Front are shown watering their horses in the Elbe, the river line that would mark the boundary between the future East and West Germany, and along which British and American forces would meet their Soviet Allies.

(*Above*) Sputnik 200. One of the units that would enter Berlin from the south as part of the 1st Ukrainian Front was the 3rd Guards Tank Army, T-34 tanks of which are shown fording a water obstacle somewhere near Berlin at the end of April 1945. From a force of over 50,000 troops at the beginning of the Berlin Operation on 16 April, with 397 functioning T-34/85s and 12 T-34/76s and an array of tank destroyers and assault guns, by 2 May only 217 of the T-34/85s were left operational. By this point the formation had lost more than 1,500 killed out of total casualties in excess of 8,000, and prior to 2 May received only 82 replacements.[47] Having started its 'road to Berlin' below Moscow in May 1942, the army had fought its way across southern Russia and the Ukraine and into southern Poland and Germany, and would even at the end of the war send troops to fight at Prague on 9 May 1945.[48]

(*Opposite, above*) Sputnik 159. Water obstacles were an issue not only outside Berlin but also within it. The river Spree that winds its way through Berlin gave Soviet naval forces the opportunity to participate in the capture of the city. Here in this undated photograph light craft of the Soviet Dnepr Flotilla are shown ferrying troops across the river where most of the bridges had been blown by the German defenders and such boats offered the opportunity to circumvent otherwise well-defended crossings.

(*Opposite, below*) Sputnik 44994. The mortar was a valuable weapon in urban warfare as elsewhere. Here, in a photograph taken during the later stages of the fighting for the city, 160mm MT-13 Model 1943 mortars are shown in action. Such large-calibre mortars obviously had greater destructive power than their smaller counterparts, although lacked the same portability. Only 720 of these mortars had been delivered to the Red Army during 1944–1945, meaning that they do not appear in many wartime photographs.[49]

(*Opposite, above*) Sputnik 44735. The defenders of Berlin made use of a motley group of tanks that included vehicles left over from the First World War, but also some of the latest tanks in the Germany inventory. Here, in a photograph taken on 13 May after the German surrender, a Tiger II or 'King Tiger' is shown knocked out and partially buried on a Berlin street. Heavy German tanks were few in number during the fighting for the city, and were not in their element in an urban environment where they had little scope to engage enemy tanks at longer ranges.

(*Opposite, below*) Sputnik 61808. By the end of the war the Red Army not only had tanks with a main armament capable of knocking out even the heaviest German tanks, but also anti-tank guns of what by the standards of the Second World War were of a very large calibre. Here Red Army personnel are firing a 100mm BS-3 anti-tank gun within Berlin on 29 April 1945, although it is clearly not being used in an anti-tank role.

(*Above*) Sputnik 5337. The German defenders of Berlin consisted of a range of troops from elite units of the Waffen SS down to *Volkssturm* militia. The latter in particular were often equipped with weapons of First World War vintage, like the MG-08/15 machine gun shown partially on the body of the dead German in the foreground of this picture, taken towards the end of the fighting for Berlin. Behind him Red Army soldiers scurry for cover with their own equivalent of the MG-08, the trusted Maxim Model 1910. German resistance was at times fanatical, as highlighted by the pockets of resistance that did not surrender on 2 May on the orders of the garrison commander. The 1st Guards Tank Army, one of the Soviet formations fighting for the city, would record that despite the surrender early on 2 May it would suffer 63 killed and 228 wounded that day as a result of 'fighting that took place in isolated sectors because the enemy sought to put up [further] resistance and not lay down their arms'. In the process of suppressing resistance that day the army claimed to have killed 470 of the enemy. Overall, that the 1st Guards Tank Army claims to have killed more of the enemy than it captured during the period from 16 April through to 2 May 1945 – 24,192 compared to 17,573 – can also be taken as evidence of the ferocity of resistance.[50]

(*Opposite*) Sputnik 1548. In addition to weapons fired by the enemy, mines were a major threat to the Red Army even in urban fighting. Here Soviet sappers and their dogs trained to seek out mines are shown taking a break in early May within the city of Berlin from what was very dangerous work for both dog and man.

(*Above*) Sputnik 61482. The Red Army made considerable use of conventional artillery in a direct-fire role in urban fighting, with the fighting for Berlin being no exception. Here – clearly towards the end of the fighting for the city with the Reichstag visible – Soviet artillerymen engage the enemy over open sights in what is a very dramatic picture showing a key episode in the final throes of the Nazi regime.

(*Overleaf*) Sputnik 1718. This photograph of Soviet tanks and personnel taken in front of the Brandenburg Gate in Berlin at the end of the fighting for the city shows a T-34/85 tank in the foreground with improvised protection attached to the turret to protect the crew from *Panzerfaust* anti-tank projectiles. The idea was that the projectile would be detonated by the wire mesh before it hit the armour itself, therefore sparing the tank and its crew the worst of the damage it might otherwise have inflicted. Despite such measures, Soviet tank losses during the Berlin Operation were horrendous, as highlighted by the losses for the 1st Guards Tank Army alone. Total losses for the 1st Guards Tank Army from 16 April through to 2 May included over 10,000 personnel, of whom 1,833 were killed, 7,771 wounded and 489 had otherwise fallen ill sufficiently badly to be evacuated to hospital. A staggering 214 T-34 tanks had been total losses, along with 18 IS-2s – where many more would have suffered damage that could be repaired – along with assault guns and self-propelled guns that brought the total to 265 vehicles lost outright. The formation none-theless claimed to have destroyed 95 enemy tanks and 54 self-propelled guns, as well as capturing a further 35 tanks and 7 self-propelled guns and destroying 366 pieces of artillery of various calibres, some of which would have been anti-tank guns.[51]

Sputnik 2000. There are a number of iconic photographs of Red Army soldiers raising the Red Banner over the captured Reichstag, most frequently published is that taken by photographer Evgenii Khaldei. This photograph – also of 2 May 1945 but by Anatolii Morozov – has the feeling of being less staged than the iconic photograph by Khaldei, where the flag for example has in this instance clearly seen better days. Either way, the Reichstag – symbol of Nazi authority – had been captured and the war in Europe was almost over.

Sputnik 2685. German prisoners of war file past a burnt-out T-34/85 on a Berlin street on 10 May 1945. One might see the burnt-out tank as being symbolic of the bitter cost of victory for the Red Army. Certainly many Soviet towns and cities also lay in ruins, with Soviet veterans returning to the difficult task of reconstruction.

Chapter 23

Finishing off the Axis: the Soviet Union against Japan

Although victory in Europe over Nazi Germany had been achieved in May 1945, for many Soviet soldiers the Second World War was not yet over. Although the Soviet Union had signed a neutrality pact with Japan in April 1941 and was not at war with Japan for the duration of the war against Nazi Germany, Stalin had begun to consider and prepare for future war against Japan once the war against Nazi Germany was going the Soviet Union's way. At the Yalta Conference in the Crimea between the Allied leaders in February 1945 Stalin was able to extract political concessions from Churchill and Roosevelt in exchange for a Soviet commitment to join the war against Japan three months after the defeat of Nazi Germany. Although US enthusiasm for Soviet participation in the war against Japan had waned by the Potsdam Conference in July 1945 and the successful testing of the US's first A-bomb, Stalin was adamant that the Soviet Union would go to war against Japan in August 1945 to a large extent to be able to make good Russian territorial losses suffered as a result of Russian defeat in the Russo-Japanese War of 1904–1905. The first exploding of a US atomic bomb in anger over Hiroshima on 6 August added a degree of urgency to Soviet preparations for war against Japan, with the Soviet Union declaring war on 8 August – the day before a second US atomic bomb was exploded over the Japanese city of Nagasaki. Japanese capitulation would not be announced until 15 August, with the formal surrender taking place on 2 September, giving Soviet forces sufficient time to sweep across Japanese-occupied Manchuria and into Korea, as well as to reoccupy the southern part of Sakhalin and take possession of the Kurile Islands.

At this stage of the war, and with the resources required to attempt to stop the US juggernaut crossing the Pacific elsewhere, Japanese forces facing the Soviets were far from capable and well equipped, although nonetheless at times put up fanatical resistance. However, the divide between the capabilities of the Red Army and the Japanese forces in continental warfare that was apparent at Khalkhin Gol in the summer of 1939 was by the summer of 1945 a schism, and the Soviet defeat of Japanese forces in Manchuria was a resounding one. Although the Red Army had suffered more than 12,000 'irrecoverable' losses during the Manchurian Strategic Offensive Operation against Japan, the fact that only 78 tanks and self-propelled guns were recorded as having been lost outright points to the disparity in capabilities between the two sides. [GPW, p. 282]

Nonetheless, although the war against Japan brought territorial gains for the Soviet Union that have been inherited by post-Soviet Russia, thousands of service personnel had been lost in a war that lacked the existential justification of the fighting in the West.

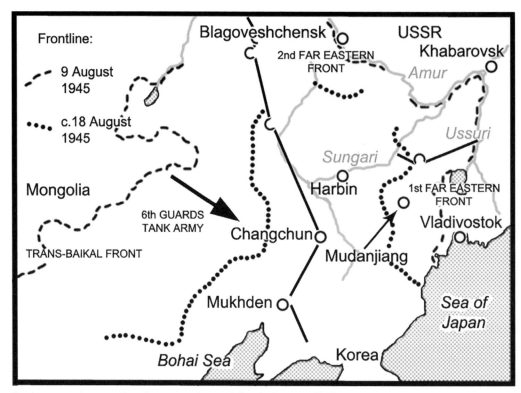

Soviet operations against Japan on the mainland, August 1945.

Sputnik 136014. Although the Soviet Union was not at war with Japan for most of the Second World War, there was plenty of bad blood for Soviet propagandists to focus on when the time came to try to rally elements of the Soviet population for more war in August 1945. This Soviet propaganda poster by Nikolai Dolgoruchkov (1902–1980) clearly links the war against Germany with the war against Japan, stating that 'and in the Pacific – their advance was halted!' Perhaps more potent for mobilising animosity towards Japan than the limited links between Germany and Japan as members of the Axis alliance are the references on the Japanese bandages to the fighting against the Japanese at Lake Khasan in 1938 and Khalkhin Gol in 1939. The bandage reference to the Soviet Volochaevsk Operation of 1922 when Red forces defeated the Whites in the Far East in the Volochaevsk region would perhaps only have had meaning to those in the Far East, although it was the population of that region that was probably the primary audience for this poster.

(*Above*) Sputnik 171533. One of the Soviet axes of attack against the Japanese in Manchuria – for the Trans-Baikal Front – was through the Greater Khingan mountains from Mongolia. Here elements of that force are shown in a valley in the mountains on 8 August. In the lead here are T-34/85 tanks, followed by a fairly motley collection of other vehicles. The advance on this axis was something of a logistical achievement, with fuel having to be flown in to maintain the advance and with older T-26 and BT-5 tanks soon being left behind for want of fuel. The 6th Guards Tank Army was in the vanguard of the Soviet advance on this sector of the front, and as expected met little resistance during the initial phase of operations when clearly there was little Japanese expectation of Soviet activity. In fact, between 9 and 19 August the 6th Guards Tank Army would encounter Japanese forces numbering only in the hundreds, with the 7th Mechanized Corps for example killing or wounding 216 enemy troops and disarming a further 1,327 for the loss of 5 killed and 11 wounded, and where numbers for those evacuated owing to sickness and other non-combat losses far exceed those from combat.[52]

(*Opposite, above*) Sputnik 171532. This second picture was taken on the same day as the above, and not only shows the motley collection of vehicles involved but also provides a good shot of some of the mountainous terrain. In the foreground is a US-supplied Studebaker truck towing a ZiS-3 gun. Having secured the passes through the mountains, forces of the Trans-Baikal Front were to push on towards Changchun.

(*Opposite, below*) Sputnik 67353. Much of the advance of the Trans-Baikal Front further to the south-west towards Mukhden in the direction of the Bohai Sea and Korean Peninsula would be across very open and sparsely populated terrain, both semi-arid plains and desert. Some idea of the vast expanses over which Soviet and Mongolian forces ranged on that sector of the front can be gained in this picture, also of 8 August 1945, of Soviet tanks with accompanying infantry advancing with a liaison aircraft overhead. On 18 August, when Japanese forces ahead of the 6th Guards Tank Army agreed to surrender, forward detachments raced forward to secure territory far from their current positions and occupied by far more significant Japanese forces, including Port Arthur and objectives on the Korean Peninsula.[53]

(*Above*) Sputnik 1315. A second Soviet advance, this time by the 1st Far Eastern Front, would take place from near Vladivostok westwards towards Harbin, Mudanjiang and ultimately Changchun. This picture of a Soviet ISU-152 assault gun crossing a water obstacle was taken on 14 August 1945 not far from Mudanjiang. The Japanese had spent some time fortifying this sector of the front, although their plan was to fall back into positions in the hinterland after initial resistance on the border. Fortified Japanese positions combined with heavy rain on the eve of, and at times during, operations meant that the advance by the 1st Army of the Front in a series of columns was relatively ponderous. The advance was led by small groups of tanks, sappers and infantry, supported where required by self-propelled guns such as the one shown in this picture. The loss of a T-34 tank on 13 August was something of a rare occurrence for the 1st Army in Manchuria, in considerable contrast to the Soviet experience in the West.[54]

(*Opposite, above*) Sputnik 63869. A third prong of the Soviet advance was along the Sungari river towards Korea by the 2nd Far Eastern Front, with additional penetrations of Manchuria across a wide front over difficult terrain in far from ideal weather conditions. This photograph shows a Soviet monitor of the Amur River Flotilla; it seems to be a pre-revolutionary 'Shkval' Class monitor, possibly the *Sun-Iat-Sen*. The monitor is shown landing troops somewhere on the Amur or Sungari, the longest tributary of the Amur that snaked its way from the Soviet border in a loosely south-westerly direction. A number of monitors of this class were used on the Amur and its tributaries during the opening phases of the war against Japan, both for landing troops and fire-support.

(*Opposite, below*) Sputnik 839212. The Soviet Pacific Fleet would also play a role in the war against Japan, and in particular in operations to recapture South Sakhalin and to take the Kurile Islands, both tasks the responsibility of the 2nd Far Eastern Front. Here Type 7 destroyers of the Pacific Fleet are shown under way at some point during August 1945, apparently heading out on a mission. Soviet naval forces could operate with relative impunity given that the Japanese Navy had almost ceased to exist, and Japanese air power in the region was extremely limited and easily dealt with by the Soviet VVS and air forces of the Pacific Fleet. There were, however, sizeable Japanese garrisons to contend with on South Sakhalin and the Kurile Islands, with the 2nd Far Eastern Front recording 63,841 enemy prisoners taken by its 'Northern Direction (South Sakhalin and the Kurile Islands)'.[55]

(*Above*) Sputnik 6051476. Soviet forces used some of the latest and some of their most outdated equipment in the war against the Japanese in 1945, with the former tending to feature in photographs taken at the time. Here Soviet troops engage the Japanese using a BS-3 100mm anti-tank gun in a direct-fire role at the start of the campaign on 9 August 1945. By this time the Red Army had had plenty of practice at using overwhelming firepower to subdue enemy defensive positions. Some of the older equipment used during the fighting in Manchuria included pre-war BT-series and T-26 tanks, as in the case of the 6th Guards Tank Army in Sputnik 171533 (p. 284). [GPW, p. 275]

(*Opposite, above*) Sputnik 67315. Curious locals gather round a Soviet US-supplied Sherman tank somewhere in Manchuria on 19 August 1945. The 1st Far Eastern Front alone committed almost 2,000 tanks to operations against the Japanese, who despite having on paper more than 1,000 tanks available in the theatre, in reality had little that could stand up to the by now formidable Soviet anti-tank capabilities. [GPW, p. 275]

(*Opposite, below*) Sputnik 60196. The relatively slow rate of advance for forces of the 1st Far Eastern Front is highlighted in this picture of a Soviet gun crew engaged in fighting for the city of Mudanjiang a week into the war and only a little over 100km from the Soviet border near Vladivostok on 16 August 1945. The 1st Army did not conduct a frontal assault on the city, but sought to envelop it before clearing it of enemy troops who had not escaped the encirclement. During the brief fighting for the city that day much of the 1st Army's artillery was still en route through the difficult terrain over which it was advancing.[56] By this time Soviet forces of the Trans-Baikal Front were hundreds of kilometres into the Japanese rear where, according to historian David Glantz, 'only logistical difficulties limited the Soviet advance' and where Japanese forces were unable to form a viable defensive line. [cited in GPW, p. 279] Although the gun being used is a wartime ZiS-3 piece, note that the soldier on the left directing the gun crew is still wearing a pre-war Model 1936 helmet!

(*Opposite, above*) Sputnik 64204. In this picture Soviet troops are shown in Mudanjiang on the same day as Sputnik 60196 was apparently taken. The enthusiastic greeting on the part of the local civilians is no doubt genuine. Notice that there are a number of Korean flags in the crowd – flags representing the Provisional Government of the Republic of Korea. This provisional government-in-exile had operated from Shanghai and later Chungking from 1919 onwards.

(*Opposite, below*) Sputnik 839285. In this photograph of 30 August Soviet troops are shown passing through the city of Mudanjiang after its liberation from Japanese occupation by the Red Army. The artillery pieces being towed in this case seem to be of late-Tsarist vintage, their being pulled by horse teams seeming very appropriate!

(*Above*) Sputnik 66026. Here Japanese troops are surrendering to the Red Army somewhere in Manchuria on 18 August 1945 – the day on which the widespread surrender of Japanese forces in the theatre began. As in the case of the 6th Guards Tank Army in the caption for Sputnik 67353 (see p. 285), the Red Army would transport troops by air or send forward detachments ahead of their main force at around this time in order to try to speed up the surrender of Japanese forces and occupy territory.

(*Opposite*) Sputnik 5822475. There were still many Japanese troops in Manchuria to be rounded up after the formal Japanese surrender of 2 September 1945. Here large numbers of Japanese troops – relatively lightly guarded – are being marched away on 3 September 1945 by troops of the Soviet 1st Far Eastern Front. From 9 August to 1 September 1945 the 1st Far Eastern Front would report the capture of 257,225 enemy troops, of whom 236,216 were Japanese. Most of these were captured after the fighting had died down, with only 7,000 reported as having been captured 'during the actual fighting'. [GPW, p. 281]

(*Above*) Sputnik 834147. Revenge for the Russo-Japanese War: Soviet naval infantry look at their Soviet naval flag over Port Arthur (now Lüshun Port) in a photograph taken in mid-October 1945. Soviet liberation of the nearby northern part of Korea – mirrored by US occupation of the south – would lay the foundations for the subsequent Korean War.

Chapter 24

Counting the Cost, Reconstruction and Commemoration

The Great Patriotic War was a defining event not only for the Soviet regime but also for so many of the Soviet people. The German invasion that had threatened to topple the Soviet regime and, as soon became apparent, lead to the enslavement of the Soviet peoples had been repulsed. Not only had the Soviet regime survived and been shown to be resilient in crisis, but it had gone on to spread its particular brand of revolution well to the west into Eastern Europe to an extent that earlier Soviet leaders could have only dreamt of. A Soviet Union sidelined in international affairs during the 1920s and 1930s was now a permanent member of the new United Nations Security Council and the dominant power on the Eurasian land mass. Such success, however, came at a terrible cost, not only in terms of death and injury, but also in material terms. In the immediate aftermath of the war Stalin and the Soviet leadership were silent on the true costs of the war, and it would be decades before figures of 20 million and then 27 million lives lost due to the war would surface and become accepted. These figures do not of course include the further millions physically and mentally scarred by an ordeal that touched the vast majority of Soviet families in some meaningful way.

From children who became orphans and tens of thousands of soldiers with long-term disabilities, to women who would never marry and have families because so many young men had been killed, the knock-on effects of the war for Soviet society were considerable. From the rubble of the war many rebuilt their lives as best they could, but even if physical wounds had healed over time the mental damage would for many inevitably resurface in some form in a society where mental illness was rarely discussed and was seen as a sign of particular weakness. Any expectations by Soviet citizens of some sort of peace dividend would frequently be dashed when returnees from the front or dislocation found living space in even shorter supply than had been the case before the war, and where Stalin's government continued to pump resources into heavy industry and defence rather than agriculture, housing and light industry – the latter a long-neglected Soviet consumer sector. It would take Stalin's death for things to start to change, and the late 1940s and early 1950s were a time of hard work for little material reward for many who had contributed so much to victory.

The war was a collective trauma for Soviet society, but nonetheless also a cause for pride. For some the war even provided opportunity, where so many male peasants, for example, were able to break away from the collective farm and its second serfdom thanks to their having been mobilised into the Red Army. For the Soviet government victory in the war in many ways superseded the revolution as *de facto* justification for its continuation. This focus on the war, which would permeate the Soviet arts and media to such an extent, is understandable not only from the regime's perspective but also given that for Soviet citizens pride in their contribution to the war effort was something sanctioned and even encouraged by the regime that so many could participate in with enthusiasm. Titles and awards, memorials and anniversaries relating to the war became a core part of Soviet social and political life. Such traditions have endured into the post-Soviet period in Russia, in particular as Vladimir Putin's Russia seeks to become the heir to a Soviet past where Boris Yeltsin had threatened, metaphorically speaking, to throw the baby out with the bath water. The number of surviving veterans of the war may be dwindling, but interest in and commemoration of the war in Russia has had a new lease of life. Victory Day parades under Putin have provided a spectacle of which many of his predecessors would have been proud, and Soviet victory in the Great Patriotic War looks set to remain a significant component of the Russian national myth long after those who participated in it have passed away.

(*Opposite, above*) Sputnik 594370. Whilst the scene here is not as raucous as, for example, in the famous photographs taken at Piccadilly Circus in London the day before, the joy on the faces of those in this crowd in Red Square on 9 May – Victory Day for the Soviet people – is evident.

(*Opposite, below*) Sputnik 60177. Although for some of the Red Army's personnel the war was not over in May 1945, for the vast majority it was. Within weeks many had returned to what was often a hero's welcome back in the Soviet Union, even if subsequent life may not have seemed fit for heroes. Survival was of course reward in itself for many. In this photograph of 10 July 1945 Red Army troops are seen returning to the Soviet Union by train from Berlin. The text on the sign on the front of the train – 'Our cause is just. Victory is ours!' – is a reference to part of Soviet Foreign Minister Viacheslav Molotov's radio address to the Soviet people of 22 June 1941, in which he suggested that 'Our cause is just, the enemy will be defeated, victory will be ours!' – sentiments repeated by Stalin in his address to the Soviet people of 3 July, in which he noted that the Soviet population and others could see that 'our cause is just, that the enemy will be beaten, and that we must be victorious!' Molotov's wording appears on a sign being passed by Red Army soldiers on their way to the front in Sputnik 662773 (see Chapter 4, p. 49). In 1945 'Our cause is just. Victory is ours!' appeared on medals celebrating victory over Nazi Germany, and indeed as the sign here suggests, elsewhere as well!

(*Above*) Sputnik 346. The caption for this picture of a Red Army soldier being greeted by his wife or girlfriend at Moscow's famous Belorussia station sometime in June 1945 reads 'Belorussia Station. Tears of joy – the happiness of meeting'. Tears of joy might also have been tears of relief, as well as tears for those who did not make it back.

(*Opposite, above*) Sputnik 153. Those who did not make it back. In this photograph junior lieutenant and sniper of the 61st Army Aleksandr Lebedev is shown by the grave of a fallen comrade on the Briansk Front in June 1943. Lebedev was credited with 307 enemy 'kills' before himself being killed on 14 August 1944. He would be posthumously awarded the title of 'Hero of the Soviet Union'.

(*Opposite, below*) Sputnik 48516. Demobilisation from the army at the end of the war was not an exclusively male affair, and in fact proportionally more women were demobilised in 1945 than men as women were largely deemed to no longer be needed in the post-war Red Army. In this photograph female medical personnel – already in civilian clothes – board a lorry as part of their journey back home to the Soviet Union from Austria. The Soviet leadership was particularly concerned that young women such as these should marry and have children in order to start to make good the demographic deficit in the Soviet Union caused by losses in the war.

Sputnik 58699. At the end of the war much of the European part of the Soviet Union still lay in ruins. Here, on 18 April 1945 in the capital of the Belorussian SSR, Minsk, debris from a ruined building or block of buildings is being removed – a small part of the titanic job of reconstruction of the Soviet Union.

ТЫ ХРАБРО ВОЕВАЛ С ВРАГОМ—
ВОЙДИ, ХОЗЯИН, В НОВЫЙ ДОМ!

Sputnik 136601. 'You fought bravely against the enemy, now – man-of-the-house – enter your new home!' reads the text of this 1945 Soviet poster by artist Nina Vatolina (1915–2002). Unfortunately, this was not the reality for the vast majority of returnees in 1945, or indeed over the next few years, with those returning more likely to be living in so-called 'communal' accommodation than their own house or apartment. It would not be until the period of Nikita Khrushchev's premiership of the Soviet Union that many Soviet couples would get to enjoy their own apartment that did not share cooking and washing facilities with others.

Sputnik 37795. Cleaning up after the war not only meant clearing up debris, but also making safe the many millions of unexploded pieces of ordnance across Soviet territory. Here a Soviet sapper is shown in September 1964 sweeping for ordnance on the territory of the Brest Fortress on what had been the German-Soviet border in June 1941. Even today it is not unusual to unearth unexploded ordnance in the fields and even more so the forests of the former Soviet republics in the west.

Sputnik 2684043. During the Soviet period considerable effort was put into public memorialisation of those who lost their lives during the war, with those sites continuing to be focal points for remembrance to this day. One of the most famous such sites is the Mamaev Kurgan memorial complex overlooking what was Stalingrad, and is now Volgograd in contemporary Russia. The large statue in the background is 'The Motherland Calls!' by sculptor Evgenii Vuchetich (1908–1974), that in the foreground the equally well-known 'Fight to the death!' This photograph was taken in May 1972.

Sputnik 2842229. Annual Victory Day parades on 9 May continue to be a feature in the post-Soviet calendars of many former Soviet republics, including of course Russia. Here a Victory Day parade is under way to mark the 71st anniversary of victory over Nazi Germany on 9 May 2016, in this case on Palace Square in St Petersburg, formerly Leningrad. Although historical vehicles and uniforms have been increasingly in evidence in recent years, the dwindling numbers of veterans of the war have always been and remain a core part of the festivities. A display of current military hardware has historically been a feature of such parades, with contemporary hardware playing a prominent role in recent parades under the Putin administration. Pictured here are T-72B3 tanks of the Russian armed forces – an updated version of a late Soviet-era tank, adding that additional element of continuity with the past.

Sputnik 5967667. Although celebrations on 9 May are to a significant extent concerned with remembering those who lost their lives in the war, such events are also about celebrating the achievements of those who survived. The final photographs in this chapter provide pictures and a few key details about some of the veterans recently celebrated in the Russian press, starting with a veteran who, although surviving the war, paid a high personal price in the war in losing a hand and part of his arm. Stepan Anufriev was born on 30 May 1923 in the village of Pravie Lamki in the Tambov region. Before the Great Patriotic War he worked as an electrician in a factory in the Moscow region before volunteering for military service in 1941. On 15 October 1941 he began his military education at a communications school for the armoured forces in Ul'ianovsk on the Volga. In May 1943, with the rank of lieutenant, he was sent for field service with the 3rd Guards Tank Army, serving as the commander of radio communications for a tank corps. Having participated in the battle of Kursk and the crossing of the Dnepr, he was wounded during the liberation of Kiev and ultimately ended up losing his hand and part of his arm to gangrene, and was demobilised as a Class 2 Invalid. After being demobilised Stepan Anufriev had a full working life that included being the headmaster of a school near where he was born and working for the railways in the Tambov region, and at the time this photograph was taken on 3 August 2019 he was living in Tambov. For his service during the war Anufriev was awarded the Order of the Red Star and the Order of the Great Patriotic War 1st Class.

Sputnik 5870755 & 5870436. Maria Limanskaia was born on 12 April 1924 in the village of Staraia Poltavka of what is now the Volgograd region. She was sent to the front in 1942 and for the duration of the war served in a reserve regiment, in which she sewed uniforms for Soviet soldiers. Ultimately she and her friend were selected to become traffic controllers, for which they received three days of training. On 2 May 1945 Maria Limanskaia was directing traffic in front of the Brandenburg Gate in Berlin, where was subsequently photographed by Evgenii Khaldei in a photograph given the caption 'Traffic controller of victory'. After the war Maria Limanskaia worked as a nursing sister and school librarian in the Volgograd region. From 1994 until the date this photograph was taken she lived in a village in the Saratov region, in a district in which in honour of the 74th anniversary of victory over Nazi Germany it was decided to erect a monument to her. For her military service she received numerous honours, including medals for the 'Liberation of Warsaw' and the 'Capture of Berlin'. She is pictured here in the contemporary picture with fellow veteran and signaller of the 98th Guards Tank Regiment Nikolai Ilinev in the village of Zvonarevka, Saratov region, in May 2019. The second picture shows her back in 1945 directing traffic in front of the Brandenburg Gate in Berlin.

Sputnik 6060300 & 6060307. Nikolai Fadeev was born on 27 November 1925 in the village of Nikitino in the Kurgan region that borders what is now Kazakhstan. In December 1943 he volunteered to serve at the front, and after finishing the appropriate courses became a gunlayer for a ZiS-3 gun and was sent to the Volkhov Front near Leningrad. After serving as a ZiS-3 gunner and having reached the rank of sergeant, Nikolai Fadeev became a gunner in a T-34 tank of the 3rd Belorussian Front. It was in this role that Fadeev served until victory day, on which he was in Königsberg in East Prussia. Fadeev's war was not, however, over at this point as he was then sent to the Far East for the war against Japan. He is shown here in a recent picture taken in October 2019 in the Cheliabinsk region of Russia as well as in a wartime photograph taken with fellow crew members of their T-34 tank, in which he is in the centre of the picture. For his wartime service he received a number of honours including the medal 'For Bravery' received directly from Soviet Marshal Vasilevskii. In 1946 as a member of the Kantemirov Division he took part in the Victory Parade in Red Square.

Notes

1. Svetlana Alexievich (ed.), *The Unwomanly Face of War: An Oral History of Women in World War II* (New York: Random House, 2018), p. xiv.
2. Put' boevikh deistvii 70-i Ordena Lenina s.d./Kratko/. 21 May 1942 or earlier. Central Archive of the Ministry of Defence of the Russian Federation (hereafter TsAMO RF) f.1148.o.1.d.28.ll.46–8.
3. Roman Karmen, *Pod pulemetnim ognem. Zapiski frontovogo operatora* [*Under Machine Gun Fire – Notes of a frontline cameraman*] (Moscow: Algoritm, 2017), p. 25 [Google Play version]
4. A.G. Soliankin et al., *Otechestvennie bronirovannie machini. XX vek. Tom 1. 1905–1941* [*Armoured vehicles of the Motherland: XX Century, Vol. 1, 1905–1941*] (Moscow: Izdatel'skii tsentr' 'Eksprint', 2002), p. 17.
5. A.G. Soliankin et al., *Otechestvennie bronirovannie machini. XX vek. Tom 1. 1905–1941*, pp. 16–17.
6. Zhurnal boevikh deistvii 1-go Gvardeiskogo kavaleriiskogo korpusa. 11-12.7.41g. TsAMO RF f.3465.o.1.d.78.l.17.
7. A.G. Soliankin et al., *Otechestvennie bronirovannie machini. XX vek. Tom 1. 1905–1941*, p. 214.
8. A.G. Soliankin et al., *Otechestvennie bronirovannie machini. XX vek. Tom 1. 1905–1941*, p. 18.
9. Donesenie. O Poteriakh Lichnogo Sostava 44 kavaler. divizii s 16 noiabria po 21 dekabria 1941 g. TsAMO RF f.301.o.6782.d.14.l.35 and Donesenie. O Poteriakh Konskogo Sostava 44 kavaler. divizii s 16 noiabria po 21 dekabria 1941 g. TsAMO RF f.301.o.6782.d.14.l.35ob.
10. Boevoi put'divizii (sentiabr' 1939 g.-sentiabr' 1942 g.) [printed] TsAMO RF f.1316.o.1, d.2, ll.1+ (pp. 15, 19, 22).
11. Alexander Hill, *Soviet Destroyers of World War II* (Oxford: Osprey Publishing, 2018), pp. 44–5.
12. A.V. Platonov, *Entsiklopediia sovetskikh nadvodnikh korablei, 1941–1945* [*Encyclopedia of Soviet Surface Vessels, 1941–1945*] (Saint-Petersburg: OOO 'Izdatel'stvo Poligon', 2002), p. 59.
13. Ibid., p. 93.
14. Ibid., p. 143.
15. Ibid., p. 64.
16. V.V. Litvinenko, *Liudskie poteri na frontakh Velikoi Otechestvennoi voini. RKKA i Vermakht. Mifi i pravda istorii* [*Human losses on the Fronts of the Great Patriotic War ...*] (Moscow: Veche, 2015), pp. 60–3.
17. Lev Lopukhovsky & Boris Kavalerchik (trans. Harold Orenstein), *The Price of Victory: The Red Army's Casualties in the Great Patriotic War* (Barnsley: Pen & Sword, 2017), p. 161. This book offers a detailed discussion of figures for Soviet losses during the war.
18. A.N. Lepekhin & Iu.A. Lepekhin, *Pervii Gvardeiskii kavalerskii korpus* [*First Guards Cavalry Corps*] (Dedilovo: 2016), pp. 560–8 [Google Play edition, Litres, 2017].
19. Zhurnal boevikh deistvii 1-go Gvardeiskogo kavaleriiskogo korpusa. 7.12.41. TsAMO RF f.3465.o.1.d.78.l.62.
20. Prikaz o sformirovanii zhenskikh aviatsionnikh polkov VVS Krasnoi Armii No. 0099. 8 oktiabria 1941 g., in V.A. Zolotarev (gen. ed.), *Russkii arkhiv. Velikaia Otechestvennaia. Prikazi Narodnogo Komissara Oboroni SSSR 22 iiunia 1941g.-1942g. T.13 (2-2)* (Moscow: Terra, 1997), pp. 112–13.
21. Immenoi spisok bezvotvratnikh poter' nachal'stvuiushchego sostava... TsAMO RF f.58.o.18001.d.683.l.65.

22. Svetlana Gladish, *Sobaki na frontakh Velikoi Otechestvennoi* [*Dogs of the Fronts of the Great Patriotic War*] (Moscow: Kuchkovo pole, 2012), p. 192.
23. Chlenu Boennogo Soveta ZF tov. Bulganinu. Shtab 1 gv. kk., … 16:00 3.12.41g. TsAMO RF f.3465.o.1.d.10.l.296.
24. P.F. Gladkikh & A.E. Loktev, *Sluzhba zdorov'ia v Velikoi Otechestvennoi voine 1941–1945 gg.* [*Medical Services in the Great Patriotic War 1941–1945*] (Saint-Petersburg: 'Dmitrii Bulanin', 2005), p. 118.
25. Ibid., pp. 190, 213, 235.
26. Nagradnoi list. Passar Maxim Aleksandrovich. 5 sentiabr 1942 g. TsAMO RF f.33.o.682525.d.182.l.134. Immenoi spisok bezvotvratnikh poter'… 117strel'kovogo polka 23 strel'kovoi divizii s 19.1 po 29.1 1943 g. TsAMO RF f.58.o.18001.d.92.l.88.
27. Shtab Iuzhnogo fronta. Nachal'niku operativnogo otdela. Informatsiia k 15:00 12.3.43. Nach operotdela shtaba 4 Kub gv kkk. 12.3.1943. TsAMO RF f.3470.o.1.d.155.l.232.
28. Zhurnal boevikh deistvii [246 Rifle Division]. 17.6.42. TsAMO RF f.1528.o.1.d.45.ll.49–51.
29. Zhurnal boevikh deistvii [246 Rifle Division]. 18.6.42. TsAMO RF f.1528.o.1.d.45.l.52.
30. V.N. Shunkov, *Artilleriia Krasnoi Armii i Vermakhta Vtoroi Mirovoi voini* [*Artillery of the Red Army and Wehrmacht in the Second World War*] (Moscow: AST, 2005), pp. 127, 130–1.
31. Alexander Hill, 'The Bear's New Wheels (and Tracks): US-Armored and Other Vehicles and Soviet Military Effectiveness during the Great Patriotic War in Words and Photographs', in *The Journal of Slavic Military Studies*, Volume 25, Number 2 (2012), pp. 208–9.
32. Ibid., p. 211.
33. Ibid., pp. 216–17.
34. Ibid., p. 216.
35. Zhurnal boevikh deistvii 2-i tankovoi armii s 1 iiulia po 8 avgusta 1944 goda. TsAMO RF f.307.o.4148.d.1.ll.165–6, and Zhurnal boevikh deistvii 2 tankovoi armii s 8 avgusta po 10 sentiabria 1944 g. TsAMO RF f.307.o.4148.d.280.l.100.
36. David Cesarani, *Final Solution: the fate of the Jews, 1933–1949* (New York: St Martin's Press, 2016), p. 626.
37. K.A. Pakhaliuk et al. (eds), *Kontsentratsionnii lager' Maidanek. Issledovaniia. Dokumenti. Vospominaniia* [*Majdenek Concentration Camp: Research, documents and recollections*] (Moscow: 'Piatii Rim', 2020), p. 76.
38. Ibid.
39. Ibid., p. 81.
40. Yefim Gordon & Dmitri Khazanov, *Soviet Combat Aircraft of the Second World War. Volume One: Single-engined Fighters* (Leicester: Midland Publishing Ltd, 1998), p. 96.
41. Ibid., p. 143.
42. Grib Mikhail Ivanovich. http://www.warheroes.ru/hero/hero.asp?Hero_id=6036 [accessed 10 February 2021].
43. Yefim Gordon & Dmitri Khazanov, *Soviet Combat Aircraft of the Second World War. Volume Two: Twin-engined Fighters, Attack Aircraft and Bombers* (Leicester: Midland Publishing Ltd, 1999), pp. 115–16, 156.
44. Ibid., p. 147.
45. Zhurnal boevikh deistvii 3-go Gvardeiskogo kavaleriiskogo … korpusa za ianvar' m-ts 1945 goda. TsAMO RF f.3468.o.1.d.194.ll.10–11.
46. Saul Friedländer, *The Years of Extermination: Nazi Germany and the Jews, 1939–1945* (New York: HarperCollins, 2007), p. 36.
47. Colonel-General Ribal'ko et al, Deistviia 3-i Gvardeiskoi tankovoi armii v Berlinsko-Prazhskoi operatsii 1 UF. 16 aprelia-9 maia 1945 g. [Prepared May–June 1945]. TsAMO RF f.315.o.4440.d.538.ll.58–64.
48. Map. Boevoi put' 3 gv. TA v Otechestvennoi voine s 28.5.42 po 9.5.45. TsAMO RF f.315.o.4440.d.508.l.71.
49. V.N. Shunkov, *Artilleriia Krasnoi Armii i Vermakhta Vtoroi Mirovoi voini*, p. 244.

50. Zhurnal boevikh deistvii 1 Gvardeiskoi tankovoi armii s 1 ianvaria 1945 g. po 9 maia 1945 goda. 2 maia 1945 goda. TsAMO RF f.299.o.370.d.799.ll.201–2 and Uron nanesennii protivniku voiskami armii v boiakh s 16.4.45g po 2.5.45 goda. TsAMO RF f.299.o.370.d.799.l.203.

51. Zhurnal boevikh deistvii 1 Gvardeiskoi tankovoi armii s 1 ianvaria 1945 g. po 9 maia 1945 goda. 2 maia 1945 goda. Uron nanesennii protivniku voiskami armii v boiakh s 16.4.45g po 2.5.45 goda and Poteri armii s 16.4.45g. po 2.5.45 goda. TsAMO RF f.299.o.370.d.799.l.203.

52. Nastupatel'naia operatsiia 6 gv. TA ZabF. Otcheti o boevikh deistviiakh. Data sozdaniia dokumenta 31.08.1945 g. TsAMO RF f.339.o.5179.d.130.ll.1+, pp. 21–32.

53. Ibid., pp. 29–32.

54. Zhurnal boevikh deistvii 1 A v period 9.8-20.8.45g. Data sozdaniia dokumenta 5.10.1945 g. TsAMO RF f.294.o.6961.d.120.ll.28–76.

55. Natupatel'naia operatsiia Vtorogo dal'nevostochnogo fronta, provedennaia v period 9-31 avgusta 1945 goda. "31" ianvaria 1946 g. TsAMO RF f.238.o.1584.s.170.l.1+, p.101.

56. Zhurnal boevikh deistvii 1 A v period 9.8-20.8.45g. Data sozdaniia dokumenta 5.10.1945 g. TsAMO RF f.294.o.6961.d.120.ll.76–81.

Further Reading

This section is for those looking for more information on some of the events and themes covered in the chapters in this book. In addition to following up on the references in and taking a look at my *The Red Army and the Second World War* (Cambridge University Press, 2017) and *The Great Patriotic War of the Soviet Union, 1941–1945: A documentary reader* (Routledge, 2009), the following titles are recommended for particular topics and themes, with this further reading section beginning with some more general titles that cover the war as a whole. Those books marked with an * are ideal introductory works, typically very readable and accessible, through to those marked with an *** that are very detailed and often operational in nature or very much academic works for the more committed. This reading list is far from exhaustive, and I have deliberately not included multi-volume works on a single battle or campaign such as David Glantz's four volumes on the Battle of Stalingrad – books that it is assumed offer far too much detail for the more casual reader, and may already be known to those with particularly deep interests in a topic.

General Histories of the Great Patriotic War

*Chris Bellamy, *Absolute War: Soviet Russia in the Second World War* (Macmillan, 2007). An engaging single-volume history of the Great Patriotic War that is more than just an operational history.

**John Erickson, *The Road to Stalingrad* ... and *The Road to Berlin* ... (Weidenfeld & Nicholson, 1975 and 1983 respectively). Although published before the end of the Cold War and the opening up of Soviet archives, Erickson fully exploits the Soviet literature and the personal testimony available at the time to produce a lucid history that has stood the test of time.

**David Glantz & Jonathan House, *When Titans Clashed: How the Red Army Stopped Hitler* (University of Kansas Press, 1996). Very much focused on military matters, this single-volume operational history offers an introduction to David Glantz's voluminous work on the Great Patriotic War in an accessible form, aided by Jonathan House's clear writing.

**Evan Mawdsley, *Thunder in the East – The Nazi-Soviet War 1941–1945* (2nd edition) (Bloomsbury, 2005). First published in 1995, this second edition updates to some extent this excellent operational and strategic history of the war.

*Catherine Merridale, *Ivan's War: Inside the Red Army 1939–1945* (Faber & Faber, 2005). This 'soldier's view' social history of the war provides an often useful addition to the operational accounts by Glantz and Mawdsley, for example, that tend to be 'top down'.

*Richard Overy, *Russia's War – A History of the Soviet War Effort: 1941–1945* (Penguin, 1998). Although primarily a specialist on Germany, Overy provides an excellent and very readable synthesis of the literature at the time this was written in this useful single-volume history.

**Geoffrey Roberts, *Stalin's Wars: From World War to Cold War, 1939–1953* (Yale University Press, 2008). Considering a slightly longer period than the above books, this engaging wider history of Stalin's military and diplomatic leadership spends much of the book on Stalin and the Great Patriotic War.

*Alexander Werth, *Russia at War* (Barrie & Rockliff, 1964). First published in 1964, Russian-born British journalist Alexander Werth reported from the Soviet Union during the war, and this insightful and very well-written history of the war drawing on his own experiences has been reprinted many times for good reason.

Key Biographies and Memoirs for the Great Patriotic War

* Artem Drabkin & Oleg Sheremet (eds), *T-34 in Action* (Pen & Sword, 2006). This book provides sometimes revealing eyewitness accounts of the war by some of those who served in the ubiquitous Soviet T-34 tank. Drabkin has published a number of similar collections, others of which have also been translated into English.

* Geoffrey Roberts, *Stalin's General: The Life of Georgy Zhukov* (Random House, 2012). The best English-language biography of the Soviet Union's most famous wartime general (later Marshal), who appears in three photographs in this book.

** Harold Shukman (ed.), *Stalin's Generals* (Weidenfeld & Nicholson, 1993). Although published back in 1993, this is still the best single-volume on the Soviet Union's wartime military leadership. Military biographies are provided for twenty-six generals and marshals, many of whom feature in this book.

* Boris Sokolov, *Marshal K.K. Rokossovsky: The Red Army's Gentleman Commander* (Helion & Company, 2015). An engaging biography of another one of the Soviet Union's wartime marshals, and one of the few Soviet commanders to appear in more than one photograph in this book.

* David Stone (ed.), *The Soviet Union at War, 1941–1945* (Pen & Sword, 2010). A useful collection of essays on different themes relating to the war.

* Ivan Yakushin, *On the Roads of War: A Soviet Cavalryman on the Eastern Front* (Pen & Sword, 2005). Selected as an example of the growing number of Soviet memoirs by junior personnel translated into English, this particular memoir concerns cavalryman Yakushin's wartime experience of the war from Leningrad to Berlin. Mansur Abdulin's *Red Road from Stalingrad: Recollections of a Soviet Infantryman* (Pen & Sword, 2005) is another worthy example of a memoir written by a junior member of the Red Army.

** Georgii Zhukov, *Marshal of Victory: The Autobiography of General Georgy Zhukov*, edited by Geoffrey Roberts (Pen & Sword, 2020). Marshal Georgii Zhukov's memoirs are a valuable source for understanding much of the Soviet military decision-making of the war, even if readers have to be wary of Zhukov's self-promotion!

Chapter 1: The Red Army Prepares for War

** Roger Reese, *Stalin's Reluctant Soldiers: A Social History of the Red Army, 1925–1941* (University Press of Kansas, 1996). This academic work looks at the development of the Red Army from the late 1920s through to the beginning of the Great Patriotic War, with particular reference to the people serving in it.

*** David Glantz, *Stumbling Colossus: The Red Army on the Eve of War* (University Press of Kansas, 1998). A detailed assessment of the state of the Red Army on the eve of the Great Patriotic War that provides many reasons as to why the Red Army was not ready to face the Axis invasion in June 1941.

Chapter 2: Preludes to the Main Event

Here in particular I encourage readers interested in learning more to look at Chapters 4–6 of my *The Red Army and the Second World War* (Cambridge University Press, 2017).

*** Alvin D. Coox, *Nomonhan: Japan Against Russia, 1939* (Stanford University Press, 1990). A very detailed account of the fighting at what for the Soviet side was known as Khalkhin Gol, although with an emphasis on the Japanese side. Coox certainly gives many pointers as to why the Red Army was so successful in this engagement.

** Stuart Goldman, *Nomonhan, 1939: The Red Army's Victory That Shaped World War II* (Naval Institute Press, 2012). A more accessible Japanese-orientated analysis of the Khalkhin Gol battle put into a wider diplomatic context. This is based on a PhD thesis written well before 2012, so like Coox's book not written in the light of post-Soviet Russian language accounts.

*** E.R. Hooton, *Spain in Arms: A Military History of the Spanish Civil War, 1936–1939* (Casemate Publishers, 2019). Another very detailed military historical work, this time focusing on a number of key military engagements in the Spanish Civil War.

Chapter 3: Débâcles in Poland and Finland

*** Alexander O. Chubaryan & Harold Shukman (eds), *Stalin and the Soviet-Finnish War, 1939–1940* (Routledge, 2002). This is an edited translation of the surprisingly informative official Soviet 1940 dissection of the experience of the war in Finland.

** Carl van Dyke, *The Soviet Invasion of Finland, 1939–1940* (Routledge, 1997). Perhaps the best academic monograph on the Red Army in the war against Finland.

Chapter 4: Barbarossa

** Artem Drabkin & Aleksei Isaev (English text by Christopher Summerville), *Barbarossa Through Soviet Eyes: The First Twenty-Four Hours* (Pen & Sword, 2012). Personal testimonies are woven into this account that focuses on the first day of the Axis invasion of the Soviet Union by two of Russia's most prominent younger popular military historians.

** David Stahel, *Operation Barbarossa and Germany's Defeat in the East* (Cambridge University Press, 2009). The often ferocious nature of Soviet resistance during the first weeks and months of the war is very much apparent in this excellent otherwise German-focused analysis.

Chapter 5: On the Moscow Axis

* Roderic Braithwaite, *Moscow 1941: A City and Its People at War* (Profile Books, 2006). A well-written book by a former British ambassador to Russia considering not only the military side of the Battle of Moscow, but also the lives of Muscovites behind the front line.

*** Lev Lopukhovsky, *The Viaz'ma Catastrophe, 1941: The Red Army's Disastrous Stand against Operation Typhoon*, trans. and ed. Stuart Britton (Helion & Company, 2013). A detailed examination of the large-scale encirclement of Soviet forces as German forces resumed their push on Moscow in October 1941.

** David Stahel, *The Battle for Moscow* (Cambridge University Press, 2015). This book gives a very good idea of the nature of Soviet resistance before Moscow in October and November 1941 from a German perspective, including by encircled Soviet troops whose continued resistance did so much to slow down the German advance.

Chapter 6: Leningrad Besieged

** David Glantz, *The Battle for Leningrad, 1941–1944* (Lawrence, KA: University of Kansas Press, 2002). A good single-volume operational history of the fighting around Leningrad.

* Harrison Salisbury, *The 900 Days: The Siege of Leningrad* (Harper & Row, 1969). Although looking a little dated in terms of source material, this very readable work that draws on Salisbury's own visit to Leningrad as a journalist late in the war is still widely considered a 'classic' account of the siege.

Chapter 7: The Soviet Navy at War

* Alexander Hill & Felipe Rodríguez (illustrator), *Soviet Destroyers of World War II* (Osprey Publishing, 2018). Although focusing on a particular type of warship, this book provides an appreciation for the many operations in which the Soviet Navy was involved during the Great Patriotic War.

** Friedrich Ruge, *The Soviets as Naval Opponents* (Patrick Stephens, 1979). Relatively little has been written in the West on the Soviet Navy during the Great Patriotic War, with this assessment by former German naval officer Friedrich Ruge retaining its value over the years.

Chapter 8: Counterattack

David Stahel, *Retreat from Moscow: A New History of Germany's Winter Campaign, 1941–1942* (Farrar, Strauss & Giroux, 2019). Picking up where his *The Battle for Moscow* left off, this account leaves the reader with little doubt as to the scale of the damage that the Red Army inflicted on the German Wehrmacht during the winter of 1941/1942.

Chapter 9: In the Enemy Rear

***John Armstrong (ed.), *Soviet Partisans in World War II* (University of Wisconsin Press, 1964). A valuable and detailed study of the Soviet partisan movement across the Soviet Union based on captured German materials.

*Alexander Hill & Johnny Shumate (illustrator), *Soviet Partisan versus German Security Soldier* (Osprey Publishing, 2019). A well-illustrated look at three vignettes in the partisan war in north-west Russia from 1941 to 1943, with a good introduction to the topic.

***Ben Shepherd, *War in the Wild East: The German Army and Soviet Partisans* (Harvard University Press, 2004). An excellent academic study of German responses to the partisan threat in their occupied territory of the USSR, focusing on Army Group Centre.

Chapter 10: Soviet Women and the War Effort

Svetlana Alexievich (ed.), *The Unwomanly Face of War: An Oral History of Women in World War II* (Random House, 2017). Originally published in Russian in 1985, and then first in English in 1988, this version of a classic work sheds light on the roles of Soviet women in the Red Army during the Great Patriotic War through their own testimonies.

Roger Marwick & Euridice Cardona, *Soviet Women on the Frontline in the Second World War* (Palgrave, 2012). A wide-ranging examination of the front-line roles of Soviet women during the war.

Chapter 11: 'All for the Front!'

*John Barber & Mark Harrison, *The Soviet Home Front: A Social and Economic History of the USSR in World War II* (Longman, 1991). A slightly dated but nonetheless very useful introduction to the Soviet war effort.

**Wendy Goldman & Donald Filtzer, *Fortress Dark and Stern – The Soviet Home Front During World War II* (Oxford University Press, 2021). An excellent academic study of the Soviet home front that draws on a wealth of archival and other materials that have become available since 1991.

***Mark Harrison, *Accounting for War: Soviet Production, Employment, and the Defence Burden, 1940–1945* (Cambridge University Press, 1996). A detailed analysis of the Soviet Union's wartime economy by the prominent Western economic historian of the Soviet Union during this period.

Chapters 12: 'Not a Step Back!' and 13: The Turning Tide

*Anthony Beevor, *Stalingrad: The Fateful Siege, 1942–1943* (Penguin, 1998). Although he is prone to exaggeration, Beevor's acclaimed account of the Stalingrad fighting is well-written and engaging.

*Geoffrey Roberts, *Victory at Stalingrad: The Battle that Changed History* (Pearson Education, 2002). A very readable and yet still scholarly introduction to the battle for Stalingrad and its significance.

**Alex Statiev, *At War's Summit: The Red Army and the Struggle for the Caucasus Mountains in World War II* (Cambridge University Press, 2018). An excellent academic account of the fighting for the Caucasus region from a primarily Soviet perspective.

Chapter 14: The Bitter Road back to Smolensk and Beyond

**Svetlana Gerasimova, *The Rzhev Slaughterhouse: The Red Army's Forgotten 15-month Campaign against Army Group Center, 1942–1943*, trans. and ed. Stuart Britton (Helion & Company, 2013). A very good book for gaining an appreciation of the horrific slaughter on the central sector of the Eastern Front during 1942 and 1943.

**David Glantz, *Zhukov's Greatest Defeat: The Red Army's Epic Disaster in Operation Mars, 1942* (University Press of Kansas, 2005). A detailed account of the Soviet failure to repeat success on the scale of that achieved in the Stalingrad region in a major operation further north near

Rzhev in late 1942. This operation was led by Zhukov, who predictably downplays its relative importance in his memoirs.

*** David Glantz with Mary Glantz, *Battle for Belorussia. The Red Army's Forgotten Campaign of October 1943–April 1944* (University Press of Kansas, 2016). A detailed account of Soviet operations on the central axis during late 1943 and early 1944 that saw only limited success, prior to the successful Operation 'Bagration' in the summer of 1944.

Chapter 15: From Kursk to the Dnepr

** David Glantz & Jonathan House, *The Battle of Kursk* (Lawrence, KA: University Press of Kansas, 2004). An excellent operational introduction to the fighting in the Kursk region in 1943.

*** Valerii Zamulin, *Demolishing the Myth: The Tank Battle at Prokhorovka, Kursk, July 1943: An Operational Narrative*, trans. and ed. Stuart Britton (Helion & Company, 2010). A detailed account and analysis of the fighting near Kursk, and in particular the famous tank battle of Prokhorovka.

Chapter 16: Allied Aid and the Soviet War Effort

** Vladimir Kotelnikov, *Lend-Lease and Soviet Aviation in the Second World War* (Helion, 2018). A comprehensive and very well illustrated assessment of the contribution that Lend-Lease made to the Soviet Air Forces during the Great Patriotic War.

* Steven Zaloga & Henry Morshead (illustrator), *Soviet Lend-Lease Tanks of World War II* (Osprey Publishing, 2017). This book gives the reader a good idea of the sort of tanks sent to the Soviet Union by the Western Allies and their use by the Red Army, in a very readable and well-illustrated format.

Chapter 17: The Axis Undermined

*** David Glantz, *Red Storm over the Balkans: The Failed Soviet Invasion of Romania, Spring 1944* (University Press of Kansas, 2006). Another detailed Glantz operational study, this time of Soviet attempts to seize Romania in the spring of 1944: the precursor to eventual success that summer.

*** Kamen Nevenkin, *Take Budapest! The Struggle for Hungary, Autumn 1944* (The History Press, 2013). A detailed operational history of the fighting in Hungary during the autumn of 1944 prior to the protracted siege of Budapest.

** Krisztián Ungváry, *The Siege of Budapest: One Hundred Days in World War II* (Yale University Press, 2005). This work details the fighting for the Hungarian capital, Budapest, that dragged on from late 1944 into February 1945.

Chapter 18: 'Bagration'

* Steven Zaloga, *Bagration 1944: The destruction of Army Group Centre* (Osprey Publishing, 1996). A good overview of Operation 'Bagration' in a clear and well-illustrated format.

** Charles Dick, *From Victory to Defeat: The Eastern Front, Summer 1944* (University Press of Kansas, 2016). A good analysis of how the Red Army was able to inflict such a crushing defeat on the Wehrmacht during 'Bagration' in particular.

Chapter 19: The Air War

** Von Hardesty & Ilya Grinberg, *Red Phoenix Rising: The Soviet Air Force in World War II* (University Press of Kansas, 2002). An excellent overview of Soviet air operations during the war, but with analysis likely to be of interest to those with more knowledge as well.

Chapter 20: The War in the North

** Pritt Buttar, *Between Giants: The Battle for the Baltics in World War II* (Osprey Publishing, 2013). A German-orientated overview of the fighting for the Baltic Republics, primarily in 1944–1945.

*** James Gebhardt, *The Petsamo-Kirkenes Operation: Soviet Breakthrough and Pursuit in the Arctic, October 1944* (Leavenworth Papers, Number 17) (Combat Studies Institute, US Army Command and General Staff College, 1989). One of the few substantive accounts in English of this Soviet operation, and one that is surprisingly readily available from a number of sources in book and ebook form.

Chapter 21: From the Vistula to the Oder

*** Richard Harrison (ed. and trans.), *Prelude to Berlin: The Red Army's Offensive Operations in Poland and Eastern Germany, 1945* [Soviet General Staff] (Helion & Company, 2016). There are a number of volumes of Soviet General Staff Studies and materials available edited either by Richard Harrison or by David Glantz and Harold Orenstein. These are typically fairly detailed and not written in flowing prose, but can be very informative for those interested in operational details.

Chapter 22: The Prize

* Anthony Beevor, *The Fall of Berlin, 1945* (Penguin, 2003). Similar to his book on Stalingrad, Beevor's account of the fall of Berlin is well-written and engaging, even if he sometimes stretches the evidence available in his sources for dramatic effect.

*** Richard Harrison (ed. and trans.), *The Berlin Operation, 1945* [Soviet General Staff] (Helion & Company, 2016). Another very detailed study originating from the Soviet General Staff.

Chapter 23: Finishing off the Axis

*** David Glantz, *August Storm: The Soviet 1945 Strategic Offensive in Manchuria* (Leavenworth Papers, Number 7) (Combat Studies Institute, US Army Command and General Staff College, 1983). As with the earlier Leavenworth Paper by Gebhardt mentioned above, this provides a good operational summary of Soviet operations, in this case in Manchuria at the end of the Second World War. It can be obtained from a number of sources.

Chapter 24: Counting the Cost, Reconstruction and Commemoration

*** Jonathan Brunstedt, *The Soviet Myth of World War II: Patriotic Memory and the Russian Question in the USSR* (Cambridge University Press, 2021). An academic study of war and memory in Russia.

*** Mark Edele, *Soviet Veterans of the Second World War: A Popular Movement in an Authoritarian Society, 1941–1991* (Oxford University Press, 2008). Examines the demobilisation and trials and tribulations of veterans seeking reintegration and recognition in post-war Soviet society.

Index

Holocaust, see Final Solution
Hungary, 200, 207, 212–14, 217–19, 255, 266–7

Iassi, 208
Il'men (lake), 173
infantry weapons (Soviet use) (excluding most
   common types): DP (LMG), 68–9, 86, 115,
   148–9, 172–3, 180, 197–8, 212, 216–17,
   226–7, 229, 260–1; DShK (HMG), 152–3, 200;
   flamethrower, 74; Maxim Model 1910/1930
   (HMG), 25, 50, 53, 56, 90–1, 170, 192, 228–9,
   256–7, 264; MP 40 (captured), 104, 165;
   PTRD (anti-tank), 60–1, 98, 184–5, 192,
   258–9, 210–11; StG 44 (captured), 271;
   Thompson (SMG), 203
Iran, 42, 149, 196, 205
Italy, 18, 90, 183, 204

Japan, 1–2, 17–20, 23, 25, 28–9, 31, 55, 79, 93,
   150, 160, 196, 206, 242, 281–4, 286, 288–9,
   291, 293, 307
Jews, x, 231, 260, 262

Kalinin, 44, 94, 102
Kaluga, 74, 101
Karelia, 39, 67–8, 250–2
Karmen, Roman, 18
Kazakhstan, 4, 307
Kerch', 44, 96, 160
Khabarovsk, 282
Khaldei, Evgenii, xi, 279, 306
Khalkhin Gol (1939), 23–9, 281, 283
Khar'kov, 44, 160, 138, 160, 245–6, 170–1, 183,
   190, 196
Kherson, 160, 192
Khrushchev, Nikita, 301
Kiev, 10, 14, 55, 67, 115, 184, 194, 207, 241
Kirkenes, 208
Kishinev, 208
Komsomol (Communist Party youth
   organization), 13, 27, 119–20, 122, 124, 127,
   129, 165
Konev, Ivan, 267
Königsberg, 256, 258, 264, 269, 270, 307
Korea, 281–2, 286, 291, 293
Košice, 217
Kovpak, Sidor, 115
Kraków, 208, 260–2
Krasnoarmeisk, 160, 189
Kronstadt, 76, 85
Kurland, 245, 254

Kursk, 68, 115–16, 142, 160, 183–7, 190, 207–8,
   233, 236, 305
Küstrin, 268
Kuznetsova, Masha, 129

Ladoga (lake), 44, 67–8, 73, 76
Lake Khasan (1938), 19–21, 26, 283
Latvia, 17, 208, 253
Lebedev, Aleksandr, 298–9
'Lend-Lease' aid (to the Soviet Union), 52, 88,
   90, 136, 138, 146–7, 181, 195–206, 211, 215,
   225, 234, 245, 249, 252–3, 284–5, 288–9
Leningrad, 16, 31, 52, 64, 67–77, 79, 85, 96, 98,
   100, 118–20, 122, 134, 136, 145, 171, 173, 245,
   250, 304, 307
Lenino, 130, 160, 180
Levitan, Iurii, xi
Limanskaia, Maria, 126, 306
Liskow, Alfred, 45
Lithuania, 1, 17, 34, 44, 208, 253
Litviak, Lidia, 129
locomotives, railway (Soviet), 136–7, 296–7
lorries, see motor vehicles (un-armoured)
Lublin, 226, 231
Luga, 118
L'vov, 208

Majdanek, 208, 281
Manchuria, 2, 17, 19, 281–93
Mannerheim Line (Karelia), 11, 37
maskirovka (camouflage/concealment), 22–3,
   26–7, 184–6, 225
medical services (Red Army), 47, 119, 124–5,
   131–5, 234–5, 298–9
militia/*opolchenie* (Soviet), 51, 61, 67–8, 70, 118
Minsk, 48, 193, 221, 224–5, 300
Moldavia, 50
Molotov, Viacheslav, 48
Mongolia, 17–18, 23, 28, 282, 284
Moscow, ii, 9–11, 32, 48, 53, 55–64, 67–8, 74,
   90, 93–6, 100, 102, 105, 119, 121–2, 130, 138,
   145, 171, 173, 179–80, 193, 196, 200, 206, 231,
   234, 236, 272, 298, 304
motor vehicles (un-armoured, in Soviet
   service): Ford GPA (amphibian), 200, 265;
   'Jeep', 142–3, 189, 202; motorcycles
   (various), 58, 211; US-supplied trucks,
   142–3, 200–1, 253, 284–5
Mozhaisk, 58, 200
Mudanjiang, 282, 286, 289, 291
Mukhden, 282, 284